Person-Centred Counselling Training

Dave Mearns

SAGE Publications

London • Thousand Oaks • New Delhi

First published 1997

SAGE Publications Ltd
6 Bonhill Street
London EC2A 4PU

SAGE Publications Inc
2455 Teller Road
Thousand Oaks, California 91320

SAGE Publications India Pvt Ltd
32, M-Block Market
Greater Kailash – I
New Delhi 110 048

British Library Cataloguing in Publication data

A catalogue record for this book is available
from the British Library

ISBN 0 7619 5290 X
ISBN 0 7619 5291 8 (pbk)

Library of Congress catalog record available

Typeset by Photoprint, Torquay, Devon
Printed in Great Britain by Biddles Ltd, Guildford, Surrey

Dr Charles Devonshire

This book is dedicated to Chuck Devonshire, whose tireless work over twenty-five years is responsible for developing person-centred counselling training in fifteen European countries.

Contents

Introduction

I have been researching this book for many years, reflecting on my own experience as a person-centred counselling trainer, sharing the experiences of my colleague trainers and taking particular note of the experiences of course members. This book is equally written for trainees and trainers – it seeks to illustrate and learn from the lived experience of both. It should also be useful for person-centred practitioners because it extends and develops current thinking within the approach.

This is the fifth book I have either individually or jointly produced. Hopefully, this one learns from those that have gone before it. *Person-Centred Counselling in Action* (Mearns and Thorne, 1988) sought to lay out in a clear fashion the principles and practices of person-centred counselling. This was followed by *Experiences of Counselling in Action* (Mearns and Dryden, 1989), which researched the experiences of clients and counsellors equally. That book was my first venture into exploring the experiences of the client which, in turn, led to my continued fascination with the large 'unspoken relationship' between client and counsellor. *Developing Person-Centred Counselling* (Mearns, 1994a) sought to introduce the person-centred practitioner to some new ideas and re-shaping of old ideas within the approach. Much of this material was drawn from experiences within person-centred counselling training. The most recent book, *Issues in Professional Counsellor Training* (Dryden et al., 1995), was not restricted to the person-centred approach but laid out central principles and practices of counsellor training which would cross all mainstream approaches. The production of that book helped me to clarify and sharpen my thinking on essential features of counsellor training and how the person-centred approach could articulate with these.

To my knowledge this is the first book devoted to person-centred counselling training. Indeed, it is surprising to see how little has been produced on the subject since the early work by Truax and Carkhuff (1967) and others of their genre. Indeed, in the first 11 years of the specialist person-centred journals, *Person-Centered Review* and *The Person-Centered Journal*, there have been only two papers on the training of client-centred therapists (Combs, 1986a; Thayer, 1987). It is not before time that the approach presented and debated its pedagogy. This need to explore the requirements for person-centred training is emphasised by the fact that person-centred counselling is extremely dangerous for practitioners who have insufficient training. Professional complaints procedures are littered with insufficiently trained 'person-centred' counsellors whose attraction to the approach is matched only by their incompetence. Carl Rogers was fond of pointing out that it was the personal and relational qualities of the counsellor which made the difference in effectiveness and that these were not necessarily generated by psychology training of the time. In other words, it would be possible to find someone who possessed the appropriate qualities without training. Unfortunately, for every person for whom this may be true there are a thousand who believe it to be true of themselves. Personally, I have never met this fictional person who needed no specialist training. The danger of working with insufficient training is that the approach involves highly volatile elements such as empathy, therapeutic congruence, working within the client's existential world, a deep relational connection and a kind of loving. With powerful elements such as these, there is a danger of lightly trained practitioners using the person-centred approach as a licence for their own disorder rather than as a disciplined professional way of working.

Person-centred counselling probably requires more training and a greater intensity of training than most other mainstream counselling approaches because of the daunting personal development objectives which require to be met. Chapter 7 details these objectives and gives the reader an indication of the intensity and duration of training which is likely to be required both in terms of the basic training course and also the extended 'training period' which follows that initial training. It is of crucial importance to establish a high degree of simultaneous support and challenge on the training course for the attainment of the personal development objectives. It is for this reason that person-centred trainers emphasise the necessity of a coherent initial course rather than one which practises a system of Accreditation of Prior Learning, whereby bits of training are added together from different contexts without an intensity of relating being maintained throughout the training.

There are three main levels and applications of person-centred counselling training. The *Introductory Course* might range from a 15-hour weekend to a 30-hour course spread over 10 weeks meeting one evening per week. These courses are excellent for people who have no prior training in the approach but who have a strong interest born of experiences in their working or social life. The second level of course is the *Certificate in Counselling Skills*, which should properly be 120 hours in length if it is conforming to the principles of university accreditation. Such a course will likely be distributed across a period ranging from 6 months to 12 months and may involve half-day or whole-day meetings as well as perhaps some weekends or a whole week of intensive work. There are two main purposes of this Certificate level course. Firstly, the Certificate course can help people to develop person-centred counselling skills which they are then going to apply in their non-counselling work settings. A lawyer described the dividend which his Certificate course training had given him:

> Previous to the training I was completely lost when any emotional content came up in my work with clients. Remember that emotional content arises more with lawyers than even with doctors. After the training I found that I had the skills to exert a *choice* in relation to my client. I now had the ability to respond to the feeling content either by giving a large space or, more practically, by giving a small space with good quality 'contact'. Also, the skills helped me to know how *not to* open up to the emotional content when that was my wish. I think another benefit of the training has been to increase my sensitivity to my clients' distress and to help me to know that I can't properly deal with that – I now keep a number of professional counsellors busy with referrals!

A second purpose for the Certificate level course is as preliminary training for those who are considering a full-scale Diploma level counselling training. The Certificate course provides a solid beginning which can help the person to become sure that this is the right profession for them and also provides a springboard into the qualifying course. Many of the chapters in this book will be relevant to course members and tutors on Certificate level courses but Chapter 12 specially addresses that context.

The third level of training is the *Diploma in Person-Centred Counselling*. Diploma courses are usually between 400 and 450 tutor-contact hours in duration. This amount of time is needed because person-centred counselling training is not simply a matter of 'learning how to do it' but requires considerable attention to personal development since it is the 'Self' of the counsellor that is the central ingredient in the endeavour. There are three main structures for Diploma level training. Firstly, there is the *day release* model, where the course members meet for one day per week, usually for a period of two years with added weekends or whole weeks. In practice the 'day' is more often an afternoon and an evening, such that both the employer and the course member contribute a little of their time towards the venture. The main advantage of this model is that it allows the course member continually to come back and forward from his or her work existence to the training course and to inter-relate the two. The disadvantage is the relative loss of intensity – the course member has to 'start again' each week which can make it difficult to sustain momentum. The second structure is the *full-time* model whereby the course is literally a full-time activity, usually for an academic session from October to June. The central advantage of this model is the intensity which it creates. Issues arising on the course cannot simply be shelved for another week, they tend to be addressed more urgently and immediately. A kind of 'greenhouse' effect can develop whereby the rate of growth can feel unbelievably fast. The disadvantage is the loss of the more extended period offered by the other models. It can be important for the graduate of the full-time course to pay careful attention to the supportive structures he has in place for the year following such an intensive training experience. The third main structure for Diploma level training is the *block release* model. This course might be spread over two or three years with several residential weeks, or longer blocks, plus scattered weekends in between blocks. This design offers a productive combination of intensity and length which has the additional benefit of being more accessible to those in full-time employment who may find it easier to find two free weeks each year rather than a half-day every week. The disadvantage is the greater cost involved in the higher residential element. While universities tend to favour the day-release or full-time structures because these fit their timetabling conventions, private training institutes have the flexibility to opt for the block release model.

The prospective counselling trainee should not presume that all courses labelled 'Diploma' are of sufficient scale. Some courses carry remarkably little tutor content, even as low as 150 hours, yet they are given the label 'Diploma'. This practice is derived from courses in other subject areas where the emphasis is on using a minimum of class contact to stimulate considerable private study on the part of the student. While this model would fit a course *about* counselling, it is inadmissible as a *training* in counselling, which requires considerable human contact between trainers and trainees as well as among trainees, in addition to private study. As a guideline, prospective trainees might look for a full-time course to offer 90–100 days, each with $4\frac{1}{2}$ contact hours; while a day-release part-time course might offer about 67–70 days, each with 6 contact hours; and a part-time residentially based course should have a minimum of 50 days, since it is impossible to achieve more than 8 contact hours even in a residential based day. Recently I challenged a course which offered a residentially based 'Diploma' in 22 days: there is no way that such a training would win accreditation with professional bodies who are, after all, interested in training counsellors, not somnambulists!

I have the same amount of experience working with all three structures, full-time, day release and block release, and find that each has advantages and disadvantages. I also have experience of university-based courses and courses derived from an independent professional counselling training institute. There has been a distinctive movement over the past ten years towards a public preference for university-based courses, a fact which appears to bear no relation to the quality of the training provision. Counselling trainers based in universities face a continual struggle for provision of good student:staff ratios and recognition of the difference between providing an academic course *about* counselling and offering a thorough *training* in counselling which adequately embraces the dimension of personal development. Although I am now based entirely in university, I would still urge the prospective trainee to explore those independent courses associated with specific core theoretical models and offered by experienced professionals who put the profession of counselling to the fore. I fondly remember a six-year period of collaboration between the Westminster Pastoral Foundation and Person-Centred Therapy (Britain), two of the earliest courses in Britain to win accreditation with the British Association for Counselling (BAC). Though these courses represented quite different core theoretical models, psychodynamic and person-centred, communication was easy because both were established in the needs of the profession of counselling and found themselves drawing the same kinds of priorities. Professional counselling organisations will protect the profession more surely than universities. Despite my prejudice towards independent professional counselling training institutes, the reader will find that most of the examples in this book are drawn from the university sector. There are two reasons for this leaning: firstly, most of the *conflicts* which arise for trainers relate to working within a university context. For example, the questions, Can we individualise the curriculum? Can we operate self-assessment? and Can we include a large personal development component? are simple matters of choice for those in the independent sector, yet they may represent major policy and validation battles within the university. The second reason for the bias in this book towards universities is that if person-centred counselling training is to become fully established in the mainstream, it must justify itself within mainstream tertiary education. This is *not* the choice which Carl Rogers made in moving from the University of Wisconsin to Western Behavioral Sciences Institute in the late 1960s, and I believe the approach within the mental health profession in the USA has suffered as a result.

Virtually the whole of this book is relevant to the various facets of Diploma level training, including 'Central dynamics in person-centred counselling training' (Chapter 3), 'Selecting and supporting trainers' (Chapter 4), 'Selecting course members' (Chapter 5), 'Counselling experience supported by supervision' (Chapter 6), 'Personal development during training' (Chapter 7), 'Skill development' (Chapter 8), 'The large group meeting' (Chapter 10) and 'Professional issues' (Chapter 11), as well as the concluding Chapter 13 entitled 'Looking back and looking forward', which is structured as an interview with the author on critical questions for person-centred counselling training.

Chapter 9 'Understanding theory', requires a 'health warning' for the casual reader, but it should prove useful to trainers and practitioners. It researches possibilities for a theory curriculum and in the process it reviews more than 200 academic works.

While this book offers separate chapters on these various issues such as personal development, skills, theory, those separations are misleading. Essentially the person-centred approach is so integrated that it does not divide neatly into chapters. Probably the best example of this abstraction into categories, historically in the approach, is the apparent distinction created among *empathy, unconditional positive regard* and *congruence*. The abstraction and artificial separation of these three 'conditions' has been understandable for the approach which sought to communicate its principles and to research its essentials. However, the separation also represents a misleading reductionism. The reality is that the therapeutic conditions are integrated and inseparable, becoming a part of what we might call *'working at relational depth'* and *'meeting the client at his existential level of functioning'*. This integrative notion, which seeks to re-discover the essence of person-centred working, is explored in Chapter 2.

Outlining the 'contents' in the introduction to this book would be misleading if I did not also include some extracts on the *experiences* of those involved in person-centred training, because those experiences are integral to the book. To this end, Box 1, entitled 'The Joys and Frustrations of Person-Centred Training', presents a few self-reports of former course members. The issues

Box 1

The Joys and Frustrations of Person-Centred Training

Later encounters with former course members yield some of their views on the joys and frustrations of the training experience:

The joys

- 'The whole thing was a *challenge* from beginning to end – every day offered new opportunities.'
- 'In the very first week it brought me closer to myself than I have ever been, and it held me there for a year.'

The frustrations

- 'It would have been nice if they [the staff] had looked after me more – I felt that it was up to me whether I sank or swam.'
- 'Person-centred training is *so* dependent on self-development and that, in turn, is so dependent on us, the course members, that they [the trainers] can only offer us "opportunities" – they can't actually guarantee to "train" us. They said that in the first week, but it took me half the course to understand it – I wasted a lot of time being scared to use the opportunities.'

Sometimes the joys and frustrations are wrapped up together

- 'I think my learning about *congruence* sums up the whole experience – at first I was frustrated that the staff wouldn't simply tell me how to do it – how to be congruent – then I realised that the real value of this approach was the very fact that it wasn't easy – it needed genuine personal development on my part. I was going to have to face my inner hopes and fears before I could properly release my congruence.'
- 'They [the staff] consistently refused to take responsibility *for* me. I *hated* them for that – why wouldn't they let me play my usual 'Child–Parent' games? I am grateful that they held that line so firmly – it meant that my "Adult" simply had to stay involved. That meant that for the first time I actually learned to succeed instead of my usual pattern of succeeding in failing.'
- 'I got so used to being close with the other people on the course that it became the norm in my life. I had forgotten that the so-called "real" world was so "unreal". When the course ended I had to remember how to be unreal again. Fortunately, my clients still need my realness.'

to which they refer may give further glimpses of some of the important processes and dynamics of the training.

The quotes in Box 1 are used with the permission of the former course members. That is the pattern for the majority of quotes in this book. In some cases the quotes are real but disguised to ensure the anonymity of those involved. In a few cases, where the real example could not help but identify even in disguised form, the construction is fictionalised but the heart of the statement is preserved.

Rather than embark upon clumsy notations such as 'he/she' or repeated presentations of 'him or her' I shall attempt to simplify communication in this book by using only one pronoun. The convention I have picked for this is fairly arbitrary but, if anything, it is designed to contradict the stereotypical inference that it is the male who is in the more powerful position. To that end, in most references, the *trainer* will be female and the gender of the *course member* will alternate with chapters. The alternation is necessary since there are many more references to course members. Despite the convention adopted, readers are encouraged to stretch their imagination to translate any or all of these examples as far as gender is concerned. Where the gender is genuinely important, that will be preserved. References to 'counsellors' and 'clients' will be randomised for gender.

A difficult decision in the drafting of this manuscript concerned the use of the terms 'trainee', 'course member', 'student' or 'participant' to denote the customer of the training course. The word 'participant' would have been misleading because, in person-centred training, the staff are also participating. The terms 'trainee' and 'student' are accurate, though they are often imbued with negative connotations because they appear to sharpen the distinction with 'trainer' and 'teacher'. Personally, I like the terms 'trainee' and 'student' – I like to emphasise to myself those times when I am a learner, so that I can open to that endeavour and not try to hide my naivety. However, many people do carry negative feelings about these terms, so to cause least offence I have tended to use 'course member,' with recourse to the other terms as a means to introduce variety.

With the exception of the theory curriculum within Chapter 9, most of this book is written in the first person. That is an unconventional choice in academic texts where the norm is to de-personalise the endeavour. However, I am of the view that academic writers would present a more accurate image of their work if the personal pronoun was used. The use of impersonal language cloaks in objective terminology a range of opinions, judgements, conclusions and prejudices which are highly subjective. As a student of Carl Rogers in 1972/73, I was introduced to the work of Michael Polanyi on the intrinsic subjectivity of the whole of scientific endeavour (Polanyi, 1958). Since that time I have preferred to emphasise rather than mask my subjectivity in academic work. This book is a highly subjective enterprise, comprising my personal opinions, judgements, conclusions and prejudices.

Three chapters in the book are re-drafted from previously published papers. Chapter 2 is based on the paper 'Working at relational depth with clients in person-centred therapy', *Counselling*, 7(4): 306–11 (Mearns, 1996c). Chapter 3 is substantially re-worked from the paper 'Central dynamics in client-centered therapy training' *The Person-Centered Journal*. 4(1): 31–43 (Mearns, 1997a). Chapter 7 is a re-working of 'Achieving the personal development dimension in professional counsellor training', *Counselling*, 8(2): 113–20 (Mearns, 1997b). The re-working is extensive in all three cases.

A final note in this introduction asks the course member to be aware that his own training course will not do all the things mentioned in this book, or take the same approach as the trainers quoted. Trainers must paint their own canvas when designing their course – the course must be congruent with the trainers.

With the introductions complete it is time for the party to begin. If this book is successful it will introduce the reader, fairly personally, to some of the 600 course members and 20 trainers with whom I have had the pleasure to work most closely. Our shared endeavour was to aid the development of 'person-centred' counsellors. A first step, in that regard, must be to explore what 'person-centred' means.

1
What Does 'Person-Centred' Mean?

Box 1.1

The Answer from Alison, a New Trainee

'Person-centred' means something I have had to change my life for. I thought I had got my working life in order – I was a pretty good CPN [Community Psychiatric Nurse] who presumed that I was qualified to be a counsellor and quickly found that I wasn't. Yet I had a *sense* of what would be helpful for my patients – I could *feel* the difference between the patient who was gently helped to find portions of strength in her Self and the patient who was hooked on other people's pills, whether chemical or 'advice pills'. The change in one patient was permanent and in the other it was transient. Now I have to do this training – I guess by the end of it I'll know what else 'person-centred' *really* means.

Different Labels for the Approach

The approach, devised and developed by Carl Rogers over 50 years of his life and by others in the time which has followed his death, has had numerous changes of name. Although he had not formulated his theory of therapy to any degree in his first book, *The Clinical Treatment of the Problem Child*, in 1939, Rogers does refer to his approach as a 'relationship therapy'. By the time of his 1942 book *Counseling and Psychotherapy* (Rogers, 1942a), he was using the term 'non-directive therapy'. While the therapy remained non-directive, and does so to this day, by 1951 Rogers had re-focused the title to 'client-centred therapy' in a book of the same name (Rogers, 1951). It is in that book that the main propositions of his theory are espoused for the first time. 'Client-centred therapy' continued to be the label which represented the approach universally right up until the 1970s and including the notable 1970 book by Hart and Tomlinson, *New Directions in Client-Centered Therapy*. The term 'person-centred' crept in during the 1970s as the therapeutic approach began to be applied to other settings including 'student-centred' learning, 'person-centred'

group work, the 'person-centred approach applied to management' and the 'person-centred approach applied to conflict
resolution'. For a time the two labels, 'client-centred' and 'person-
centred', stood side by side, the first to denote the therapy and the
second its wider applications, as exemplified in the 1984 book by
Levant and Shlien, *Client-Centered Therapy and the Person-Centered
Approach*. Perhaps the cumbersome nature of that book title
showed that some resolution had to take place. A major step in
that regard was made by the journal of the approach, begun in
1986, and called *Person-Centered Review*. This journal, and its
successor, *The Person-Centered Journal*, retained the term 'person-
centred' which had by now become the generic name for all the
applications of the philosophy. Some parts of the world then
opted for 'person-centred therapy' as the specific label for the
application to therapy, while those places such as the USA where
research, practice and training had been in place for some time
retain the term 'client-centred therapy' to this day.

While this analysis suggests that there was no specific conceptual reason for the evolution from 'client-centred therapy' to
'person-centred therapy', apart from the broadening of the application to other contexts, there were, in fact, other contributing
factors. By the early 1970s, Carl Rogers, as well as others, was
more and more emphasising the fact that the 'person' of the
therapist was an active ingredient in the therapeutic process.
Rather than being seen as merely a shadowy reflector, greater
emphasis was being placed on the therapist's congruence in the
therapeutic relationship. While the therapy still remained centred
in the aims and process of the client, it actively attended to the
presence of both persons in the relationship, hence the term
'person-centred therapy' may be seen to acknowledge the fact that
this therapy embraced the personhood of the therapist as well as
the client (Rogers, 1987).

This evolution of labels for the approach may seem strange to
the new reader but it is a healthy evolution in that it helps to
retain a question on the focus of the approach. Even the fact that
in the present day there are practitioners who call themselves
'client-centred therapists' and others who use the label 'person-
centred therapist' is not unhealthy. Personally, I find something
useful in both labels: 'client-centred therapy' emphasises to me the
fact that the whole focus of this endeavour should rightly be on
the experiential process of my client while the term 'person-
centred therapy' also reminds me that as a therapist I must attend
to my own personhood in order to be a healthy contributor to the
process of my client.

The use of the term 'counselling' or 'therapy' within the person-centred approach reflects cultural variations rather than any functional difference between the terms. Whether the practitioner is adopting the label 'person-centred therapist' or 'person-centred counsellor' makes absolutely no difference to what we expect of her – with both labels we expect her to be able to meet her client at considerable relational depth and work with whatever existential content she finds there.

Misconceptions of Person-Centred Counselling

Some people are attracted to person-centred counselling because they do not understand it well. A common misconception is that the person-centred counsellor is not particularly *active* in the process and that she is simply a passive companion on the client's journey. This conception therefore attracts the counsellor who is not confident about her presence or interventions. It may even attract the counsellor with low self-esteem. In fact, person-centred counselling requires the counsellor to achieve considerable self-confidence, self-esteem and self-acceptance, not to mention a quality of 'presence' which can allow her to relate with the client at existential depth, with confidence and without fear.

Another fairly widespread misconception of person-centred counselling relates to its effects upon clients. Some counsellors think too narrowly about the impact of person-centred counselling, imagining that its effects on clients are purely 'positive' in terms of helping them to become less defensive, more expansive, more open to their experiencing, more able and willing to be empathic with others, more self-accepting and accepting of others. While person-centred personality theory would certainly predict that clients, given a sustained experience of the therapeutic conditions which they can symbolise, can be expected to move towards a greater integration of their self-structure and experience, leading towards the kind of changes mentioned above, we must be aware of the huge individual difference among clients with respect to:

- the *pace* of that integration;
- the *process* of that integration;
- the *immediate behavioural consequences* of that integration.

If our naive counsellor is attracted to the approach because it promises the birth of 'beautiful people' then she should think again and become aware of how slow the pace towards integration can be, how rough, how confusing and at times how devastating can be the process and how the immediate behavioural consequences of that integration may not be pleasant for people around the client or even for the client himself. The portraits of the clients Pam and Paul offered below both illustrate a fairly effective person-centred therapeutic process and skilful work on the part of experienced counsellors, but the prospective person-centred counselling course member should be aware that Paul is as representative of the process as Pam.

Pam

Pam came into counselling at a time when she was really 'ready'. She had 'tried' counselling twice previously but had stopped after a few sessions on both occasions. At those previous times she had been fearful of what might be the consequences of counselling for her relationship. This time she did not have that fear, for the inevitable had happened – her relationship had gone to the Bahamas with his secretary.

Pam still had fear – fear of what she would discover about herself. It was comfortable to hate her husband, but she knew that *she* had been a part of the relationship as well.

In fact, what she found, in even the first session, was that, in a real sense, she had not been *in* the relationship. She had never really occupied space in the relationship – instead, she had 'made space' in the relationship for her husband. She had placed no demands – she had exerted no presence. She had not sought to be *active* in this partnership: 'I was like a little girl, so pleased to have found her prince. From the start of our relationship all I did was try to hold on to him – no wonder I lost him.'

Pam's counsellor found the relationship fairly easy – 'It is a pleasure to work with someone who is so ready.' Pam had come to a turning point in her life and could use counselling as a reliable 'sounding board' and a 'place of safety'.

Fairly quickly, Pam identified the basis in her own personality for her tendency to try to make relationships into fairy tales. She could identify the conditions of worth which had taught her that she was only valuable insofar as she could please others. She hated the way she had constantly, as a child, obeyed her mother's bidding in trying to please her father. Yet, she could also empathise with herself – she could understand her young Self and that young Self within her present woman. That understanding brought an acceptance of Self which gave her considerable strength in *all* relationships. Her counsellor reflected on that strength in their relationship – on how Pam took responsibility for herself and how she was able to express intimacy.

During her counselling work Pam established another relationship in which she exercised a more congruent expression of her Self. She used counselling to monitor how different she felt in this relationship and the other things which this relationship was helping her to discover in herself.

Paul

Paul had initially come into counselling with his wife and later, after that relationship had dissolved, he entered counselling on his own.

Throughout the first three months of the work Paul was aggressively resistant to virtually everything the counsellor did. Frequently, he was personally insulting to the counsellor about her 'incompetence', about her 'inability to help him', and even about her clothes. Paul seemed to enjoy the counsellor's discomfort when that came and probed more when it didn't.

Paul kept coming to counselling.

On one occasion Paul asked his counsellor to hold him. The counsellor's response was perfectly congruent and quite detailed. She said that, in principle, she had no difficulty with the idea of holding him. However, she felt uncomfortable with his request at this moment – she could not understand where it had come from – it did not seem to fit anything that had gone before. Paul smiled at this response and confessed that if she had held him he would have spat in her face.

Three months into the work Paul cried, congruently. It was difficult to know exactly what had shifted to allow this to happen. There were occasions in the previous three months when Paul had cried but he had later identified that crying as being 'a manipulative tactic I have developed with women'. But this time his crying was completely different and quite uncontrollable. When he did speak he apologised sincerely for the way he had behaved over the past three months. He spoke in detail about the way he had treated the counsellor and explained how he had often felt strongly ambivalent in relation to her. He had loved the way she seemed to value him and how consistent that was. Yet, at the very times he felt that affection he had to push her away. The 'prizing' which the counsellor offered to him was about the most fearful thing that could have happened because it was something he wanted but did not dare to want.

During the next two months Paul and his counsellor worked at sustained relational depth on existential material, and, as often happens, when that level of contact is established, enormous ground was covered not only in relation to Paul's awareness about himself but also in the ways he was able to begin to change his response to people and events.

Suddenly, the counselling stopped. Paul missed three consecutive appointments. In each case the counsellor phoned him and on the first two occasions he said that he had been 'too busy' but that he would 'come next week'. On the third occasion he said that 'counselling is no good for me' and that his life was 'as bad as ever'. He reported that the consequences of counselling for him were that he had been publicly rude to his boss and was likely to lose his job; he had told his new partner exactly what he thought of her and she had left; he had started drinking again to excess; and that he couldn't even face living in his own home – he had left it empty and was living in a rented caravan in the country. Although the counsellor was experienced enough to know that it was important not to be frightened off by her client's process it was also difficult to retain contact in that telephone conversation – the important thing she could offer him was to continue to not judge him.

Three months later Paul returned to counselling. During the next six months in counselling they were able to unravel a lot which helped Paul to understand himself and helped his behaviour to be understandable. Perhaps it is easiest to describe Paul's process using the language of person-centred personality theory. The early 'conditions of worth' under which Paul had tried to develop were oppressive in the extreme and reflected the ideology of an extreme Protestant religion that translated a doctrine of original sin into a form of parenting which emphasised to the child that he could *only* be bad – that not one single thing he did could, in any spiritual sense, be 'good'. No matter how he had tried, as a child, his father's lack of acceptance and critical judgement were unshakeable. Under any conditions of worth the 'actualising tendency' works on the Self to help it to make the best job of the circumstances in order to maintain and enhance its· existence. Thus, Paul's skill and faculties helped him to develop his emotional insensitivity, his hardness, his invulnerability to apparent intimacy and a portfolio of sophisticated ways of keeping other people away from him – hence, his array of destroyed relationships.

However, Paul carried with him enormous existential fear: fear of intimacy; fear of 'free relating'; fear of *really* becoming close to someone; fear of really being *seen* by others. One of the chilling discoveries which Paul made was that his fear of others seeing his own self-hate or his own existential despair was life-threatening. If people saw his abject self-hate or despair his whole edifice would crumble – he would be exposed. Paul actually identified that he protected that possibility of exposure with the fantasy of suicide. If he had been exposed he could have committed suicide.

However, Paul's 'actualising tendency' was not silenced – at times, and at some level, he also wanted to be open and to love and to be congruently intimate, though his full awareness of that only arose in the last six month period of counselling.

Hence, Paul was experiencing a classic conflict between the actualising tendency and the Self as it has actualised under the conditions of worth. That conflict explained his 'approach/avoidance' relationship with counselling. As part of him, activated by the actualising tendency, would move towards expression and integration, the Self as it had actualised had to resist else it would be inviting its own annihilation.

Pam and Paul look entirely different as clients and yet they both reflect a pattern which we might expect in person-centred counselling. As mentioned earlier in this section, 'clients, given a sustained experience of the therapeutic conditions which they can symbolise, can be expected to move towards a greater integration of their self-structure and experience . . .'. However, as is also mentioned earlier in this section, the *pace* of that integration, the *process* of the integration and the *immediate behavioural consequences* of the integration can vary enormously. Our first client, Pam, showed a fast *pace* towards integration and a fairly clear and even *process* towards that integration. Also, that increased integration manifested itself in behavioural consequences which were clearly 'positive' in most systems of values: she achieved more 'presence' in her relationships, took greater responsibility for Self, exercised more congruent functioning, and was more easily able to be intimate within relationships.

The pace, process and immediate behavioural consequences of Paul's move towards integration were different in every respect and can only really be understood if we grasp his phenomenal perspective and understand something about the nature of his existence. His *pace* of movement was much slower than Pam's – perhaps he was coming earlier in his changing process than Pam, but certainly his slower pace might fit with the daunting existential fear he had to face. Also, the process of his integration was much more complex, with a long period where he was both 'testing' the counsellor and also trying to get her to reject him. His own words give us a phenomenal insight and describe his process most accurately:

> If I was 'testing' her then I was testing her 'to destruction' the way a piece of metal is stressed until it breaks. She was meant to break. I couldn't understand why she didn't break. No, it wasn't really 'testing' her – I needed to destroy her to preserve my Self.

When his counsellor did not oblige by rejecting him (see 'The Spiral of Rejection', p. 61 in Mearns and Thorne, 1988), he took what for him was a dangerous step – he became open to all his experiencing. Again, Paul describes it better:

> I literally 'fell open' – like a scallop shell I fell open and exposed all my soft parts. I could be eaten. I was terrified – but I also had *hope*. I guess the balance of hope and fear had changed, and for the first time in my life I went with the hope. But it felt really scary. In *my* world behaving this healthy was psychotic.

What followed for Paul was two months of his life when he was open and when he met his counsellor at existential depth (Mearns, 1996c). We must be thankful for his counsellor's considerable experience in that she was not thrown by the next stage in the 'roller coaster' process. In theoretical terms, as mentioned earlier, Paul had found himself responding to the urges of his actualising tendency against the commands of his actualised Self. But the campaign for the Self was not over. There were many other conflicts to follow in the three months during which he stopped counselling. Part of that process may have been his 'self concept fighting back' (Mearns, 1992a, 1994e), where he seemed to do things in his life which reinforced the fact that he could not change and had to retain his self-concept as it was: he sank into drinking; he was verbally cruel to his partner; he insulted his boss and he rejected counselling. Yet, the process was not even that definable – again we need to learn from his phenomenal experience:

> What I was doing was a strange mixture. I was so torn with conflict – I think it was conflict between *wanting to love* and *needing to hate*. I think that everything I did in those three months reflected that conflict. It wasn't simply a negative 'retreat'. Part of it was negative – like cutting things out of my life to make me alone again. I had dreams of slashing hidden parts of my body with a hunting knife. I cut out my therapist. I cut out my partner. I tried to cut out my job. I even cut out my home. But it wasn't just that simple – in a way I was also forcing myself to move on.

Here, Paul describes a complex conflict between the Self as it is actualised and the actualising tendency. The Self as it is actualised wants to cut things off to return to the safety of the known, but his actualising tendency – his motivation for enhancement, is also pushing him. His growth has gained momentum during those previous two months and it is difficult to stop growth.

As well as his pace of integration being elongated and its process resembling a roller coaster, the *immediate behavioural consequences* of Paul's early moves towards integration do not resemble the 'rose garden' which many clients and even counsellors envision (Green, 1967). The immediate behavioural consequences included virtually losing his job and certainly endangering his future in that work; losing his partner; and nearly giving up his house entirely. Most 'outcome' research would take these as indicators of failed counselling, yet they were, in fact, part of an effective process.

These contrasting clients, presented so early in this book, are intended to give some indication of the range of experience which the professional person-centred counsellor might expect. Some of the most worrying 'person-centred' work can be found in the untrained practitioner, attracted to the approach by its conception of the person, but unwilling and unable to cope with clients who do not move readily towards that idealised view. In fact, such a counsellor offers a highly *conditional* relationship: 'Be like my ideal of how people should develop or else I will feel unsure/unsafe and will withdraw from you.' The approach still suffers from such untrained counsellors who like to call themselves 'person-centred' but have not embarked upon the kind of training challenge described in this book.

A Person-Centred Training Relationship is not the same as a Counselling Relationship

A mistake made by some course members and occasionally also by trainers is to expect the same kind of relationship between trainer and course member as exists between counsellor and client. There will be some similarities in these two relationships. The very fact that the training reflects a person-centred emphasis means that the trainers will expect to ground the training in each developing course member. In practice this usually means that around two-thirds of the course, or even more, is devoted to structures that permit the course member the opportunity to focus upon and consult with others on her development. Some structures that lend themselves to the course member setting the agenda include personal development groups, supervision groups, experiential workshops, skills practice groups, community meetings and personal therapy. The course member, like the client, might also expect the person-centred trainers to be able and willing to empathise, to value the course member as a person of worth and to be congruent in relating. However, the course member should not expect these conditions to be manifested in the same form as she may have experienced in a counselling relationship because the two relationships have important differences.

Firstly, the counselling relationship is highly *exclusive*. That exclusivity is important to the client and is often necessary for him to feel sufficiently safe to explore. The training relationship cannot be so exclusive because trainers have responsibility to *all* the course members, equally. If a trainer forms an exclusive relationship with one course member then considerable dangers ensue and the trainer might properly be challenged on over-involvement.

A second difference between training and counselling relates to *confidentiality*. The training staff need to create a network of communication about the course members. If one staff member holds back important information about the development of a course member, she is asking her colleagues to work in the dark and is taking on an exclusive rather than networked supportive function in relation to the course member. Hence, it is healthy in a training staff for important information about course members to be shared but to be held as confidential within the staff group. If this is the approach taken to confidentiality by the staff, it is important that it be made clear to course members at the outset of the course lest they presume separate confidential relationships with each of the staff as would occur in a counselling relationship. Course members are different from clients and it is reasonable to expect course members to be able to function openly with trainers even though they are not being offered exclusive and confidential relationships. Trainees can be expected to be more advanced than clients in their ability to take risks in that regard.

A third difference between course members and clients is that course members can be expected to *share responsibility* in the trainer–trainee relationship. Hence, the course member can reasonably be expected to voice difficulty or discontent directly. Person-centred training courses encourage this direct action because it is seen as a way of exercising responsibility. Courses, typically, have various large and small group formats which offer sufficient openness in their structure to allow such direct expression. When one course member said 'throughout the two years you never realised what I needed', the trainer would be concerned with this experience of the course member but might also challenge her on her failure to express her needs openly and her expectation that the staff should be able and willing to guess at her needs. Such an expectation would often occur in counselling but would not be particularly appropriate to a training relationship where greater responsibility is expected of the course member.

A fourth difference between the training relationship and the counselling relationship is that while the counsellor has responsibility to the client but is strict in refusing to take responsibility for the client, trainers inevitably have at least a small degree of *responsibility for* the course member insofar as the trainer is explicitly or implicitly conferring some commendation of the course member's work to the rest of the profession and to current and future clients. Chapter 3 goes into this issue of responsibility in more detail and looks at how person-centred trainers endeavour to minimise the degree to which they take responsibility for the course member, but cannot avoid it entirely.

Hence, the trainer's empathy, valuing and congruence in relation to the course member are set within the context of a different relationship to that which we can expect in counselling. If the course member expects that the trainer will be exclusively attending to her in the same fashion as her counsellor then her expectations are unrealistic and need to be challenged, hopefully by herself.

Setting the Person-Centred Training Framework

An easy mistake to make as a person-centred trainer is to presume that the structures of our own successful training can be transposed to other contexts and will work just as well. The development of person-centred training is littered with such disasters where the trainers thought that 'being person-centred' meant doing things in a particular fashion without regard to the context. The examples which follow represent the kinds of disasters which can ensue.

- I remember, with continued discomfort, and an inclination to edit this text, an occasion nearly 30 years ago when I thought I was 'being person-centred' when I responded to a request to give a guest lecture on the person-centred approach by abandoning the lecture and moving into an unstructured large community meeting. I suspect that few people at that meeting retained any connection with the person-centred approach thereafter!
- Then there was the other trainer who began his weekend introductory course in person-centred counselling skills with a time-unlimited, unstructured encounter group without giving any prior warning or explanation.
- Another, almost apocryphal, entry in the catalogue of person-centred training disasters was the trainer who tried to run a counselling training course *entirely* on student-centred principles. She gave no input or suggestions and offered no framework. That kind of approach can be made successful but not in this case where the participants were given no prior warning or induction. Half of the participants left that two-year course within the first 48 hours. In fact, the course made something useful for itself with the people who were left, but at what human cost?

These disasters came from well-meaning rather than neglectful trainers. The mistake which was made was the same in every case – the trainers were taking practices which were successful in one context and applying them to another without attention to the suitability and preparation of the context. Sometimes there is dogma which develops in the person-centred approach – a dogma which says that all person-centred work must be student-led, or a dogma which demands that unstructured encounter groups or large groups must always be employed in person-centred training. This kind of dogmatic thinking errs because it takes a *structural* rather than a *functional* perspective. 'Being person-centred' is not defined by the structures we impose but by the functions served by these structures. I recall a very clear example of this in a 'free school' I visited in Los Angeles in the early 1970s. The school was designed along person-centred principles as far as the teaching staff were concerned. But the regime was in fact an autocracy where the staff insisted that the whole curriculum had to be derived from the interests and expressions of the students. In fact, person-centred functions were not being met by that regime because the students were confused, disinterested and disempowered. More than that, the students actually felt that they were not regarded as important by the teaching staff who were perceived as 'wanting to do their own thing'. A training system is not person-centred because it includes particular structures – it is 'person-centred' if its effects are to empower its course members to maintain and enhance their functioning. It is extremely difficult to establish an atmosphere of empowerment, chiefly because conventional expectations about education and training, in any discipline, are that it will be disempowering, even disrespectful, of the naivety of the trainee. Students enter the training context *expecting* to be oppressed. Indeed, this is the reason that terms such as 'student' and 'trainee' are problematic in a text such as this. Such is the power of the negative connotation of the education endeavour that these terms are in themselves taken to denote oppression, subservience and disempowerment. Box 1.2 illustrates the conflict a new course member experiences between her expectations of disempowerment and what seems to be being offered by the trainers.

In setting the training framework our aim is to devise a system which will have the best chance of being empowering. To do that we shall certainly embrace the *central dynamics* of person-centred training discussed in Chapter 3, but we also need to take into account a number of variables relating to our course members so that we can set structures which have the best chance of meeting the desired functions. For example, we need to consider the *expectations* which our course members are likely to carry into the training. What expectations are they likely to have on the training methods we shall use on the course? Will they be expecting us to be very unstructured or highly structured in our approach to training? Will they be expecting a system of tutor-assessment or self-assessment? Even if they have been told about the system of

---

Box 1.2

It helps that I know you care . . .

It was difficult to believe what the trainers were offering. It was a mixture of a serious *challenge* but also intensive *support* of my person. They kept 'pushing' me to take risks, to put myself forward, to try new things. Yet, they simultaneously offered just as intense a support to who I was as a person. They repeatedly encouraged me to 'be gentle with myself', to 'stay close to who I *am* as a person', to feel OK about making 'mistakes'. I remember being shocked and also getting a frog in my throat when my group supervisor responded to a dreadful piece of work with a visible tear in her eye and a deep recognition of my struggle to 'portray' a perfect counsellor which had fallen flat on its face. She didn't stop challenging me, but it helped that I knew she cared.

---

self-assessment, will they really believe it? Another consideration in structuring the course is the likely *level of fear* among the course members. It is important that course members are not selected if their level of fear is too high because virtually all training structures are very challenging. But, even at levels of fear which are still suitable for training there can be a big variation. If the course member's fear is high, unstructured training settings will be difficult. Also, the trainee with great fear will find it difficult to volunteer for testing situations, like showing a videotape of her practice. Another variable within the cohort of course members is the *level of commitment*. Courses will have taken what measures they can to ensure that those recruited to the course have a high degree of commitment because the trainers will know how necessary this is in person-centred and indeed in any approach to counselling training. However, even with fairly high levels of commitment the variations affect the way course members can use the structures of the course. For example, a supervision group may be operated in a highly unstructured fashion if the members are very committed to the process. Where commitment is very low, the group supervisor might find that the empowering function is better served by creating a minimal structure whereby, for example, she ensures that each person has an opportunity to present her work during each of the early meetings.

These variables describe conditions of facilitation for the trainers which will vary in 'favourability' (Fiedler, 1978). A highly unfavourable combination is where the course members have expectations for high structure, high fear and low commitment.

The opposite profile describes a highly favourable situation for the trainers. A major aim of the selection procedure is to procure as highly favourable a profile as possible. However, it is important for trainers to assess the degree of favourability of the profile so that they can consider the structures they are to use. It is vital to note that an unfavourable profile does not mean that the trainers should immediately resort to highly structured procedures in order to meet the course members' expectations. On the contrary, the trainers will likely want to move the unfavourable profile towards the favourable direction and will challenge course member expectations rather than comply with them. However, having considered the favourability of the pattern in advance allows the trainers to take care in the way they set up their structures and organise communication with the students so that this movement of the profile may best be encouraged.

A concrete example of this kind of decision-making is reflected in our own University of Strathclyde Diploma in Counselling. For the first few years we would begin our personal development groups by forming them initially as encounter groups and running these for two full days near the start of the course. The idea was good in theoretical terms – we could familiarise course members with the idea of giving and receiving feedback and being as immediate and responsive to their feelings as possible. However, it did not work as well in practice. Our analysis of the situation was that the level of fear was too high for the encounter groups to go through sufficient process in those two early days of the course. We considered a number of solutions. An obvious possibility is to alert trainees to this structure well in advance of the course so that they know what to expect. However, it is extremely difficult to alert someone to the nature of encounter groups if they have not had that experience before. Another possibility would have been to run the encounter groups for six days rather than two. This would almost certainly have resulted in the initially slower process speeding up considerably over the last few days. That policy might have worked but it would have been a risky decision to give so much time to a highly feared activity. In the end we decided that the encounter groups at the beginning did not really represent a sacred cow and we replaced them with 'autobiography groups' in which course members spent the initial two days of these personal development groups discussing material from their specially constructed auto-biographies. In general, that training procedure induced much less fear and carried the same bonding function which we sought for this beginning to the personal development groups. Interestingly, these training groups used encounter groups very well indeed when they appeared much later in the course.

There are many different ways of deriving the functions which are sought by person-centred training. The onus on trainers is not to stick to any dogma on the structures which define a training as 'person-centred' but to consider how their course members vary so that structures are chosen and presented in such a way as to present a challenge, but an attainable challenge. 'Person-centred' means attending to the 'persons' who are our clients or our course members.

2
Meeting the Client at Relational Depth

Before we set out to design appropriate training processes we need to be clear on the kind of work expected of our person-centred counsellors. A common misconception among practitioners of other disciplines is that person-centred counselling is a fairly superficial endeavour where the counsellor simply contrives to portray empathy and acceptance, thereby offering 'support' to the client – indeed, within psychodynamic circles the approach is often classified as mere 'supportive counselling'. If this caricature was accurate, then training person-centred counsellors would be a fairly straightforward endeavour. Probably a single evening would be sufficient to train such counsellors in basic acting skills, giving them a catalogue of 'stock' responses by which they might portray incongruent empathy and warmth as well as various ways to hide their lack of understanding and strategies by which they might learn to swallow their judgements of the client and present a fixed smile in any doubtful circumstances. An advanced training course filling an extra evening might make the acting skills and strategies more subtle so that the counsellor actually appeared not to be acting, but being congruent.

Of course, this fictional farce is far from the reality of our training aims. In this chapter we shall explore the issue of *meeting the client at relational depth*. In this conception of person-centred counselling the counsellor is willing and able to meet the client at sufficient depth to work at the existential level of the client's experiencing. The word 'existential' might be difficult for the new reader, but it is a useful concept once developed. When I am working with my client at the existential level of his experiencing it means that he is giving me access to his innermost feelings and thoughts about his Self and his very existence. He is not giving me a false picture layered with defences and pretences – he is including me in the dialogue he has with himself. This level of meeting lies far deeper than the level of transferential relating. Indeed it is striking to see how transference phenomena are totally absent at this depth of working – this is the level of the client's very existence in the world. Often the transferential level of relating has been broken through to reach this level – both counsellor and client have fought to establish congruence rather than transference. There exists a beautiful paradox in showing willingness to meet the client at relational depth and work with the existential issues which present at that level: the person-centred counsellor is *not* setting that existential agenda – it is perfectly possible for the client to maintain the agenda at a more superficial level. Yet, if there *are* tensions at that existential level, the fact that the counsellor is able and willing to go there provides such safety and support that the client is inclined to make that choice.

Before we move on too quickly, we must set out the case for 'meeting the client at relational depth' being a fundamental ability for the person-centred counsellor and explore the demands this makes of the training we are to design.

Establishing Psychological Contact

For two people to be in relationship with one another the essential prerequisite is that they be in psychological 'contact'. This is the first of six 'therapeutic conditions' laid down by Rogers in defining his therapy (Rogers, 1957a). Psychological 'contact' may be viewed as a binary phenomenon whereby it is either present or absent. However, the phenomenological reality of psychological contact to both clients and counsellors is that there are *degrees* of contact. A counsellor might experience a considerable depth of psychological contact in relation to one client, a much more superficial contact with another and, indeed, a sporadic loss of contact with a third. If they could compare their experiences, clients would also testify to variations in the psychological contact which they had managed to establish with their counsellors!

The crucial work published in recent years in the area of client-centred pre-therapy (Prouty, 1994; Van Werde, 1994a, b) gives the person-centred counsellor an evolved way of working with clients whose profound learning difficulties or psychoses make the establishing and maintenance of psychological contact problematic even though the quality of that contact, once engaged, may be rich. Having explored this lower end of the contact dimension so fully, it is appropriate that we begin to look at the other end of the contact spectrum – relating with the client at very high levels of psychological contact or, as labelled in this chapter, *meeting the client at relational depth*.

A year before his death Rogers wrote about what he called a quality of *'presence'* which he found valuable in his relating with clients. From the oft repeated quote which follows, it appears that he is speaking of his own experiencing at times of working at considerable relational depth with clients (Rogers, 1986):

> When I'm at my best, as a group facilitator or a therapist, I discover another characteristic. I find that when I am closest to my inner, intuitive self, when I am somehow in touch with the unknown in me, when perhaps I am in a slightly altered state of consciousness in the relationship, then whatever I do seems to be full of healing. Then simply my *presence* is releasing and helpful. There is nothing I can do to force this experience, but when I can relax and be close to the transcendental core of me, then I may behave in strange and impulsive ways in the relationship, ways which I cannot justify rationally, which have nothing to do with my thought processes. But these strange behaviors turn out to be *right* in some odd way. At those moments it seems that my inner spirit has reached out and touched the inner spirit of the other. (p. 199)

Some readers have taken this as evidence of Rogers' growing mysticism or even spirituality in the later years of his life. My own view is that he would have been equally interested in the theoretical and empirical exploration of the phenomenon he observed. It is to that end that I shall endeavour, in this chapter, to explore illustrative experiences of clients and counsellors working at relational depth and to tease out some of the theoretical and training issues which are of relevance.

Lace Curtains and Safety Screens

Most of our human relating does not take place at depth. Perhaps that is why we tend to place great value on relational depth when we experience it or read about it from others, even attributing the basis for such relating to 'spiritual' or otherwise mystical aspects of our being. Perhaps we should regard it as a pity that we have to reserve such special labels for those instances where we manage to relate with another human being at depth. Is it relational depth which is the special issue, or should we be turning the coin over and asking serious theoretical questions on why this phenomenon is so rare? Is it, for example, because we are too afraid of others or perhaps of our Selves, or both, to risk meeting each other at relational depth? Perhaps Schopenhauer's old analogy liking humans to hedgehogs (Foulkes and Anthony, 1957) best describes the extent of our evolution in relational terms: that, like hedgehogs, we desperately want to be close enough to feel each other's warmth, but not so close that we feel the prickles!

Most of our relating as humans is not conducted openly and at depth but carefully with a screen between us and the other person. If we are lucky, that screen might be likened to a lace curtain allowing a degree of permeability and at least the comfort of an illusion that we are perceiving and relating with each other at depth. At the other extreme, perhaps for reasons of our pathology and existential need to protect our Self, our safety screen has to be virtually impermeable lest we be destroyed by our experiencing of the other or of our Self reflected in the other (see Lambers, 1994c).

Sometimes our screen is not strictly necessary for our own protection from the other or from a reflection of our Self, but that screen has become a *habit* which we find difficulty in breaking through. In counselling training we see many examples of course members struggling to break through screens put up at a much earlier age to protect them in relating, for example:

- The *incongruent smile* that does not reflect an inner feeling of warmth or appreciation but exists as a defence to portray one of these to the other person in order to pre-empt even the possibility of any negativity in the other's response.
- An *over-effusiveness* is such an obviously incongruent protective device that it is usually challenged very early in training. The sadness of this and most other screens is that the subject genuinely cannot understand the difficulty which others are having with him – after all, this way of behaving has always succeeded before in preventing relational depth – how dare these others ignore that convention?
- On his first visit to Britain and after his first day in an encounter group set in a quiet corner of England, Carl Rogers, with some despair, wondered if British people could ever become client-centred therapists because 'they have to be so damned *polite* with each other!' (Rogers, 1979). He genuinely thought that it would be extremely difficult for people to meet at depth if the rules of their communication were governed by such strict and pervasive considerations of politeness.

But these are just a few of the most common lace curtains or safety screens with which person-centred counsellors struggle in the early days of training. Such lace curtains tend to be further enshrined by the rationalisation that they provide safety for the other person in the relationship by mediating and moderating the communication which that person will receive from us. Of course, the lace curtain also prevents the other person from truly experiencing us and vice versa, which may be to their deficit and ours.

Even in counselling, most of our relating with each other is at a level which is removed from our direct experiencing of the other. The dynamics of this for both counsellor and client are explored in the theory on the 'unspoken relationship' between counsellor and client (Mearns, 1991a, 1994n, o). For our present purpose let us focus only on the part played by the counsellor and leave the client on one side.

The likelihood is that in any therapeutic exchange the counsellor will be 'experiencing' a great deal in relation to the client. However, the vast bulk of that experiencing is filtered and translated into a considered response – a response which is judged to be more likely to be helpful than unhelpful to the client and a response which will be protective rather than risky for the counsellor. The counsellor may further complicate her communication by adding a curtain of *portrayed* warmth or interest to the filtered response.

The resultant counsellor response could relatively easily be analysed into *surface relational competencies*. This is as far as NVQ/SVQ* attempts in Britain have gone to isolate the competencies of therapeutic counselling and part of the problem of defining human processes simply in terms of behavioural objectives. Indeed, the enshrinement of surface relational competencies in the NVQ/SVQ framework may serve to keep counselling and counsellors further removed from meeting the client at relational depth. Simple surface relational competencies defining the level of relating outlined in the previous paragraph might include:

- *Partial or even accurate empathy* – perhaps up to point 3 on the Carkhuff five-point scale (Carkhuff, 1969) and point 2 on the Mearns and Thorne 0–3 scale (Mearns and Thorne, 1988).
- *Warmth* – this would not necessarily be congruent warmth – it could be portrayed warmth expressed perhaps through tone of voice, pace, facial or bodily expression and word choice.
- *Attention* – perhaps implying 'interest' and evidenced by catching changing client meanings and changes in client expression.
- *Communication of understanding* – through the counsellor's repetition, paraphrasing or interpretation.

However, working at relational depth with clients in person-centred counselling goes far beyond such surface relational com-

---

* In Britain, the government has encouraged the development of 'National Vocational Qualifications' and 'Scottish Vocational Qualifications' in counselling. These qualifications seek to be 'competency' based but draw criticism from senior trainers on the naivety of their construction and assessment.

petencies. Perhaps it is best, first of all, to introduce the subject through the *experiences* of clients and counsellors working at relational depth.

Experiences of Working at Relational Depth

The following quotes are derived from earlier research into clients' and counsellors' experiences of counselling (Mearns and Dryden, 1989) and more recent reports by counselling trainees. At this point in the chapter they are presented together to give the reader a general *feeling* for the experience of working at relational depth. Many of the quotes will be re-visited and investigated more closely in later sections.

Clients' experiences

- 'It felt as though he [the counsellor] was right there, in the garden, with me – like he could see it as well.'
- 'It felt as though she was right *inside me* – feeling *me* in the same moment that I was feeling myself.'
- 'The *space* she created for me was huge. It made me realise how little space I usually felt in other relationships.'
- 'She met me fully and openly right away. There were no embellishments – she just quietly opened to me.'
- 'I knew he felt my terror. But it wasn't just that – it was one of those *I knew he knew I knew* . . . things – like we were communicating at a lot of different levels at the same time.'
- 'The depth at which she met me scared me.'

Counsellors' experiences

The first three of the quotes which follow come from experienced person-centred counsellors, whereas the last three come from counsellors during training. Not surprisingly, counsellors are more verbose than clients in describing their experiences!

- 'After the first few minutes I wasn't aware of myself at all – I was right there *with* him [the client], at the edge of his experiencing.'
- 'I spend a few minutes before every session really slowing down my own tempo. If *I* am moving too fast then my client and I will likely stay at a superficial level of relating – talking *about* his experiences rather than experiencing it with him. If *I* can slow down then it can help my client to slow down so that we can meet in a different way than people normally meet.'

- 'I find that I *say* very little when I am really "with" the client. There is no need to say much – he *knows* that I am "with" him so there is no need to remind him of that – also, it is *the very being with him* which is useful, rather than any clever things I might say.'
- 'I had not been *in* that far with a client before . . . I think it happened by accident really . . . I felt so relaxed and at ease with myself. Instead of thinking one step ahead, I just found myself responding to him in the moment – sometimes in ways which were unusual for me. It was amazing how powerful, yet simple, the process was.'
- 'Things are changing quite rapidly for me with clients. There are some with whom I am still a bit "stiff" but I am much "freer" with most of them – with these I find that I don't need to *think* about what I am doing so much – also, I am less *afraid* of them . . . maybe I am less afraid of *me* too.'
- 'I can work with people's very personal material and I can even be very open myself with clients, but in comparing myself with other students' tapes I notice that I don't engage really *deeply* with the client. I think I am scared . . . but I don't know what I'm scared of.'

Early Theory on Working at Relational Depth

A first, and obvious, theoretical point is that working at relational depth does not mean that *all* the psychological contact is at this level. The interaction between counsellor and client will move around the contact spectrum, at times engaging very deeply and on other occasions much more superficially. A 'good' therapeutic relationship should not be seen as one which takes place entirely at a very deep level of contact but, rather, it is one which can easily flow both ways along the dimension of psychological contact. At times the counsellor and client will be at a low level of psychological contact with one or both parties withholding most of their actual experiencing in that moment. That withholding is a perfectly normal and functional part of human relating. However, the essence of a strong person-centred therapeutic relationship is that the counsellor is both willing and able to move to deeper levels of relating. Perhaps the client is also able to do that even early in the counselling process but with other clients that movement may only be possible later in the therapeutic process.

Of course, the person-centred counsellor would not be steering the client into a deeper level of relating or taking him back from that level when the counsellor judges that the client has had enough. As always with the person-centred mode of facilitation the counsellor's task is to show a *willingness* to meet the client at that deeper level through her manifestation of high degrees of the therapeutic conditions (as discussed below). Similarly, the person-centred counsellor would not be making a judgement on when the client has had enough at that level, but awareness of how power-ful this experience usually feels for clients makes the counsellor sensitive to the client's needs when he backs off and moves to a lower level of psychological contact.

It is clear even from the few client and counsellor experiences presented in the previous section that one of the ingredients involved in the counsellor's ability to work at relational depth is a coming together of high levels of the therapeutic conditions of empathy, unconditional positive regard and congruence, as has been discussed in the exploration of the quality of 'presence' (Mearns, 1994k).

> . . . there is a blending together of high degrees of the three core conditions of empathy, unconditional positive regard and congruence. In conceptual terms these three concepts come close together when we look at their extremes, particularly empathy and congruence . . . (p. 7)

The crucial therapeutic condition here is *congruence*. While the aforementioned surface relational competencies might be 'por-trayed' rather than being congruent, working at relational depth cannot be achieved through portrayal. Counsellors may think that they can fool clients with incongruent portrayal and that may even be fairly effective at superficial levels of psychological con-tact, but clients are not going to be prepared to meet counsellors at relational depth when the counsellor is not willing to go there herself. There will be exceptional cases where the client's particu-lar pathology will make him vulnerable to the incongruent coun-sellor. That is a recipe for abuse.

The sixth *therapeutic condition* postulated by Rogers in his famous paper (Rogers, 1957a) was stated thus:

> The communication to the client of the therapist's empathic under-standing and unconditional positive regard is to a minimal degree achieved. (p. 97)

One of the fascinating things about working at relational depth is that both clients and counsellors regularly report that this com-munication is particularly subtle.

The third counsellor quote in the previous section illustrates this:

> . . . There is no need to say much – he *knows* that I am 'with' him so there is no need to remind him of that . . .

This is a most interesting phenomenon. It is as though two people working at relational depth do not need the same 'proofs' or 'reassurances' which may be required when the work is at a lower level of psychological contact. At a lower level of contact we need these proofs to confirm the other's attention but at a higher level of contact there may be other, perhaps more subtle, means of communication which confirm the close contact. When the client feels that close contact, he or she has no doubts about the counsellor's empathy or unconditional positive regard. An example of this was discussed in the experience of the client Terry in Mearns (1994k).

> All the way through the session I was filled with such a wide range of emotions – it felt like I was exploding. Watching that on the video, it doesn't really come across. Another thing was that it felt like Dave was doing an enormous amount right through the session. Again, when watching the video he seems to be very quiet and there were a lot of silences. But 'silences' isn't a word that I would use. It felt like – at points it was unbearable, the amount of emotion and the intensity of the interaction between the two of us. (p. 7)

Although there may not be the usual and obvious ways of communicating empathy and unconditional positive regard when working at relational depth, 'communication' is certainly going on, and at a fairly intense level. For example, in the session with Terry mentioned above the counsellor described his experience in the commentary:

> We were communicating intensely in the session but most of it wasn't happening at the verbal level. I was sitting so close to him that I could feel his body reflecting his emotions. I am quite sure that, because I was feeling so 'present' with him, my body was responding to his through my breathing, my sighs . . . and at times, my forgetting to breathe for long periods! (Daly and Mearns, 1993)

There is a wealth of opportunity for the counselling researcher to explore the perhaps different ways in which communication is operating between counsellor and client working at relational depth. Some practitioners might be inclined to attribute the quality of interaction and communication to the spirituality of the two persons, but such hypothetical constructs tend to foreclose on the issue and do not leave much scope for empirical investigation and further discoveries of an even more fascinating nature.

Looking at communication more broadly and not just in terms of the counsellor's empathy and unconditional positive regard, both clients and counsellors working at relational depth at times report the experience that communication is occurring at many levels of perspective. The fifth client quote in the previous section illustrates this point:

> I knew he felt my terror. But it wasn't just that – it was one of *those I knew he knew I knew* . . . things – like we were communicating at a lot of different levels at the same time.

For students of interpersonal perception, it may not simply be a matter of 'communication' occurring at different levels of perspective, it is likely that *conjunction* is occurring across and between the different levels of perspective of the client and the counsellor. For those interested in exploring this phenomenon of interpersonal perception across different levels of perspective, the key text in the area continues to be Laing, Phillipson and Lee (1966).

The second counsellor experience in the previous section emphasises the importance of the counsellor *preparing* herself or himself to meet the client. For that experienced counsellor this involved 'really slowing down my own tempo'. However, for other less experienced practitioners much more may be involved in preparing to be open to meeting the client at relational depth. For a start, the counsellor must be able to lay to one side her own existence for herself and become quite *still* inside. In meeting the client at relational depth the counsellor will be putting that 'still' Self into relationship with the client's experiencing. Reference is made to this in the exploration of 'presence' (Mearns, 1994k):

> . . . the counsellor is able to be truly *still* within herself, allowing her person fully to resonate with the client's experiencing. In a sense, the counsellor has allowed her person to step right into the client's experiencing without needing to do anything to establish her separateness. This second circumstance is made much easier for the counsellor if she is not self-conscious. (p. 8)

Perhaps we might add a little to the theory by suggesting that a prerequisite to achieving this personal 'stillness' in relationship with the client is not merely 'unselfconsciousness', but also that the counsellor is not *afraid*. To a new reader it may sound strange to think of counsellors being afraid in relation to clients, but most practitioners will recognise the feeling and will know how pervasive and limiting it can be.

The counsellor may either be afraid of the client or of what she may discover about herself. Fear of the client commonly has to do with concern over the client's judgements or misjudgements, for example, fear of the client's judgements of the counsellor's competence or fear of the client's misjudgement of the counsellor's motives. When working at relational depth the counsellor is making herself much more vulnerable in relation to the client because any judgements which will be made by the client are being formulated on the basis of the counsellor's congruent functioning and cannot easily be dismissed. In a sense, the counsellor is putting herself 'on the line' in the work rather than merely risking a superficial portrayal. It is one thing to have my surface relational competencies judged, but can I risk my congruent self being judged?

The second area of fear for the counsellor is related to what she may discover about herself. Perhaps the counsellor will discover that she cannot *sustain* relational depth with clients or, even worse, that she cannot *trust herself* when working at relational depth, or there may be a lurking fear that she will get lost in her own emotionality when fully entering the affective realm of the client.

These are just some of many fears which the counsellor may harbour – fears which might severely inhibit or even prohibit her ability to become 'still' enough in herself to engage the client at relational depth.

When considering the difference between the counsellor preparing herself to work at relational depth compared merely to using her surface relational competencies, we might draw a metaphor with the difference between so-called 'method' acting as against 'scripted' acting. In 'method' acting, the actor will endeavour not to be restrained by a conventional script but will endeavour to project and immerse herself fully into the role to explore how it feels and the variety of responses which are engendered. Similarly, the counsellor who is willing to work with the client at relational depth tries to leave aside conventional ways of responding and projects herself fully into the client's experiencing. Sometimes the counsellor is surprised at the *novelty* of the responses evoked in that way of working. The metaphor of method acting also holds with respect to the *control* exerted, both by the actor and by our counsellor. At any moment the person-centred counsellor may step out of the client's experiencing to function just as effectively at other levels of psychological contact. In early stages of development the person-centred counsellor may have to attend to this boundary in a disciplined fashion, perhaps by leaving space after sessions for reflecting and focusing, just as our method actor, early in her development, may have to attend to her de-roling. Interestingly, person-centred counsellors tend to leave slightly longer spaces between sessions – perhaps there is a developed wisdom which has come ahead of our theory.

This theory section has emphasised very personal dimensions of the counsellor, including her congruence and 'stillness' not to mention fears. This begs the question of how we train person-centred counsellors to be able to work at relational depth with clients. Appropriately, that is the focus of the final section of this chapter.

Training to Work at Relational Depth with Clients

Early in training it is perfectly understandable that many person-centred counselling course members will go through what can be a fairly lengthy phase of developing their surface relational competencies. This is usually part of the progression which begins with a growing awareness of one's incompetence and helps the course member to feel better about his functioning having seen his development from *unconscious incompetence*, through *conscious incompetence* and on to a degree of *conscious competence* (Clarkson and Gilbert, 1991). In developing the surface relational competencies there is a fairly natural tendency towards *portrayal*. The course member strains to portray himself as a warm, empathic, accepting counsellor no matter how testing the client may be. The important challenge, and one which can separate low-level competency based person-centred training from training appropriate to working at relational depth, is to help the course member to begin to challenge the long-term veracity of portrayal and so begin his graduation from 'conscious competence' to 'unconscious competence'. That graduation is facilitated by the fostering of the course member's *congruence*. This is not an easy process and it is usually lengthy. Indeed, it should not necessarily be expected to be complete during the basic training course but, if the course member is helped to continue development during the rest of the 'training period', then his fostering of his own congruence can continue to develop. In this regard the concept of a 'training period' extending for some three to five years regardless of the length of the actual training course is a useful notion (Dryden et al., 1995).

Given the ongoing support and challenge from a lengthy or intensive training course, the course member will eventually find that it is basically untenable to maintain the portrayal. The course member will ask 'How can I possibly feel warm towards *all* my clients?', 'How can I possibly be expected to be empathic all the time?' and 'How could I feel accepting to every single client who comes to see me?' The course member might feel somewhat despairing in asking questions like these, but his trainer would be delighted that he was coming to the point where he realised that a simple portrayal of therapeutic qualities which were not fully integrated into the Self and in that sense congruent, could no longer be sustained. Logically, the course member would see that the answer to all three questions is 'I can't'. Now the course member is thrown back on who he is as a person rather than trying to portray some ideal Self. Loosened up in this way the person-centred course member finds that he becomes a little more natural and perhaps more often spontaneous in his work with clients and also in relation to other members of the training course. Now he is testing out his own congruence and finding that if he is more himself then the sky does not fall down, fellow course members do not despise him, trainers do not throw him off the course and clients do not evaporate. Indeed, course members are often both excited and amazed by the fact that congruent relating tends to lead to quite opposite consequences.

While the course member is moving from portrayal to early congruence in actual counselling work, other aspects of the training designed to foster personal development will also be contributing. One of the reasons why person-centred training places more emphasis on group work than personal therapy for the attainment of personal development objectives (Mearns, 1994c; see also Chapter 7) is that the various groups present more personally *challenging* interpersonal encounters than does therapeutic contact with one other person. Once course members realise that conventional 'politeness' is an insufficient basis on which to sustain intense relationships amongst them, there develops an increasing challenge to incongruent ways of relating with each other. That challenge is enhanced by the generally supportive climate and, hopefully, by the consistent congruence of the trainers.

As the personal development process unfolds for each course member there will develop a greater awareness for each person of their 'lace curtains and safety screens'. Gently, and with the support of colleagues, the trainee counsellor will be helped to step beyond those lace curtains which are no longer needed for protection but have become habitual. Screens which are still needed for safety can be noted and respected. Now that he has gained awareness of the screen perhaps he can work around it while continuing, gently, to challenge the basis of the screen. An important dimension of person-centred training and also of person-centred counselling practice is respect for our self-protective structures: whether or not they are needed in the present, they have probably helped to save our life in the past, so they merit some respect.

This movement away from the collective pathology of incongruence to the fostering of the development of congruence increases the course member's *trust* of himself. In the theoretical language of the person-centred approach, the direction of movement of the course member is one of enhancing self-acceptance which brings with it an internalising of the locus of evaluation, a decrease in the need to defend oneself and consequently a reduction in the counsellor's vulnerability and a reduced self-consciousness. These shifts help the counsellor to feel secure enough and free enough in himself to engage with the client at relational depth. Now the counsellor is not operating at a level of portrayed conscious competence but has attained that kind of congruent 'unconscious competence' which allows him to function fluidly and creatively in relation to the client.

These last few paragraphs on the process of personal development within person-centred training may give the illusion of foreshortening what is a lengthy and intense process. Chapter 7 should dispel that illusion in the greater detail and slower pace it offers on personal development during training. Hopefully the pace of the present chapter gives a sense of the overall process of personal development as well as its centrality to person-centred training. Our next chapter considers some dynamics which are also central to the training.

3
Central Dynamics in Person-Centred Counselling Training

The word 'dynamic' is frequently used in psychotherapy literature. I think it took me about ten years to learn what 'dynamic' meant. Of course I hid my ignorance – that is why it took me ten years. Once it is grasped, 'dynamic' is a wonderfully rich concept. It denotes something which is essentially in perpetual conflict, but in that conflict it has life and vigour and powerful impact on people. Counselling trainers work with 'dynamics' all the time: How challenging should we make this experience? How fully congruent can I be in relations with my trainees? How much of my Self can I give? With all these dynamics there is argument and counter-argument. Creative balances are established only to be challenged and revised at some later time. Perhaps it is that lived conflict which is important – perhaps we must never find an enduring balance to the conflict.

In my work as a person-centred counselling trainer I find dynamics which never go away or submit to easy resolution – that must mean that they are important. This chapter is devoted to an unravelling of these dynamics central to person-centred counselling training:

- The 'responsibility dynamic'
- The development of self-acceptance
- Individualisation of the curriculum
- Individualisation of assessment

These are crucial areas of potential conflict and struggle for course members and trainers alike. They are not independent of each other – indeed, each of these dynamics interacts with every other. That is precisely what we should expect in person-centred counselling training, for it is an integrated whole fundamentally derived from the trainee counsellor's evolving personality.

The 'Responsibility Dynamic'

An essential dynamic within person-centred counselling itself is that the counsellor maintains a professional responsibility *to* the client while not accepting responsibility *for* the client (Mearns and Thorne, 1988; Mearns, 1994l, m). Similarly, in person-centred counselling training, the trainer will maintain a responsibility to the course members but will endeavour not to take responsibility for them. Empowerment of clients and course members alike is not engendered by taking responsibility away from them, but by creating a context where the course member or client more and more takes responsibility for herself.

Being Responsible to the Course Member

Maintaining a professional responsibility to the course members in person-centred counselling training means being clear about the *contract* which defines their relationships with staff and, thereafter, being consistent in meeting the trainer's part of that agreement. Hence, the trainer would be maintaining her responsibility to the course members by consistently fulfilling agreed aspects of their contract such as the following:

- attending scheduled meetings;
- preparing promised workshop introductions and lectures;
- giving feedback on written work;
- giving feedback on the trainer's view of the course member's progress;
- enquiring about client work in supervision;
- integrating the therapeutic conditions, including congruence, appropriate to a training (not a counselling) relationship;
- maintaining the boundaries between the course and the training institution;
- taking responsibility in the selection of course members.

Different person-centred counselling training courses might take issue with some of these areas of responsibility deemed to be appropriate to trainers. For example, it might be argued that it is 'not person-centred' for trainers to take responsibility for the selection of course members and that self-selection is more consistent with the model (see Chapter 5), or that the trainer should leave the structuring of the supervision relationship entirely to the course member, or that the trainer should desist from giving feedback unless that is requested by the course member. All these possible areas of responsibility can be argued and different groups of trainers will work out their own balances. In creating that balance, new trainers should be wary of making generalisations from the counselling relationship to the training relationship. Course members are not clients and the responsibilities of the trainer to the course member are different from those of the counsellor to the client. For example, if the training course is making *any* statement to the public about the training graduate, such as conferring its qualification on the graduate, then it bears a responsibility to that public. The only way to escape this responsibility is to decline to offer qualifications or references. I shall return to this issue of inferred responsibilities later in the section, but while I am emphasising the importance of the trainers' being clear about their responsibilities to the course members and consistent in meeting these responsibilities, I need to warn against slavish adherence to responsibilities. It is one thing to be diligent in meeting our responsibilities to course members but we are human beings and as such we cannot always *be* there, physically or metaphorically. If we make too much of a sacrifice of ourselves we are actually slipping from an adult to a parental way of relating with our course members. We have become the self-sacrificing 'parent' who always must put the other person first. Not only does this develop an inappropriately parental position on the responsibility dynamic, but it is a dreadful model to present to counsellors struggling to establish their own responsibilities in relation to clients. It is important that the trainer models the ability to look after herself.

Not Being Responsible for *the Course Member*

Having listed some of the ways in which the person-centred counselling trainer might hold her responsibility *to* the members of a training course, there will also be many areas where the trainer would avoid taking responsibility *for* the course members. The following represent just a few of the demands which course members might make on the trainer to take responsibility for them:

- tell me how I should start my sessions with clients;
- tell me how I should work with this client;
- tell me why my client is doing this;
- look after me more during training;
- tell me how to behave in the different training groups;
- protect me when I am under attack from other course members;
- don't be so 'hard' on me with your feedback;
- organise my counselling experience for me;
- tell me whether I should 'pass' or 'defer'.

In training for other therapeutic approaches the trainer might happily fit into the 'parental' role in response to demands such as these. However, the person-centred trainer would be inclined to push such responsibilities back to the course member, inviting her to exercise more centrality in her locus of evaluation. Following the concise yet symbolic language of Transactional Analysis, the person-centred counselling trainer is endeavouring to maintain an unswerving Adult–Adult relationship with the course member and resisting demands to slip into Parent–Child.

This firm line on the responsibility dynamic may demand some accommodation for person-centred counselling training on the part of accrediting bodies, who, influenced by other traditions, may generally expect trainers to take more responsibility *for* course members. For example, unless informed by the different responsibility orientation of the person-centred approach, accrediting bodies might carry expectations such as the following:

- a training course should expect *reports* from the individual counselling supervisors of course members rather than regard the supervisory relationship as confidential;
- a training course should organise counselling opportunities for course members rather than expecting course members substantially to do that for themselves;
- a training course should operate a system of tutor-assessment rather than student self-assessment.

Rather than run away from the inappropriate demands of such accrediting bodies, it behoves person-centred counselling trainers to make their case for practices consistent with their own model. For example, in Britain, person-centred counselling training courses have established their case so well that investigating panels from the main accrediting body, the British Association of Counselling (BAC), would generally *expect* course practices like the above to be consistent with the model. If, for example, a person-centred counselling training course operated a system of tutor assessment, the panel might want the course to justify that deviation from the practice of self-assessment which would be more consistent with the model. This accommodation, relevant in different ways to all therapeutic approaches, is achieved by dialogue with institutions rather than by withdrawing from them.

In counselling training we can never fully escape responsibility *for* the course member because it is a logical derivative of having some responsibility *to* the course member's clients, *to* the profession and *to* the public. An extreme example serves to illustrate the point. If it was clear from her counselling audiotapes that a course member was being abusive to certain clients then the trainer would feel both a responsibility to the course member but also, in some regard, to the client, the profession and the public. Once any responsibility is felt *to* other parties then the derivative is that the trainer has an element of responsibility *for* the course member. In this extreme situation the trainer would want to help and support the course member as much as possible and in that way be responsible to her, but the trainer would also be intent on stopping the abuse, which is a different kind of responsibility. Person-centred counselling trainers cannot adopt a simple position on the responsibility dynamic whereby they are consistently responsible *to* course members but never responsible *for* them. However, equally, an exceptional case such as this does not remove the central importance of the responsibility dynamic for person-centred counselling trainers. The challenge for trainers is to draw the line of responsibility very close to the course member rather than too close to the trainer, so that it will only be in the exceptional situation that the trainer must intervene by taking responsibility to protect the client or the profession, and even then only after helping the course member to identify her own responsibility in the matter.

Maintaining the Tension within the Responsibility Dynamic

Course members frequently find difficulty with the responsibility dynamic within person-centred counselling training because it can challenge many deeply held cultural presumptions. This is particularly true in Britain where education at all levels is dramatically authority-oriented. Even mature students are generally expected to fit into a ubiquitous child-like sycophancy in relation to the 'teachers'. It can be difficult for people coming from such a culture to make the transformation whereby they will take responsibility for themselves in an educational relationship. This is a genuine difficulty for course members. Such is the perverseness of 'the teacher taking responsibility for the student' in British culture that course members may understandably interpret a refusal to take such responsibility as neglect. Box 3.1 illustrates this experience of a course member, contributed by her from her personal journal.

Maintaining the tension within the responsibility dynamic by refusing to take responsibility *for* the course member is not

---

Box 3.1

Confusion

I am really confused. I have never felt more positive about anything in my life than I do about this course. I also feel really positive about the staff. And yet, I wonder if they don't care about me. If they cared about me they would look after me more – they wouldn't let me go through this pain. I really don't understand – they *seem* very loving people and they seem to like me, but they don't care for me – they don't look after me. I am really confused – I see the *quality* of their meeting with me but I would also expect someone meeting me that way to offer more.

'comfortable' for either party, but it does encourage the further internalisation of the course member's locus of evaluation. In a training relationship we can expect the course member to have a locus of evaluation which is at least fairly internalised from the outset, otherwise she should be a client rather than a trainee counsellor. As the course member takes more and more responsibility for her own development and her own assessment of her development in all areas of the training across personal issues, therapeutic skill and understanding of theory, she is constantly being encouraged by the very process of the course to internalise her locus of evaluation. Hence the internalisation process is continually being exercised to a point where the course member can become the *reflective practitioner* so valued within the profession (Dryden et al., 1995; BAC, 1996c).

Holding the tension within the responsibility dynamic and thereby encouraging the further internalisation of the locus of evaluation also contributes to the course member's development in relation to her self-acceptance explored in the next section.

The Development of Self-Acceptance

The major consideration within the personal development dimension of person-centred counselling training is the course member's advancement in relation to self-acceptance. Many factors contribute to the development of self-acceptance and many more derive from it. For example, we might consider that the trainee counsellor's *conditionality* in relation to certain client groups would demand work specifically in relation to those groups. Such work is certainly appropriate but also the counsellor's degree of self-acceptance will be relevant to her prejudice. This causal link between self-acceptance and other-acceptance is well described in Proposition 18 of Rogers' personality theory (Rogers, 1951):

> When the individual perceives and accepts into one consistent and integrated system all his sensory and visceral experiences, then he is necessarily more understanding of others and is more accepting of others as separate individuals. (p. 520)

Interpersonal Challenge in the Context of the Therapeutic Conditions

Intensive personal development work within person-centred counselling training faces the course member with herself more surely and effectively than any amount of individual therapy (see Chapter 7). The course member becomes aware of the *introjections* which have been formative in her past and those which continue to have life in the present. The interpersonal challenges of both large and small training groups inevitably raise not only a number of *blind spots* for the course member but those much more common areas which, though not wholly blind, are dimly illuminated and substantially feared. An example of this was the course member who allowed herself to become fully aware of her presumption that *'If I really get close to people I will be dangerous for them'*. For the trainee this had been a long-held introjection about Self but one which had seldom been focused upon. For months during early training she had used her many self-protective strategies to remain ever so slightly but firmly detached from others on the course. In training such as this, however, the challenge from others continues. However, it continues alongside degrees of the therapeutic conditions whereby she is heard and valued as well as being congruently challenged. Once this powerful combination of conditions had allowed her to face her fear she found that it had little life in her present and was relatively easily laid aside. This element of personal development contributed significantly to her self-acceptance: she had faced a significant area of self-doubt squarely and had gained strength within her self-concept not only because her fear was relatively groundless in the present, but for the very fact that she had found the courage to face it.

Even in the case of those ghosts from the past which still have some life in the present, they are not usually as powerful as the fear attached to them. For example, there was the course member who discovered: 'I actually got thoroughly angry with her [another trainee] – it was painful, but the sky did not fall down –

the world did not end.' This course member had expressed congruent anger for one of the few times in her life. It was not a pleasant experience but neither was it traumatic. She could now begin to accept this part of herself rather than spend most of her relational life seeking strategies to avoid congruent spontaneity lest any angry content should be released.

The interpersonal challenging in conjunction with degrees of the therapeutic conditions is vital within person-centred counselling training and relatively unparalleled in training from other therapeutic approaches. In Gestalt training, at least that which is modelled on the example set by Fritz Perls, the challenge certainly exists but may serve to drive the fear underground in the absence of the therapeutic conditions. Object relations training also offers considerable challenge through its use of *learning groups*, but, once again, in the absence of the therapeutic conditions, the intense challenge may simply induce course members to find more sophisticated ways of hiding.

The Unconditional Positive Regard of the Trainers

Another active ingredient which contributes to the course member's development of self-acceptance is the action of the unconditional positive regard of the trainers upon those parts of the course member's personality which she may be rejecting. Just as in counselling, unconditional positive regard on the part of trainers can initiate a 'counter-conditioning' effect (Lietaer, 1984), as exemplified in the following dialogue between trainee and trainer.

> *Trainee*: I am thoroughly disgusted with myself – just because he [the client] is a *man* I seem to be ready to find that he is a bastard – all the time. I am fighting with a part of me which is angry – angry and scared – I wish I could get rid of that part.
>
> *Trainer*: I see how frustrated . . . how angry you are at your own anger. I also wonder how important that anger *is* for you, or *was* for you at some time . . . I guess it *may* have been quite an important part of you . . .

This kind of intervention is typical of the difference between a trainer's response and that of a counsellor. It includes the empathy of the counsellor but it also presumes more internalisation of the locus of evaluation on the part of the trainee in actively pointing to one part of her personality. In affirming the possibility of at least the historical importance of even the most dismissed part of the personality it opens the door to the course member's integration and a further step towards self-acceptance. With clients, whose locus of evaluation might be more externalised, a person-centred counsellor would not make such a pointing intervention because it would be in danger of leading the client and further alienating her from her own locus of evaluation. The course member, on the other hand, can be trusted to treat the trainer's suggestions as hypotheses which may or may not have veracity. For a discussion of locus of evaluation as a determining variable in the process of person-centred counselling, see Mearns (1994d).

'Coming Out'

Person-centred counselling training provides a variety of contexts in which the course member can 'come out' in relation to feared, disliked or even hated parts of her Self. Owning, publicly, these parts of Self both indicates and engenders a gain in self-acceptance. Three of the training contexts in which course members may 'come out' are:

1 Numerous one-to-one relationships among course members, between course members and staff, in practice counselling sessions and between course members and counselling supervisors.
2 Small groups, designed to focus on group supervision and personal development.
3 Unstructured large group meetings involving the whole course membership including staff.

Course members may use these as three *levels* of 'coming out'. The more private one-to-one relationships provide the security and exclusivity which allows the first awareness or at least the first public mention of feared, disliked or hated parts of the Self. With the confidence arising from this first voicing, the course member may then disclose the issue and explore its ramifications in a small group context. The unstructured large group, which can be very large with perhaps 40 members, offers a more spectacular arena that may be used by the course member who wants to 'come out' to this part of her Self in as public a way as possible. These various levels of public disclosure may reflect a progression within the course member's integration of this part of the Self. Certainly, when course members use the large group in this kind of way the consequent gain in self-acceptance is clearly apparent.

When the feared or hated parts of the Self are publicly exposed and the 'public' genuinely does not reject or pillory, and when those same feared or hated parts are faced as legitimate parts of the Self with a basis and a function in the historical development and survival of the Self, they become accepted and integrated into the Self. Some may still be disliked, but the person no longer dislikes her whole Self because of them – thus self-acceptance has progressed.

This internalised self-acceptance may make its major movement even very late in the training in some course members for whom the internal battle has been memorable. No matter how late such gains are made, it is the fact that they happen which is important.

Individualisation of the Curriculum

The person-centred approach has a special awareness of the importance of the course member being at the centre of her learning. It would, of course, be impossible to design a training entirely around the evolving needs of each and every individual course member unless the course included only one student, but careful design can maximise the possibilities for that individualisation of the curriculum.

Limits to Individualisation

The limits on this process are not only created by the fact that there will be an inevitable competition of needs, but also because professional training confers some expectation in the mind of other professionals and also prospective clients that the person-centred counsellor will have covered, or at least been introduced to, those areas considered to be important for professional practice. Hence, a dynamic is created between the person-centred principle of an individualised curriculum and the need to ensure a degree of core and comprehensive coverage. An extreme person-centred learning perspective would say that the whole matter can be left entirely to the individual course member who will be sufficiently aware and responsible to ensure that her coverage is up to professionally acceptable standards. This is an arguable position but it might also be suggested that any professional training course should take responsibility for at least *introducing* the course member to both the breadth and the depth of the area of study so that the student became aware of what existed in the field as a guide to future choice.

A classic mistake in person-centred training is to throw the whole decision-making process about the curriculum open to the student body in the naive belief that this is a 'person-centred' way to proceed. This approach *is* appropriate to certain learning contexts, for example in person-centred experiential large group work *or* in person-centred encounter group learning. In these learning contexts there is no defined curriculum beyond the experienced and evolving needs of the participants, hence the relevance of an entirely open-learning approach. However, it is both pedagogically naive, not to mention professionally irresponsible, simply to transpose this methodology on to other learning contexts such as professional counselling training, where the learning needs are not entirely open and where there *are* limiting features felt both by trainers and professional bodies around issues such as:

- course members should have experience of actual counselling work with clients;
- course members should engage 'counselling supervision' in relation to that client work;
- course members should look at the issues of their personal development which impinge, or are likely to impinge, upon their client work;
- course members should be aware of the elements within their core theoretical model of practice.

Individualising within the Limits of the Field

These are concerns which define the *field* in which the trainee counsellor and trainer are working – they cannot simply be ignored. However, it is eminently possible to individualise the curriculum *within* these boundaries by creating learning contexts where course members can bring to the fore those issues which are of greatest relevance to them. Hence, individual supervision relationships, supervision groups, personal development groups and the unstructured large group are contexts where any individual participant can strongly influence what happens. Although many of these have a defined area of relevance, in total they offer openings to any personal or professional area of concern or interest for the trainee counsellors and actively encourage the course members' structuring of events rather than these being dictated by the trainers.

In most training courses that seek to find a workable position in relation to this dynamic of the individualisation of the curriculum, there would be a 'moving feast' of lectures, workshops, videos and visiting specialists which would run alongside the less structured individual and group contexts. Though the presentation of this material may be systematised in a way that makes sense to tutors and course validators, there is no serious expectation that each element will be being introduced at its optimal time for every course member. However, the aim in this presentation is not that it should represent meaningful learning on presentation for every course member but that it will help the course member at least to become aware of the boundaries of the core model and the many elements which it includes. Such information is power: in this case it is the course member's power to return to any of these now known areas once they become closer to her needs. For example, when the course member is introduced to the theoretical distinction between self-actualisation and the actualising tendency along with the possible conflict which can arise between these, the matter may be of a purely theoretical concern and not at all 'meaningful' in terms of her present needs. However, failing to introduce the course member to this crucial dynamic within client-centred personality theory does her the enormous disservice of not offering her one of the potentially most useful of Rogers' constructions for understanding disorder and merely hoping that she 'discovers' it for herself.

Denying the course member information is not an empowering way to proceed, neither is the presumption that elements of theory will be meaningful in the order in which they are provided. Hence, a practical approach to the dynamic of the individualisation of the curriculum is not one which leaves the course member entirely to flounder on her own but one which helps her at least to become aware of the field and offers contexts in which she might operationalise an individualised curriculum. The 'teaching' of theory is considered in more detail in Chapter 9.

Individualisation of Assessment

Assessment procedures in higher education are traditionally neurotic endeavours whereby huge amounts of time are devoted to the minutiae of fairness and reliability in order to mask the much more important and problematic question of validity.

Assessment is happening all the time in person-centred counselling training. Indeed, with its considerable emphasis on feedback from trainer to course member and between course members, probably more time is devoted to formative and diagnostic assessment than in most other higher education endeavours.

Individualising Assignments

In the setting of assignment work it is perfectly possible to individualise the process by denoting the general area of an assignment but encouraging the course member to choose her own assignment title and contents from within that broad area. This methodology offers a simple yet effective way to cope with the fact that the mature entry to counselling training creates a situation where there is a wide range of prior educational background among course members, with some having completed a doctorate in a related subject such as psychology and others having had very little prior educational experience, though perhaps a considerable amount of practical experience. Hence, if we were to set one essay title within the area of, say, 'The Therapeutic Conditions' we would inevitably be setting a task which was too simple for many and too complex for many. However, if we individualise the process by inviting the course member to produce an assignment *within the area of* 'The Therapeutic Conditions' by choosing a title and task which is meaningful to her and represents an attainable challenge, then the possibility arises for each course member to use that assignment meaningfully and for it to become a medium through which she can express her attainment. Hence, one course member for whom this theoretical material was new might choose to explore the three main therapeutic conditions, examining the contributions to the area in three texts and exemplifying the conditions in relation to her own experience. Another course member, with considerable background in the area, might set a completely different task which represented a challenge for her. Her challenge to herself might be 'to evaluate research into the therapeutic conditions to explore Rogers' hypothesis of their necessity and sufficiency'. If this latter task had been set for the first student the result would be despair and if the first task was set for the second course member the consequence would be boredom, and in both cases alienation from the assessment procedure. Assessment is a means of both course member and trainer gaining and sharing information on the course member's attainment. To that end it is surprising to note that individualisation of assignments is not the norm within higher education. Perhaps because it is not the norm and course members are not familiar with the personal self-assessment demands implicit in the process of individualising assignments, some course members may initially find it frightening rather than freeing. One course member, who could not imagine herself being responsible for creating her own assignment title, begged 'please just give me a title – I can't do it'. Taking responsibility for oneself in new situations may be important for the development of the 'reflective practitioner' but it can still be painful.

Giving Feedback

Getting assignment feedback from staff can be a feared process in the minds of course members more used to the bizarre attempts within mainstream education, where scrawled comments in red pen carry little in the way of sensitivity and respect. A much more creative, less threatening and also complete way to give feedback to course members is by means of audiotaped comment where the full meaning of the speaker's words can be heard. My finding over many years of operating an audiotaped feedback system is that it is much preferred by course members and, also, that such feedback is experienced as coming from a real person rather than simply from an impersonal authority.

Summative Self-Assessment

The most problematic area for person-centred training is not diagnostic or formative assessment or even the assessment of individual assignments, but the concept of summative assess-ment. Carl Rogers was clearly in favour of dispensing with summative assessment. His argument, espoused regularly in the Center for Studies of the Person, was that such assessment gave entirely the wrong messages to the individual, implying that she had reached a point of acceptable sufficiency in regard to training or expertise. Rogers might have been slightly more in favour of self-assessment had it been prevalent at the time but he was certainly against the idea that an external judgement such as that of staff was at all relevant.

While Rogers' position here was philosophically coherent, par-ticularly when combined with a parallel refusal to confer any kind of certification, it allowed for little dialogue with conventional training and learning institutions. In more recent years person-centred counselling has attempted the greater challenge of staying within institutions of higher learning but justifying and validating the superior effectiveness of student summative self-assessment.

Some examples of courses which have obtained the approval of professional and educational institutions for their self-assessment systems include TCPA (Greece), PCT Britain, the Institute for Person-Centred Learning, the University of East Anglia Diploma in Counselling and the University of Strathclyde Diploma in Counselling.

In designing a summative self-assessment policy and procedure, trainers have to pay regard to their training institution and the conventional thinking about assessment which is prevalent within that institution. This does not mean that person-centred counselling trainers should feel slavishly required to fit into conventions laid down for other courses, simply that it is important to consider the *context* when determining the assessment policy which is to be argued during validation of the training. The validation process of any course actually encourages educators to put forward the procedures they want and to justify these by argument. Too often trainers are over-awed by validation procedures and feel obliged to accommodate to existing conventions.

In an attempt to include at least some self-assessment yet conform broadly to the conventions of tutor assessment within the institution, courses sometimes promote a case for 'an element of self-assessment' which might count for, say 20%, towards the final summative assessment decision. Another approach is to initiate a self-assessment system along the lines detailed in Box 3.2 but to cope with the conventions of the institution by introducing a caveat whereby tutors have the power, though rarely used, to veto a course member's decision. While this has the effect of taking the course members through the important processes of self-assessment it will not contribute positively to the aforementioned responsibility dynamic because, in effect, the course member is not actually being given an absolute decision-making responsibility. Even although the veto is *never* used, in the eyes of the course members it still remains a power retained by staff. It is only when the power of decision-making is actually divested to the course member that a summative self-assessment system exists.

Box 3.2 exemplifies one such self-assessment process, currently in use within a university. Among the most recent cohort of the course described in Box 3.2, nine out of 28 trainee counsellors chose to defer their award for at least one year. This is typical of one important facet of self-assessment – that there is a much higher rate of deferment than in any system of tutor-assessment. This higher rate is not caused by a self-deprecation factor on the part of course members, because that is readily challenged by other trainees and the trainers. The real reason for the higher

---

Box 3.2
A Self-Assessment System

Steps in the process:

- Course members are informed of the self-assessment system in pre-course publicity.
- A detailed description of the self-assessment system is written into the student handbook.
- The rationale for the self-assessment system is described during the first day of the course.
- Throughout the course, trainees maintain a 'personal journal' recording their progress.
- Before the start of the final term, one workshop is devoted to 'Self-Assessment Processes' where course members are taken through the remaining steps in the self-assessment system.
- Early in the final term, course members participate in a workshop on 'Personality Mapping' which includes reflection and assessment of the development of parts of their Self.
- During a residential period, and also in and around course time, course members undertake numerous consultations with peers, trainers, individual supervisor and sometimes with clients, on their progress in relation to counselling and the course.
- Over a period of weeks, course members write their 10,000 word 'Self-Assessment Statement' which details all aspects of their functioning on the course, in external individual supervision and within their counselling practicum.
- A copy of this statement is presented to the course for access to all course members and trainers.
- Each course member spends between 30 minutes and 1 hour in presenting their Self-Assessment to members of their supervision group for detailed feedback.
- The final stage of the process involves course members presenting their Self-Assessment *decision*, on whether to take their Diploma or to defer, to the whole course community, with time available for reaction to their decision.

---

deferment rate on self-assessed courses is that these rates are *realistic* – it is tutor-assessed courses which tend to produce too high pass rates because their external tutor assessment is both less valid and less reliable. As person-centred theory would predict, self-assessment gives the power to the person who is potentially in the best position to make such judgements. The course member knows better when she is not ready; the course member knows when she has not fully enough used the opportunities of the course; the course member knows when she has had a counselling practice which is somewhat too narrow to give confidence for future working; the course member knows when there are still certain 'holes' in the personality; the course member knows when her excellent assignment performance reflects an academic ability but masks difficulties in personal development. An adequate self-assessment system has released into the assessment process an assessor who has a much more intimate knowledge of the object of assessment. In tutor-assessed systems the course member is encouraged into a game of hiding weaknesses and portraying whatever she thinks the assessor will perceive as strengths. Within that process the trainee counsellor is taken away from her locus of evaluation. Looking specifically at the recent course mentioned, most of the nine course members who deferred would have passed conventional assessment systems. Indeed, their assignment work, on which tutor-assessment would be based, was extremely good in many cases. The nine course members who deferred on this counselling course will likely take their Diplomas within one, two or perhaps three years, having met their own learning or development objectives. At that time they will take a Diploma which is truly *theirs* and which will have meaning throughout their lives.

There follows a selection of comments which course members have made following the self-assessment process. The selection is not meant to be representative of all students. In fact, it is probably unrepresentative in the sense that six of these nine course members deferred on self-assessment and also three of the nine are negative about the assessment process. Nevertheless, although they are not representative, what they have to say offers description on how the process may be experienced. None of these course members was on the recent course referred to earlier.

Some course members *valued* the demanding nature of the self-assessment process:

- 'This is the first course that I haven't passed first time. Usually courses rely on written work, even if they are about people. My whole psychology training was like that. Right up to and including my PhD I sailed through. This one-year counselling course was the first assessment which asked me to look at how I worked with people from day one to the last day. It "found me out", and I am glad of that. I have spent much of this year beginning the job of developing myself. I'm on the way – another year should be enough for me to do what I want to do.

This is the finest assessment system I have encountered. The fact that I "failed" it is a mark of its success, and mine.'

- 'I didn't give myself the Diploma. What helped me was my classmates giving me negative feedback – and doing it with caring and sometimes with pain. I know now that I have a huge "blind spot" that I need to address some more before I give myself the Diploma. Actually, on my own, I couldn't have made the decision because it *was* a blind spot. I couldn't see it. In the end I said to myself, "James, these good people wouldn't all be saying this to you if there wasn't something in it!" So, I have deferred, and look forward to the next year.'

- 'The torment within myself over whether to award myself the Diploma or not was incredible. It was a battle between my need for the piece of paper and my integrity – fortunately, my integrity won.'

- 'I knew this self-assessment thing was coming, but I had no idea how *powerful* it would be. Producing my self-assessment statement was like summing up the whole of my being, not just me as a counsellor. But, I suppose that's the way it should be.'

- 'Awarding myself that Diploma was the most joyous thing I have ever done with myself. It wasn't just a matter of deserving it because I had tried very hard. In the self-assessment consultations I realised that I had also made a good *success* out of the course.'

- On reflection, the very *fact* that I really wanted to award myself the Diploma in the face of such consistent contrary feedback from my supervision group probably showed how I hadn't developed enough.'

Some course members *did not value* the self-assessment process:

- 'I did not like the process. I really *needed* to award myself the Diploma, but I couldn't do that in the face of such total opposition in the community.'

- 'I struggled at the end with not being fully satisfied with *me* being the one to award myself the Diploma. I wanted other people, the staff, to do it. It would have felt more like a "prize" if other people had done it for me.'

- 'I worked really hard – it wasn't my fault that everything in my life conspired against me that year. I wanted to take the Diploma – I deserved it for my effort. Other people didn't have to do a part-time job, look after a family and look after a husband while they did the full-time course. It's no wonder that I didn't find it easy. I deserved the Diploma for my *effort*. But I didn't take it because of other people's feedback that, although I had tried hard, I hadn't actually achieved enough and that I still had a lot to do. I am not happy with the pressure which the large group puts on you in a self-assessment system like this. I did the assignments so I should have passed the course!'

The effectiveness of self-assessment in intensive counselling training should not be taken to presume that it will be successful if transported either into shorter training or other learning contexts. As with any aspect of pedagogy, the *context* is vital. Self-assessment will certainly not work where the course members have not themselves made large personal commitments to the course, where they do not have respect for the course and where they are, otherwise, treated in a Parent–Child manner by trainers.

It is possible to 'slip through' any assessment system, but that is more difficult with self-assessment. It is easier to fool trainers than to fool oneself. Also, the prospect of the challenge of peers and trainers is a powerful experience – in self-assessment the course members realise that the decisions which another student makes for herself affect the value of their own qualification, so there is little hesitation in voicing dissent if a course member perceived as weak should be proposing to take the qualification.

Fortunately, there are occasions when, in the eyes of other course members and tutors, an individual course member chooses to take the award despite widespread disagreement. Thank goodness that there are some such instances because these prove that the system is not tyrannical – in any case, such an individual may be *correct* in her decision!

The responsibilities for the trainers are not diminished in a self-assessment system. Since so much responsibility is being put on to the course member for her own assessment and since that is usually an alien experience as far as our education systems are concerned, then it behoves the counselling trainers to be as *clear* as possible about the steps, the process and their feedback. Although the trainers do not have the final power as far as the self-assessment decision is concerned, their feedback will be important for course members. For this reason it is crucial that the staff are as open as possible in their challenging of trainees throughout the course and not just during the later stages of the self-assessment process. In giving challenging feedback to course members, both during the course and in the self-assessment phase, trainers must be aware and careful of the nature of their *inferences*. For example, it is easy, but not strictly logical, to infer that a course member who has continuing difficulties in relation to 'authority' figures and has not successfully negotiated issues of power during the training, might be inappropriate for employment as a counsellor. While that is certainly possible, it is also an inference which may be full of holes. A person who has continuing difficulties in relation to authority might still function very well as a counsellor, providing she finds a work context that does not face her with challenging clients or colleagues.

If a course is including a meaningful self-assessment process the trainers need to consider what support they are going to offer during the deferral period. In a sense a 'deferral' period is still part of a course, and the trainers may be said to have a continuing responsibility towards deferring students in their efforts to accomplish their individual objectives during the deferral period. Hence the course might offer continued individual consultation or even a regular support group for deferring students.

This chapter has gone full circle. It began with the ways in which core staff were responsible *to* course members and it has ended with another example of that form of responsibility. Thus far in this book considerable reference has been made to 'the staff', 'the trainers', but nothing has yet been offered by way of description of the people who occupy this role. Before we begin to look at the issues involved in selecting course members (Chapter 5) we shall first consider the issues involved in selecting and supporting *trainers*.

4
Selecting and Supporting Trainers

Most counsellor training courses would require staff to be trained to a standard which is required for Accreditation with the national association and currently to be engaged in ongoing counselling practice if they are to be involved in the practical elements of the training such as supervision, and skills practice. Requiring considerable training and practical counselling experience tends to increase the average age of counselling trainers, which is a pity because it is always useful to offer course members a staff who are as varied as possible. The reason for this search after heterogeneity among the staff is that the variety creates opportunities for course members to challenge some of their assumptions in relation to a range of 'authority' figures. An ideal would be to select a staff group which was representative of both genders, varied in age, sexual orientation, race and social background. However, the advantages of heterogeneity in the staff should not be over-emphasised at the expense of selecting staff who have the appropriate qualities and abilities for person-centred training.

Qualities and Abilities

Box 4.1 reproduces a selection of views of course members on what they liked or disliked in trainers. The statements in Box 4.1 are indicative of the kind of qualities and abilities which course members like in their trainers. As far as the trainers are concerned they would be happy to be judged on most, but not all, of these dimensions. For example, the person-centred trainer would be pleased with the first evaluation – that she is prepared to 'go the extra mile' while still looking after herself. The trainer might be unhappy if it was simply the first part of that statement which was being valued, because 'going the extra mile' can also be evidence of the trainer who is willing to behave like the self-sacrificing parent without regard for her own needs and balance. Also, the trainer may or may not be happy to comply with the condition implicit in statements (8) and (9) where the course member is looking for a closer relationship with the trainer. In

---

Box 4.1
What Course Members Like/Don't Like in Trainers

1   'The trainer who is willing to go the extra mile but who is still able to look after herself.'
2   'The trainer who is willing to be known as a person.'
3   'I couldn't believe it when the trainer showed her vulnerability – I reckoned she had to be pretty strong to do that.'
4   'She's non-defensive – she's even willing to apologise when she is wrong.'
5   'She's just so trustworthy.'
6   'She is thoroughly reliable – she'll be there when she says she'll be there – and she does what she says she will do.'
7   'I feel that they [the trainers] are thoroughly dedicated to this work.'
8   'He's pleasant enough, but he stands apart more than the other trainers.'
9   'I want a personal relationship with my trainers – he isn't willing to engage me fully enough.'
10   'She does not protect me enough.'

---

some cases this will indeed be evidence of the fact that the trainer is being unnecessarily detached but in other cases that element of detachment will be appropriate to the trainer–course member contract. Less equivocal is the question of whether person-centred trainers should comply with the expectation implicit in statement (10). Course members, particularly early in training, may look for more 'protection' than person-centred trainers should offer. This relates to the responsibility dynamic within person-centred training, described in detail in Chapter 3 and also considered later in this section.

Fortunately, when we look at the *abilities* appropriate to person-centred trainers, we find considerable overlap and only a few contradictions with the expectations of course members. I shall explore a number of the most important abilities before considering how the trainer might reflect on her profile across these abilities.

The Ability to Function Fluidly within 'Open Process'

Many of the training contexts within a person-centred course are only loosely structured around a general theme such as 'supervision', 'personal development', 'skills' work, and some do not even have a theme, for example, the community meeting. This relative lack of structure exists for a good reason. It is only if the structure and process is sufficiently open that there is scope to address the individual needs and experiences of the group members (the 'individualising of the curriculum' – Chapter 3). A result of this reduced structure is that the trainer must have the ability to function fluidly within 'open process' without needing to contain it through imposing structuring or retreat from it in passivity or defensiveness. This is a considerable ability and one which is not easily obtained. Personally, as a trainer, I am grateful for the 1,000+ hours I have spent in unstructured 'encounter groups' as a foundation. That has certainly helped me to develop a moderate ability to function fluidly within 'open process'.

Non-Defensiveness

Defensiveness keeps communication at the level of debate. In counselling training we want communication to be able to cross levels of experiencing so that the parties involved can explore and express the feelings which are lying below their immediate expression. For example, in group supervision, the course member says to the supervisor, 'I don't feel supported by you over that work.' A defensive response from the supervisor might be, 'Well, I certainly felt that I *was* supportive – we gave you a lot of time over it.' This defensive response keeps the communication at the level of debate over the rights or wrongs of whether the supervisor was supportive or not. The supervisor's need to defend herself is slowing down the movement of the communication to a deeper level and may even be making that movement impossible. An alternative, non-defensive response might be 'Is it that you feel that I was critical, or perhaps that you didn't get *enough* back from me, or what . . . What's the feeling?' This response does not contradict the course member's expression but seeks to clarify and expand it, and in that way to move forward. Of course, if the supervisor felt anything in herself which corresponded to the course member's challenge then the above, clarifying question, would represent the worst in incongruent obfuscation. One of the most powerful defensive tactics in the trainer is to use training skills and knowledge to sculpt ever more sophisticated personal defences. The demand on the trainer is that she responds congruently even though she does not know where that congruent response will lead. For example, the supervisor's response to the challenge might be: 'I think you're right – I *did* feel critical about parts of the work, but I didn't say that in a straightforward way . . . and I should have. Perhaps we should talk more?' This non-defensive response allows for a full consideration of the matter in question and opens the door to deepening communication on the personal responses which each person is having towards the other.

Transparency

In the previous 'non-defensive' example the trainer's 'congruence' or 'transparency' was emphasised. However, this transparency is not only important as an alternative to defensiveness but should form the foundation of all the trainer's work. There is no argument whatsoever for the trainer presenting anything other than a transparent Self. The trainer's ease with transparency will have grown through her own personal development and is more a developed 'quality' than an ability. However, an important ability of the trainer is to recognise how she may use that transparency effectively within her communication. An example of this is the trainer remembering to add the *'because'* to her statements in order to make them transparent rather than mystifying. For example, following a group review of a course member's counselling audiotape, the trainer asks the trainee, 'I'm wondering what you think about that piece of work?' Many course members could respond quite directly to this kind of question, but some would be unnerved by what looks like a 'loaded' question from the 'powerful' trainer and might wonder as to what judgement underlies the question. An alternative way in which the person-centred trainer might ask such a question, but be more transparent in the process, would be: 'I'm wondering what you think about that piece of work, because, although we were all giving you good feedback you looked more unsure of yourself?' Adding the 'because' makes the trainer more transparent and shows the course member what is actually lying behind the question rather than leaving him to make assumptions which will probably be wrong.

Empathy

It goes without saying that a high degree of empathic ability will be central to the work of the person-centred trainer. Rather than duplicate many other writings on the salience of empathy (Rogers, 1980c; Mearns and Thorne, 1988), I would like to focus on the way I think about empathy when working with trainees. My aim is to go to the heart of the person rather than the heart of the issue. Staying at the level of the issue keeps us within the world of

'lace curtains and safety screens' (Chapter 2) in our communication. The reality is that the course member, as well as the client,
will have responses at many levels of his Self to the very personal
issues with which he struggles in training. In empathising with
the course member I am seeking to touch him at those deeper
levels of Self partly to deepen the trust between us but also so that
we can engage the responses of those levels. An example of this is
taken from a training group where the course member is talking
about the difficulties he is having in working with a particular
client. Much discussion surrounds what he has done and what he
might do until the trainer changes the whole level of the interaction when she says: 'I found myself dropping out of our
discussion as it went on. I kept looking at *you* rather than thinking
about the discussion. It seemed to me that there was a whole lot
going on in you about this – a whole lot of feeling . . .' This
intervention went to the heart of the course member rather than
the issue and touched the course member's sadness and fear
which were his true responses at depth to his work with this client
and what that might mean for his future as a counsellor. He was
in real fear that he might be discovering such a depth of inability
in himself that he could not do the work.

Unconditional Positive Regard

It is important to understand what unconditional positive regard
means and to relate it to the training frame rather than a counselling context (see Chapter 1). Unconditional positive regard does
not mean giving the course member ubiquitous approval. It does
not necessarily even imply 'liking' (Mearns, 1994f). What it
does mean is that the trainer retains a fundamental unshakeable
valuing of the course member as a person of worth. The training
frame, which is entirely different from counselling, will mean that
the trainer offers judgements and challenges in relation to the
course member's work. Offering judgements and challenges in no
way contradicts the notion of unconditional positive regard. It is
perfectly possible to retain an unshakeable valuing of the course
member as a person of worth while still offering judgements
about his work. Indeed, the willingness of the trainer to challenge
the course member is actually evidence of the trainer's valuing of
the course member as a person of worth – when the trainer
withholds the challenge she is actually expressing a lack of trust
and valuing of the course member. Interestingly, as a training
course progresses, course members themselves become more and

more willing to challenge each other and realise that such challenge is evidence of regard rather than contradictory to it. In the following example it is the trainer who is offering the challenge though many similar illustrations could be drawn from course members. This example is taken from a large group meeting where the male trainer said to the female course member:

> I feel uncomfortable around you. Every time we talk together I get the feeling that you are not really seeing me or hearing me. I was beginning to find myself making less contact with you but I don't want to do that so that is why I am saying something now. I don't know what this difficulty is and it might be my difficulty rather than yours but I have wondered whether you have difficulty with me because I am a man or perhaps it's the trainer role, or maybe both?

Not making this challenge would have been evidence of a lack of respect on the part of the trainer. If the trainer had little regard for this course member as a person of worth then he might have simply ducked the challenge and avoided the course member. Offering the challenge exposes the trainer more and shows that he is willing to take that risk in relation to the course member. Many things may follow from a challenge such as that illustrated above. Sometimes it might lead to the course member becoming aware of a difficulty she has with men or with those in authority but on other occasions it could result in the trainer discovering that these were fears of his and they were not in fact being paralleled in the course member. In one case the course member learns a lot and in the other the trainer learns a lot – in either case the training is progressed, as is the relationship between trainer and course member. Unconditional positive regard is not a woolly concept in person-centred training but a vigorous and demanding challenge.

Expertise in Holding to the 'Responsibility Dynamic'

This involves two facets, as described in Chapter 3: the ability to be consistent and diligent in fulfilling appropriate responsibilities *to* course members; and, the ability to resist taking responsibility *for* course members. Various examples of both dimensions of the responsibility dynamic are discussed fully in the previous chapter, but the task for the trainer is not simply one of undertaking appropriate responsibilities. The person-centred 'responsibility dynamic' conflicts with normal societal expectations which would place the trainer into more of a parental role. Hence, the course member might bring to the training a raft of expectations of how the trainer should 'look after him'. The ability of the trainer is to resist taking that responsibility which is not contracted and to hold the tension of the responsibility ambiguity felt between her and the course member. For example, the course member may feel insufficiently supported by the trainer who firmly holds to the contract that she will not arrange the course member's counselling opportunities *for* him. The trainer needs to resist the course member's complaint that he is not being looked after and that other courses fix counselling for their students.

The ability to hold to the responsibility dynamic is also challenged when the trainer is faced by excessive demands from course members. Even though each request on its own is perfectly reasonable, the trainer must have the ability to attend to her own needs and balance. This might mean saying 'Not at this time' to quite reasonable demands. This can be difficult for the trainer who is at all insecure about her role. If we are unsure about the quality of what we are offering as a trainer then there is a danger that we will try to offer it twice as much! Particularly in the area of person-centred therapy it is important for trainers to model self-care even though that might mean not fulfilling all the reasonable expectations of course members. When issues like this arise on a course much can be learned by bringing them into the open and exploring the responses of everyone involved.

The Ability to Relate Practice to Theory

It is incumbent upon trainers to develop a sophisticated knowledge of theory to the extent that they can offer the course member theoretical frameworks and extension reading upon which he can develop his thinking about his practical counselling work. Chapter 9 details a theory curriculum from which courses may select. It goes without saying that the trainer should be fluent in that curriculum and skilled in linking it to practice.

Expertise as a 'Demonstrator'

As well as having expertise in linking practice to theory, there is also the ability to reverse the process and demonstrate theoretical principles through practical examples. For example, while talking about different levels of empathy, the trainer would be able to describe these in terms of practical illustrations. Sometimes this will involve careful preparation of class material, but most often the skill required is to think up practical examples in the moment that an issue of theory becomes discussed in the group. Trainers vary in the slickness with which they can become demonstrators.

Expertise as a 'Facilitator'

The same individual difference among trainers is marked when we look to the ability to facilitate. In the main, facilitation does not mean demonstrating, describing or informing. Instead, it means carefully helping the course member to think about an issue or consider his feelings on that matter. The task is one of helping the course member to learn rather than teaching in any direct fashion. Often people who are good demonstrators may not be such patient and efficient facilitators – that certainly applies to myself (see Box 4.2).

Abilities Profiles for Person-Centred Trainers

It is interesting for trainers to reflect upon their abilities and perhaps to seek the views of colleagues. A simple device to aid this reflection and communication is 'profiling' where the trainer may rate herself on the kinds of abilities mentioned in this chapter. In Box 4.2 I offer, as an example, my own profile at this time of writing.

I find a few interesting and contentious features in my own profile. As mentioned earlier, I believe that my considerable experience in unstructured encounter groups has helped me to feel secure in *working within 'open process'*. The one thing which detracts from that is my tendency to *defensiveness*, on which I give myself bare pass marks. This has to do with my obsession for clarification. If I am challenged on something then I can seldom resist the temptation to get closer to a shared reality of the event in question. This urge will lead me to explain the circumstances and my own actions as I saw them rather than lay that aside for a moment to focus simply on the reality for the course member and the feelings which lie behind the challenge. So, for example, when challenged recently on my slowness in responding to a request I pointed to the fact that this request competed for the same time as an existing commitment to another course member so that I could not meet both demands at the same time. This is a typical 'defensive' response and not particularly facilitative even

---

Box 4.2

A Trainer's Profile

In the profile below I offer my self-assessment across ten abilities using a skewed scale from +4 to −1. Hopefully, a skewed scale is appropriate for trainer profiling − we should not expect trainers to need to use the highly negative end of a normal scale!

ABILITY	+4	+3	+2	+1	0	−1

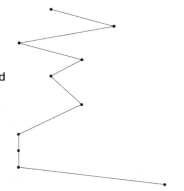

1 Working fluidly within 'open process'

2 Non-defensiveness

3 Transparency

4 Empathy

5 Unconditional positive regard

6 Not taking responsibility *for* the course member

7 Being responsible *to* the course member

8 Linking theory with practice

9 Expertise as 'demonstrator'

10 Expertise as 'facilitator'

---

although it gives some clarification. I think I would function better as a trainer if I could be more patient about giving the clarification and hear, not only the course member's challenge, but anything which underlies the challenge. I notice that I give myself the top rating for *transparency*. This was a difficult judgement to make because I had to separate my appraisal of myself from my experience of how others may see me. I believe that a number of course members would give me a much lower rating for transparency, sometimes because they would confuse it with a 'willingness to be known' (Barrett-Lennard, 1962) but, in other cases, because what they see conflicts with their assumptions (Chapter 13 explores this in some detail). I also give myself a fairly high rating for *unconditional positive regard*. Once again, some course members would rate me lower, even much lower. Part of the explanation of the difference is my inclusion of the willingness to 'challenge' as part of unconditional positive regard in a training context. I give myself lower ratings for *empathy* and *not taking responsibility for the course member*. In both cases I give myself 'pass' grades but I notice other trainers who are more able to offer a strong empathy. Also, I still have a tendency to slip into taking responsibility *for* some course members though I am much improved in this regard over the past couple of years. On the other hand, I believe that I am a reliable trainer who is pretty diligent in maintaining contracted *responsibilities to course members* and I don't hesitate to give myself top ratings on the related abilities of *linking theory with practice* and *expertise as demonstrator*. I find that my experience not only in counselling and training but also in writing helps me to make quick links between practice and theory, both in terms of drawing the course member's attention to relevant theory but also in being able to create practical examples on the spot. Finally, I give myself lowest ratings on *expertise as facilitator*. I find this to be a fascinating self-evaluation, particularly since I believe that I am much poorer as a facilitator now than 15 years ago. Paradoxically one of the factors which has contributed to this has been the growth in my understanding of person-centred counselling combined with my improvement as a 'demonstrator'. The result is that I frequently find difficulty in resisting the temptation to go into explanation or illustration when a more facilitative approach would be to stay with the course member's experience and work from that point.

The *abilities profile* can offer added staff development value if used within staff teams for self- and other-evaluation followed by discussion. Another good use is between trainer and course members while the course is in progress. This is the kind of exercise which can easily throw up important elements of the *unspoken relationship* between trainer and course member (Mearns, 1994o).

Self-Acceptance

Underlying the various abilities of the trainer are personality factors which may make it easy or difficult for the trainer to develop and maintain those abilities. The most important personality dimension is the degree of the trainer's *self-acceptance*. In Chapter 3 the issue of self-acceptance for the course member was addressed but, needless to say, it is also a critical issue for the trainer. A high degree of self-acceptance allows these abilities to emerge fluidly and consistently in a fashion which is perfectly congruent within the trainer. It is easy to see how an integrated self-acceptance helps the trainer to feel more secure to work within 'open process' and to respond non-defensively. She will find it easier to be transparent because she will not be afraid of the reflection of herself which she gets back from course members. Also, a high level of self-acceptance gives greater confidence in releasing empathic sensitivity and tends to make us more readily accepting of others. A high level of self-acceptance will reduce the trainer's tendency to take responsibility *for* the course member as a way of currying his favour. Hence, the first six of the ten abilities areas are enhanced by a high degree of self-acceptance in the trainer.

However, a trainer who does not have a high degree of self-acceptance will constantly be fighting the incoming tide of her own self-doubt. This trainer may perform well in terms of the listed abilities but it will be an enormous effort and she generally requires much more support than other trainers. Her work will tend to be 'patchy' – highly effective with some course members, but variable with those who offer some potential threat to her insecure self-structure. Also, there is a greater danger of *over-involvement* as the need for 'other-acceptance' intrudes. As well as seeking 'other-acceptance' from staff colleagues, the trainer may look for it in relations with course members. The over-involvement which might result could simply be at the level of showing a tendency to 'go the extra mile' in disregard of personal limits. Person-centred trainers frequently 'go the extra mile' in relation to participants and that is something which is often valued and respected. However, as mentioned in Chapter 3, if it happens in blatant disregard to the personal limits of the worker then it may be reflecting a difficulty. Sometimes the over-involvement takes the form of establishing exclusive relationships with particular course members. Once again, it is a perfectly normal facet of human relating that relationships within a course community will vary greatly. The person-centred trainer will not be trying to establish exactly the same kind of relationship with every course member but will be allowing relationships to develop in a natural way within the boundaries of ethical behaviour. However, there is a difference between having special qualities within a relationship and that relationship becoming *exclusive*. One of the strong symptoms of exclusivity creeping into the relationship is where the trainer finds that she is withholding confidences of the course member from her staff colleagues. Similarly, the course member may feel obliged to keep 'secrets' concerning his relationship with the trainer. It is only in a minority of cases that these exclusive relationships might breach the obvious bounds of ethical behaviour but they can still cause difficulty for the course member, the trainer and the course, long before that point.

As mentioned earlier, it is possible for the trainer with a relatively low self-acceptance to do well in the work but it tends to require an enormous effort, not to mention considerable self-monitoring and additional support.

Support

The trainer with a lower self-acceptance may need considerable support but everyone who is involved in the training role needs support. In person-centred work the trainer is not hiding behind a role or a repertoire but is more visible and involved. In that sense the *person* of the trainer is actively engaged every day in the activity. It is little wonder that person-centred trainers must pay particular attention to their support. The staff within a person-centred counselling training department of a university, for example, will be unlike that of any other university department in regard to the attention paid to maintaining the positive mental health and good functioning of colleagues. While a good functioning department in another area of the university might boast a staff who relate with each other in a friendly manner and communicate well in decision-making, the counselling department staff need to go far beyond that in the closeness of their relationships and in the degree to which they understand each other's emotional functioning. Furthermore, they need to place a considerable investment in *maintaining* that degree of involvement with each other.

Our Quality of Communication

Maintaining such closeness in relationship is more about the *quality* than the quantity of communication. For example, when my colleagues ask me how I am, I know that this is a genuine question and not simply a polite interjection. They know that I can seriously disregard my emotional state to fulfil work commitments. They also know that I tend to be too private a person and, when stressed, will tend to drift into my own private and secluded world rather than seek the company and support of others. They also know that I know they know these things and that I will take their question seriously, seeing it as an oft-repeated yet consistently genuine offer of support which I will sometimes accept.

Our Depth of Understanding of Each Other

Supporting a colleague is also about paying regard to the *whole person* and not simply the parts of her which are immediately involved in the work. Showing an interest in the colleague's life outside work and also how the colleague is developing as a person is all part of the broad and deep relationship. My life outside work is a part of me as a rounded person and will give explanation to much of my behaviour in the job. Also, my own general development as a person is crucial to our understanding and working together. For example, my colleague will understand how my passion for the work fits into my earlier development as a person. She will also understand how my reduced availability is part of my current self-maintenance.

Our Willingness to Challenge Each Other

'Supporting' a colleague means more than understanding her and holding her. It is also about being fully responsible to her – hence *challenge* is a part of support. When good relationships exist, 'challenge' is experienced with warmth, as a part of unconditional positive regard. My colleague's 'How are you?' is a challenge, as is her offer to take one of my classes when I have lost sight of my limits and become tied-up in a neurotic need to fulfil every commitment made. Challenge is a simple, loving process when we engage regularly and frequently with each other. However, if we allow the build-up of unspoken responses to each other then 'challenge', when it comes, appears to be a discontinuous phenomenon and one which can be experienced as difficult for both giver and receiver.

Specific Friendships and Exclusive Relationships

A staff will take care not to form *exclusive relationships*, while feeling free to develop specific friendships. As mentioned earlier, exclusivity in relationships introduces barriers with others. Once barriers are erected they become further strengthened by the laying down of unspoken reactions to each other and, before long, divisions have arisen such that certain staff can only work effectively with some others. Specific friendships, on the other hand, tend to strengthen a staff because of the additional degree of understanding and support provided to the individuals. There is a power difference between specific friendships and exclusive relationships as far as the dynamics of the staff team is concerned – the former empowers while the latter drains power out of the system.

As well as attending to the quality of communication in day-to-day working contacts, person-centred training course staff will often create additional special structures to aid and enhance their communication, of which the following are examples.

The Personal Training Supervisor

The practice of employing a *personal supervisor* with whom we can discuss our training work is not special to the person-centred approach. It is a logical extrapolation of the supervisory relationship in counselling. Personally, I hope that this form of support never becomes *compulsory* within the profession because I believe that it is only one way of getting the necessary support. I find it important to have this support available so that I can employ it at particular times of difficulty where the support structures put in place with my colleagues are not sufficient for my *therapeutic* need. Otherwise, I prefer to make my support needs as visible as possible to my colleagues so that we can be involved in helping each other and in that way understand each other even more fully.

Special, Focused Meetings on Staff Support

These meetings should be in addition to other normal staff meetings concerned with course planning or housekeeping. The danger in not separating support meetings is that the time may be usurped by the practical demands of the course.

Using a 'Consultant to the Staff Process'

Focused meetings on support are enhanced by the employment of an external consultant to the staff process. The consultant is someone with whom the staff team will have virtually no contact in other ways. Indeed, the consultant may profitably work from a core model of counselling which is different from that of the staff team. That difference can raise new questions and perspectives. A typical contract for the staff is to meet with the consultant for a three or four hour meeting in each term and also on other occasions if a particular need should arise. The slightly enhanced formality of having an external consultant is not only helpful for the additional perspective she brings but because she takes all the facilitation responsibility from the staff members and pays attention to each person equally.

Staff Retreats

A superb structure for focused meetings on support is the weekend staff retreat. Such residential weekends offer an intensive environment where the staff can re-establish contact with each other at a depth which could only be achieved given quality time together in a pleasant environment.

The Community Meeting

While all the above structures offer very private contexts for staff support, we should not forget that most public of arenas – the community meeting, comprising course members and trainers. It is important that trainers use the community meeting in the same way as course members. There is nothing worse than staff holding back support and challenge which they might have given each other until they are in the privacy of the staff room. In the person-centred approach to training there is no theoretical justification for maintaining a unified facade in relation to course members. It is healthy for a course staff to feel free to communicate with each other in front of course members in exactly the same ways as they would in private. Often that contact between staff members takes the form of empathising with each other, offering support but also confronting. Usually the staff have achieved such a level of understanding of each other that profound disagreements and misunderstandings seldom occur. Yet, when such dynamic material is voiced by staff in relation to each other in community meeting, the effect tends to be powerfully facilitative in a number of ways, with course members realising that the staff are willing to be individuals, willing to respect each other sufficiently to disagree publicly and willing to show considerable trust in the whole course community. Unfortunately, although these dynamic moments can be so productive, they can also not be manufactured, for congruence and absence of manipulation are paramount in person-centred training.

Having considered just some of the issues in selecting and supporting trainers it is time to turn to the issue of selecting course members and considering how that difficult process can be made as 'supportive' as possible.

5
Selecting Course Members

The Central Aim in Selection

The central aim of selection as far as the training course is concerned is to choose applicants who are at a point in their development when they are ready to approach the training in a relatively non-defensive fashion. Selection is not always used in the same way by the applicants themselves. Just as important to applicants is the issue of whether the training appears to be manageable in its practical aspects such as attendance, assignments, counselling practice, counselling supervision and reading.

Box 5.1

John: A Successful Applicant

John is 43 years of age and has worked in the same commercial sector from the age of 16. He has been a voluntary marriage counsellor for the past five years following a good experience of relationship counselling some five years prior to that time. John had entered that experience as a client with some suspicion and a feeling that it was not relevant to him. However, he had found the experience valuable in the freedom it had offered him to be himself and to become aware of his priorities in life. He and his wife had chosen to separate but John, at least, viewed that as a positive decision. During the past 10 years John has continued his own changing process and is now seeking to make a gradual career change into professional counselling. As well as his current experience in couples counselling John has negotiated, in principle, regular counselling work in a Primary Care context, with a resident counsellor as 'mentor'.

The interviewers considered that John was far enough through his own trauma of 10 years earlier and they liked the careful and gradual way in which he was moving towards a second career in counselling. They were also impressed by his decision to diversify his counselling experience into the Primary Care sector and by the fact that he had already negotiated that counselling opportunity.

Box 5.2

Kathy: Another Successful Applicant

Kathy is 23 years of age and graduated with an Upper Second Class Honours degree in Psychology some 18 months previous to this application. She had decided not to seek entry into clinical psychology but to aim for a career in counselling. Originally, she had considered undertaking the British Psychological Society Diploma in Counselling Psychology, but had laid that aside when she found that it demanded only Certificate level counselling skills training. Kathy has no prior counselling experience, though she has worked for the past year with young adults who have profound learning difficulties. This work had been challenging and she spoke at interview on how she has found herself 'simplifying my communication and making it more direct'. Kathy is uncertain how she would actually *be* as a counsellor, but she is highly motivated to find out.

Kathy's interviewers were impressed by her vitality and also by her maturity. They liked the way she spoke about the people with whom she worked – there was no hint of a patronising attitude. Kathy appeared to be a relatively non-defensive person. Her selectors wondered whether they might ask her to do Certificate level training first, but decided to take a risk by offering her a Diploma place.

Training courses find that the single most important reason for rejecting someone at application is that it is too early in the person's development to have confidence that they could make full use of the intensive training. Training at this level of personal encounter is excellent for the person who has already developed to the extent of being relatively non-defensive but it is most inefficient for those at an earlier stage in their development – it is generally more appropriate to refer the earlier applicant to a Certificate level counselling skills course, perhaps with a view to entering Diploma level training a year or two later.

'Readiness' for training is essentially a personal development characteristic. It may have been fostered by prior experience as a counsellor, but not necessarily. Boxes 5.1 and 5.2 offer illustrations of two successful but quite different applicants.

John has considerable counselling experience while Kathy has none. On the other hand Kathy has an Honours degree in Psychology while John left school at 16. Another obvious difference is that John is nearly twice as old as Kathy. John and Kathy also have some things in common: their interviewers felt that they both presented an 'aliveness' and a strong motivation towards counselling as well as both appearing to be mature and rounded persons. Because of her youth, there is inevitably less evidence to support Kathy's application but the interviewers placed considerable weight on the way she had spoken about her work experience during this past 18 months. Kathy had evidently been able to stay 'open' and actively explore and develop her communication in relation to a client group which many people would find difficult. While John was making an informed and experienced decision to opt for person-centred training, Kathy was showing the kind of personal qualities which evidenced her compatibility with the approach.

These different pen portraits of successful applicants illustrate the fact that there are many ways of evidencing 'readiness'. This fact allows us to select a fairly heterogeneous group of people for a counselling training course. That heterogeneity within the cohort is important for the learning environment.

Heterogeneity versus Homogeneity

A person-centred counselling training course relies on a rich heterogeneity within the course membership. In Chapter 7 we shall see the importance of this variety in creating a vibrant context for personal development. The hope is that course members will be faced with the task of building an intensive working environment despite differences in age, gender, life experience and cultural background. This variety will force members to face those parts of themselves, such as assumptions and values, which might ordinarily inhibit their full communication with others. Furthermore, that experience of training with a variety of people will help the counsellor to relate across the range within the client population.

It may be comfortable to relate with others who are so similar in experience and values that it makes trust-building an easier process. However, there is potentially much more to be gained in terms of our self-awareness and self-development in being faced with the task of establishing trusting relationships across a diverse group of people.

There is a danger within the counselling profession as a whole that the concept of the counsellor as a person will become ever narrower. Perhaps this is a danger which comes with our success in understanding the kind of person who will take most easily to counselling training. If we restrict our selection to that ever narrowing band of humanity then we shall, in the long term, constrain the profession and the ability of the profession to respond to changing circumstances. I remember an experience some 20 years ago of working with a seminar group of 15 students training to be primary teachers. After failing miserably during the first four weeks of term to stimulate anything in the way of debate on even the most obviously controversial issues I paused the process and asked each of the group members to say a little about their own background. One of the amazing statistics which unfolded was that 14 out of the 15 were Sunday School teachers! The way this homogeneity in that profession had evolved concerned the selection process. Competition for places was fierce – there were many hundreds of applicants who had the necessary academic qualifications. Hence, another discriminating criterion had to be introduced into the selection process. The result was that applicants were required to have prior experience of working with primary school age children. As it happens, one of the very few opportunities there are for young adults to have such experience is Sunday School teaching, hence the homogeneity within my seminar group – a homogeneity which does not encourage diversity of ideas and which can lead to the possibility of stagnation in a profession. It is important that the profession of counselling stays aware of the danger of homogeneity which can be created when a profession has many applicants seeking few places. A profession needs diversity so that it is equipped with a variety of response that will enable it both to initiate change and to respond to changed demands.

There is a growing tendency among counselling training courses to stipulate *mandatory* criteria in selection. Hence, an applicant need not apply if she does not have sufficient prior experience as a counsellor, a prescribed amount of prior counselling skills training, or previous experience as a client. Some courses even debar entry to persons under 24 or over 50. These kinds of mandatory criteria creep into selection at times when there is an over-demand for training places. Naturally, training courses find it difficult to reduce the body of applicants down to a level which can be managed at interview. Unfortunately, as well as easing the task of the selectors, the effect is to decrease the heterogeneity on the course. Consistent application of mandatory criteria such as the above will gradually yield a profession comprised substantially of female former clients aged between 35 and 45, or has it done that already?

Person-centred courses will be particularly wary of the dangers of homogeneity. They may construct selection criteria which emphasise the value of prior counselling experience, counselling training and the like but their selectors will be aware that these structural criteria do not define the whole person and they will, as far as possible, be trying to interview a fairly large and wide-ranging group of people.

Competitive and Non-Competitive Selection

Competitive selection occurs when the number of applicants interviewed is greater than the places available. We may interview 80 applicants for 30 places and find that 50 of the applicants are suitable for training. Inevitably, competition must then take place within that group of 50 by whatever process selects 'the best 30'. In non-competitive selection the course might interview applicants in the order in which they apply, offering places to suitable applicants until the places are filled. There are advantages and disadvantages in both procedures, although person-centred courses might feel more philosophically comfortable with the non-competitive process. The problem with non-competitive selection occurs when a course becomes popular. In that situation applicants may have to apply two years in advance of the course even to be considered for interview. This is an unrealistic delay between selection and entry to the course. The alternative is to establish a realistic closing date for applications and create a competitive selection procedure, resulting in the aforementioned example whereby 50 candidates may be 'suitable' after interviewing, but only 30 places are available. This is not a person-centred situation and there is no person-centred solution. We might consider inviting all 50 to take part in an event which will result in 30 embarking on the course, but I suspect that this would not so much represent a person-centred solution as a circus. There is no workable solution within the person-centred framework, so courses inevitably adopt a 'course-centred' approach such as attributing 'scores' to applicants on a variety of dimensions (see Box 5.3 for an example). A slight reassurance for person-centred afficionados lies in the fact that 'points' systems do not work well enough. A system still needs to be in place to block entry when there are doubts over mental health or the nature of the person's motivation (for example, the person who is looking for a 'growth' experience). Also, interviewers argue strongly for 'special cases' to

---

Box 5.3

Considerations in Interview Selection

In comparing meaningfully across numerous interviews the reliability may be helped by compiling 'scores' from the various selection criteria. The following represents one such system.

- Previous training, 0–20 points
- Previous counselling experience, 0–20
- Related work (but not counselling), 0–10
- Psychology Degree (or similar), 0–15
- Commitment/well-focused motivation, 0–30
- Vitality/energy, 0–30
- Willingness/ability to take responsibility for Self, 0–30
- Fit with the person-centred core model, 0–25
- Ability for the academic, 0–20
- Personal development to date, 0–20
- Counselling opportunities during course, 0–20
- Finance certainty, 0–10
- Enough space in life, 0–10

---

be made for individual circumstances – thank goodness that they do. It is a strange paradox that a person-centred system of non-competitive selection must, of necessity, fall, when it is faced with the consequences of its own success.

Selection Methods

Logically, one approach to selection could be to take an entirely 'applicant-centred' approach. This method might appeal to those who believe that within the person-centred specialism we must be entirely philosophically consistent and, in all cases, give the decision-making responsibility to the other person, be they client, course member or prospective course member. The thinking behind this approach would suggest that, given full information about the training, the person who can potentially make the best decision as to her suitability is the applicant herself. To be consistent with this approach in selection would be theoretically possible, but it would represent a *much* greater investment of resource than in conventional selection systems. Firstly, the task would have to be achieved of giving the applicant *full information about the training*. This does not simply mean giving detailed published information about the course. It would require the step of putting the applicant into an experience which duplicates that of the course so that she can make a judgement on her suitability. Hence, the applicant might spend some time engaging in mock supervision groups, personal development groups, community meetings and the like. This simulation of the course experience would have to be fairly intense and over a reasonable length of time becaue various processes would have to emerge, including the kind of confrontation which the applicant might expect to receive from other course members and staff. For example, an applicant who herself had laboured under the weight of fairly oppressive conditions of worth might learn that the incongruent ways of responding which she had evolved and which were quite functional in other life contexts attracted considerable challenge in a person-centred training environment. Only if the applicant is enabled to have this kind of experience would she have the *full information* to enable her to make an informed choice about her participation. I am convinced that this approach, perfectly con- sistent with the person-centred tradition, would be effective in most cases. There would be the minority exception where the psychological disturbance of the applicant was of a form that would inhibit her own potential for awareness. For example, an applicant whose method of protecting the Self was pre-emptively to abuse other potential sources of threat might find this training simulation process extremely difficult, but she could not also be expected to be able to take into consideration the pain and distress she was causing for others. A decision whether or not to join a subsequent training course would be made by this person on the basis of the pain which *she* might experience. She could not be expected to have the capacity for empathy.

In order to take full responsibility on the matter of her own selection the applicant would not only require experience of what to expect on the course, but she would need awareness of the aspects of her Self which might be endangered by the experience. Hence, a second requirement for the implementation of this 'applicant-centred' selection process would be the need to 'create the conditions' by which the applicant could make a choice which was also informed by *knowledge about her Self*. This might be achieved in a variety of ways but it would certainly involve a fairly lengthy experience in therapy or encounter group work in order that the applicant could become fully aware of the parts of herself which might become involved or even threatened within the training experience.

Only under these circumstances of helping the applicant to become *fully* aware of the course and of herself would we have created the necessary conditions for decision-making to be devolved responsibly.

In practice, I know of no courses which embark on the selection process in this way or which devolve the decision-making totally to the applicant. There have been some courses in the past which struggled for membership to such an extent that virtually every applicant was accepted. Often these courses suffered as a result of this impoverished selection process, finding that a high degree of pathology within even a few members of a course presents an exceedingly threatening experience for all concerned.

Some training courses are to be commended for the effort they make to help the applicant to make her decision, even though the course selectors also hold on to their selection responsibility. At the very least, courses are to be commended for preparing extremely *detailed information* about the training and for their willingness to offer *free consultation* to prospective applicants. Some person-centred training courses do even more. For example, there is the good practice of offering pre-course introductory *experiential weekends* whereby prospective applicants will, with the facilitation of course staff, engage in the kind of activities that they will meet on the course. This is an excellent way of giving applicants, who are perhaps new to the approach, a little experience of what it is like to work in an environment where all are expected to share responsibility for the process which unfolds, but it represents an enormous investment of resources on the part of the course.

Sometimes that experiental element is retained but reduced into a two-hour unstructured, *leaderless group* where the selectors observe the process. Here, the aim is not so much to give participants experience of the group process but to observe how they function in that environment and use that observation information in the selection decision. It must be said that relatively few person-centred courses employ this method, which is more often a part of selection to psychodynamic or Gestalt training.

Similarly, *personality tests* are rarely used in selection for person-centred courses. As well as offering questionable validity and reliability in gauging suitability for person-centred training the use of such tests is generally reckoned to be incompatible with the person-centred approach.

A selection method which is generally seen as a requirement for Diploma level training is the *interview*. Usually there would be two interviewers: enough to allow comparison of perspectives but not so many that might intimidate. Person-centred courses generally opt for very informal interviews where the aim is the open exploration of the 'fit' between the applicant and course.

Finally, we should not under-emphasise the importance of the initial *application form* which the applicant completes. A good application form for a person-centred course will engage the applicant in a process of *focusing* which helps her to consider many of the personal issues around entering such a training course. Open-ended questions such as the following encourage this reflection and focusing (each of these questions might have at least a half-page space for response):

- Please detail your present opportunities for practising as a counsellor. (If you do not have current opportunities for practice, please give details of your plans for the nature and location of these opportunities, and describe any earlier practice opportunities you have had.)
- Please write about your present strengths and weaknesses in the role of helper.
- Please consider, and describe, your reasons for wanting to embark on this course at this time in your life.
- Please go into detail on the ways in which the Person-Centred Approach, as you currently understand it, relates to your own personality and experience. Do not hesitate to comment on the 'conflict' as well as the 'fit'. (You are not *expected* to know a vast amount about the approach, so do not feel too threatened by this question. The asking of this question reflects our belief that the 'fit' between the person and the core theoretical approach is very important in training.)
- What are your thoughts about the financial and time commitments of the course in relation to your current life?
- What makes you confident that you can handle the theoretical parts of the course, including the reading and the written assignments? (Applicants will vary in their prior educational experience – rather than ask for specific previous attainments we prefer to consider the applicant as an individual whose confidence in this area may be derived from various prior experiences.)
- Please write here anything else you would want us to know about you.

These are the questions used in the application form for the courses with which I am involved. Sometimes people have written to thank us for this application form because the focusing it engendered enabled them to realise that this was not the point in their development to apply for a course such as this. A good selection process is one in which all parties are helped to consider the 'fit' between the person and the course.

Unsuccessful Applicants

At the start of this chapter the point was made that the central aim in selection was to check whether the applicant was sufficiently developed to make full use of intensive training. This final section explores some of the reasons for applicants being rejected because of insufficient or inadequate development to that point. I shall then close this chapter with a box which documents an error in selection. Firstly, let us look at a few of the reasons why applicants might be rejected at selection.

- *The applicant who is too 'old'* This has virtually nothing to do with chronological age but is more related to how fresh and alive the person appears to be. Specifically, I consider the question: is the applicant able to be congruently expressive with ease? Courses might well take risks on an applicant who is low in counselling experience but who has that quality of *congruent expressiveness*. Chronological age is a poor correlate with this dimension. As a selector I remember some course members who were 'young' at 65 and others who were far too 'old' at 35.
- *The applicant who cannot allow herself to be a student* Sometimes applicants are too experienced, or believe themselves to be too experienced, to open themselves fully to the training process. This applicant is seeking to enter training because of the paper qualification it will bring but only strives to use that training to confirm her already high esteem of her own ability. Sometimes this person can change her orientation to the course to use it fully but too often that change is slow to happen and much of the training time is wasted. This applicant is frequently angry when rejected for the course.
- *The applicant who has excessive difficulty in relation to people in authority* It is common to find this kind of difficulty within higher education and, to a degree, the fact that training will help to surface these problems can assist the course member to develop awareness and control. However, excessive difficulty in this regard can block the course member's active participa-

tion and willingness to take risks. Essentially, the person's excessive difficulty in relation to those in authority makes it impossible for her to take responsibility for herself and make progress in relation to the 'responsibility dynamic'.

- *The applicant who is too close to her own trauma*   Having experienced a major personal trauma can be a strength in the background of a counsellor, or it can be a constant drain. Basically it depends how far through the trauma the person has succeeded in moving before entering the training. If a person is too close to their own trauma she will constantly be faced with it during training and it may slow her progress considerably. This point should not be exaggerated because the majority of course participants will experience some of this re-emergence of earlier trauma during the course without it being disabling.

- *The applicant who does not have a sufficient degree of self-acceptance* An effective person-centred training will help the course member to develop her self-acceptance but it is inappropriate to accept applicants whose starting point as far as self-acceptance is concerned is too low (see Chapter 3). Some training structures can cope better than others as far as this is concerned – for example, more intensive structures like full-time training can accommodate lower self-acceptance more easily than less intensive courses, but all courses have limits. The great danger for a course is that it takes on as a course member a person who should really be a client.

- *The applicant who is in danger of using her power abusively*   This can cover a huge range of possibilities and it must be admitted that selection procedures cannot easily pick up this kind of tendency in an applicant. Abusiveness in counselling does not usually take the form of conscious manipulation with the systematic disempowerment and subservience of the client. That pattern of abuse is even less pronounced in person-centred counselling, which offers reduced scope for the orchestration of this kind of pathology compared to other approaches. However, a more common form of abusiveness which can be found in the person-centred approach as easily as in any other is represented by the combination of (i) invasive and exploitative needs on the part of the counsellor; (ii) a lack of awareness of these needs and the way they are articulated; (iii) a lack of awareness of the client's experience of the counsellor's behaviour. An example of this was the counsellor whose spiritual needs had become so involved in her counselling that, with one client, she had developed a practice of 'laying-on-of-hands' at the end of each session. The counsellor was unaware of the extent to which this practice was meeting *her* needs and she was also unaware of the disempowering effect this ritual was having on her client.

More space has been given to introducing this question of abusiveness because it is both extremely important to the counselling profession and it is also particularly difficult to spot in selection. Selectors might only see the mildest of clues about the possible invasiveness of the applicant's needs and her lack of awareness as to how that might be experienced by others. The reality is that selectors rarely get sufficient evidence of an abusive tendency to intervene at the point of selection. More often the applicant moves on to the course, where the problem later emerges.

In my experience as a trainer it is rare to find serious mistakes in selection. Applicants have had a fairly thorough chance to explore their own decision and that is reflected by drop-out rates of around 3%. Only rarely have I come across individuals whom we have later had to ask to leave the training. Box 5.4 describes a fictionalised example of the kind of pattern which can emerge where the selection has failed to uncover a fundamental and relatively immovable problem.

The Power of Positive Selection

Too many parts of this chapter have been cautionary and at times downright depressing. A more positive tone is needed for the end of the chapter because rigorous selection ends with a strong course. The reality is that the selection process helps the course to begin with a personnel which is heterogeneous but which shares a strong motivation towards counselling, a realistic understanding of counselling, a considerable experience in counselling or related work, a useful (regardless of age) vigour in relation to the work, an openness to personal exploration and development, a positive excitement about working with fellow 'travellers' on the course, a willingness to engage the theoretical as well as the practical, a modicum of self-doubt but not sufficient to paralyse, and a basic compatibility with the underlying philosophy of the person-centred approach.

Box 5.4

Charlene: An Error in Selection

Charlene was selected for the course, though there was some uncertainty felt by the selectors about the 'intensity' of her motivation and, indeed, her 'dedication' to counselling. Her actual counselling experience was fairly recent, having been invited to run a dedicated service for the parents of children in the Children's Hospital where she worked as a nurse. As often happened at that earlier time in the development of counselling in Britain, an interested nurse without counselling training would be invited to 'do' counselling. The way Charlene spoke about that counselling work was convincing to the selectors, though, in retrospect, they wondered if she had not been a bit 'over the top' in describing her work – perhaps too many of her needs had become entangled in the work.

It was only towards the end of Term 1 that the problem with Charlene had become obvious. As often happens on training courses, allowances are made and it is some time until a pattern emerges. Charlene could not behave *congruently* in *any* context. Her partners in skills practice found her to be 'over-effusive' and not 'present'. Members of her supervision group felt that she could not really empathise with her clients as evidenced in audiotape supervision. Furthermore, she seemed to have enormous difficulty in understanding what the supervision group members were saying to her. Her personal development group found that, as the first term wore on, Charlene had become the regular 'client' in the group. Once again, Charlene did not see the problem and was really grateful for the support she was receiving from everyone. In the community meeting Charlene was sometimes terrified and at other times she took centre stage. On one occasion she read her poetry on 'The Abused Client' and late in Term 1 she explained that the difficulty she was having with clients and also with members of the course was to do with the fact that, fundamentally, she was 'in mourning for the human race'.

Charlene did not start Term 2 of the course and that decision was not a matter of her choosing. The staff found it incredibly difficult and indeed a painful experience to explain the problem to Charlene, who could not understand what they were talking about. Charlene described a pattern within her personality which is perhaps the saddest of all. She was a person who was genuinely motivated towards intimacy yet unable to sustain or even engage that intimacy because of the threat it posed within her own personality.

Two years later the staff learned that Charlene had been accepted on an unaccredited counsellor training course which operated only an academic selection and assessment process.

Having achieved that basis through selection, the course members are now in a position to support each other in the training and in the supervised counselling practice which will be integral to that training.

6
Counselling Experience Supported by Supervision

Within the first few minutes of her selection interview, both Bron's interviewers had been confident about her suitability and readiness for professional counsellor training. That confidence continued through the early part of the course as Bron engaged confidently and enthusiastically with all its elements. Yet, coming towards the end of the sixth and final term of her training, Bron was facing the fact that she would choose to defer the award of her Diploma. Her early progress had been arrested by her lack of adequate counselling opportunities. Her self-appraisal statement describes her experience:

> I had been confident that I would be able to turn enough of my social work job into actual counselling practice. For most of the time it looked as though this would happen, but, in reality, I only had about one proper counselling client a week. About halfway through the two years I realised I might have to get counselling opportunities outside the job, but I baulked at the thought of finding yet another night away from the family, so I kept trying to develop counselling within my work.
>
> During the first half-year on the course my lack of proper counselling opportunities didn't seem to matter, but at about that point my development seemed to come to an abrupt halt. It was like a marathon runner hitting the 'wall' – everything felt laboured and in slow motion after that point. Other people in the groups were able to be fully involved – I could see how they were moving emotionally and as whole people. But for me, all I could use was my head and my imagination. I could do the theory bits but I had nothing to tie them to. Gradually my progress came to a halt.

The Necessity of Counselling Experience during Training

Bron's experience described in Box 6.1 gives a fairly representative illustration of what happens when a course member is not getting enough actual counselling experience during training. The course member may not feel the restriction of the practice deficit early in the course but there will come a time when it becomes impossible to make further gains. For example, the theory on the development of the therapeutic conditions and on the intricacies of the therapeutic process can only be held in intellectual understanding and cannot be translated into skilful behaviour unless given the orchestration through practice.

The question of *how much* counselling experience a course member should have during training is important and yet efforts at responding to that question have been naive in the extreme. The tendency is to give a *structural*, rather than *functional*, answer to the question of 'how much?' For example, the criterion may be set at 'three to five client hours per week'. Expressing the practice criterion in a structural fashion such as this gives clarity to the course member, but it is not at all person-centred, nor is it particularly meaningful. A better way to approach the question of counselling experience is to address it individually with each course member. Questions such as the following should help the course member to judge the degree to which his ongoing counselling experience is meeting his needs:

- Is the *intensity* of your current counselling experience enough to sustain you in your development?
- Are you having *too much* counselling experience – are you finding yourself 'carrying' too much from your client work into the rest of your life?
- Is your counselling experience sufficiently *diverse* as far as a range of clients is concerned?
- Is your current counselling experience helping you to *consolidate* your learning on the course?
- Is your counselling experience helping you to learn about *longer-term* as well as *shorter-term* working?

These questions get to the heart of the importance of counselling experience during training. It is not simply the total number of counselling hours a person achieves during training that is important but whether that ongoing experience is sufficiently *intense* to sustain his development. For example, on a one-year full-time course there will be only about 25 weeks available for actual counselling practice in combination with the training. In this context a criterion of 100 hours means that the trainee counsellors would be working with an average of four clients a week. For most, that should provide a fairly intense experience, sufficient to sustain their development. However, on a two-year part-time training there may be as much as 20 months available for counselling practice work. In this context a 100 hour criterion is grossly insufficient in intensity since it implies not much more than one client hour per week. Not only does this fail to offer sufficient intensity to sustain development, but it is positively dangerous for new counsellors to work with only one client a week because their professional self-esteem would be subject to the vagaries of a single therapeutic process. If a counsellor is seeing four clients a week then the fact that he may be going through a difficult experience with one client is offset by the other therapeutic processes. However, if a counsellor is working with only one client then his whole self-respect in the work arena may be coloured by that client's individual process. In those circumstances it would not be surprising if the counsellor found ways of 'keeping the client up' rather than following the client's therapeutic process.

The *diversity* of counselling experience is also relevant during training. Work which is entirely related to clients with a single presenting problem, work involving clients of only one gender, or work with clients from a very restricted age range, may not be offering a sufficiently diverse counselling experience even although it may be providing considerable intensity. One course member noted this problem:

> I had always presumed that my counselling practice was about the best you could get in the sense that it was particularly intense and involved profound existential issues. In our agency all the clients have had recent attempts at suicide. It was only late in my training that I noticed the deficit in my experience. I brought a tape to supervision of my first work in a Health Centre to which I had just attached myself. I brought the tape because I was uneasy with myself in this session but couldn't understand why. The others in the group quickly noted how detached I was with the client and how my empathy seemed to be offered at a very low level. What was happening was that I had got so used to working with clients who were at such extremes of existential despair that I found myself virtually unable to 'connect' with a client who was *not* at that existential depth. I needed to get experience not only of intensity with clients but with a broader range of clients.

It is difficult for training courses to resist framing the counselling practice criterion in terms of a specific minimum number of client hours since course members are often clamouring for that form of definition and also accrediting bodies have usually had to resort to offering a specific guideline in terms of a number of client hours. However, it is also important for person-centred trainers to note the importance of asking the functional questions and to expect students to address these as well as meeting any minimum criterion.

Counselling 'Opportunities' or Counselling 'Placements'

In Chapter 3 I used the question of counselling 'opportunities' or counselling 'placements' to illustrate the responsibility dynamic within person-centred training. Person-centred training courses usually prefer a system whereby course members organise their own counselling opportunities, albeit with whatever support and communication is necessary between the course and the counselling agency. The aim is to keep a direct bond of responsibility between the course member and the counselling agency so that any matters arising between them will be addressed in a direct fashion rather than indirectly through a third party such as the course. In person-centred theory this is a better model for communication not to mention potential conflict resolution. The term 'placement' is borrowed from the social work domain where the course 'places' the worker into a practice context and then maintains a substantially parental responsibility for communication between the course member and the agency.

The alternative approach to counselling practice, whereby the course member is principally responsible to the counselling agency and the course does not interfere between the course member and the agency, respects the professionalism of the agency with respect to direct communication with the counsellor and also pays respect to the course member as a person who can take responsibility in relation to the agency.

This approach to responsibility does not debar communication between the agency, the counsellor and the course: in certain situations it might be important for all three parties to come together to discuss specific issues. However, any such communication between the course and the agency would happen with the full involvement of the course member and not behind his back.

Supervision Supports the Counsellor

Thus far the counselling profession has developed a system of supervision which fully supports the counsellor in her practice. Indeed, it might be argued that the British Association for Counselling (BAC) takes a distinctly person-centred orientation to supervision in advocating that the primary responsibility of the supervisor is to the counsellor rather than to the employer. The supervisor is expected to hold a confidential relationship with the counsellor and should not have any line management responsibility with respect to the counsellor (BAC, 1996b). This emphasis on a direct and primary responsibility to the counsellor is at odds with supervision policy and practice in other professions, for example in social work where the supervisor is usually the line manager with primary responsibility to the agency rather than the worker.

Person-centred theory would suggest that the counselling approach to supervision would help the counsellor to feel supported and empowered by the supervisory relationship. In such a relationship the counsellor would feel able to explore her areas of greatest difficulty in the knowledge that the purpose of the work is to assist her in her development rather than to oversee her work and judge her competence. This is generally the experience reported of counselling supervision (Dryden and Thorne, 1991; Mearns, 1995) and the contrast with social work supervision is highlighted by the number of social workers who employ their own counselling supervision because that is more nourishing (Mearns, 1995).

During training it is common to offer two or three different forms of supervision to the course member. The course might expect the trainee counsellor to employ a confidential *individual supervisor*, usually drawn from a list of supervisors whose training and experience is vetted by the course staff. Courses need to be pragmatic in compiling such a list. An ideal would be to have a supervisor who was trained at depth in the person-centred approach, who had considerable experience as a counsellor and had undergone additional supervision training. However, for various reasons it is not always possible to demand all three of these criteria. The geographical distribution of well-trained and experienced practitioners is by no means perfect and courses sometimes have to be creative in responding to bad distributions. One criterion which should be held as long as possible is that the prior counselling training of the supervisor is compatible in terms of core theoretical model with the course. The supervisor needs to be aware of the person-centred approach at practical and theoretical depth else she will not so readily be able to support the course member in that regard.

Person-centred counselling training courses would generally hold to the view that the relationship between the individual supervisor and the trainee counsellor should be confidential in the same way as exists in professional counselling. However, specific exceptions are made to that confidentiality contract. For example, the course might reasonably stipulate that it should be allowed to approach the supervisor to confirm the regularity and sufficiency of the supervision provided. Another exception which might be stated is that the course or the supervisor may contact each other in the event that either is concerned about the ethical working of the course member. These exceptions should be few in number and need to be clear to the trainee counsellor from the outset, lest the value of the supervision as a confidential relationship is diminished.

It is possible that this orientation taken by counselling supervision whereby the supervisor is responsible *to* the counsellor rather than responsible *for* the counsellor simply reflects the fact that the profession is still in its infancy. Perhaps the effects of creeping institutionalisation will mean that the profession becomes governed by the need to protect itself from the isolated case and sacrifice useful ideas such as the empowerment of the practitioner. Already, signs to that effect can be noted by the fact that some counsellor training courses do not permit a confidential relationship between the individual supervisor and the trainee counsellor but require regular consultations between trainers and supervisors on the progress of the course member.

One of the problems that can arise in this confidential relationship between supervisor and trainee counsellor is that the course member uses the privacy of the supervisory relationship to explore difficulties which he might be having on the course. Supervisors might respond to this in different ways. Some may feel that it is relevant to give some time to that exploration, insofar as it may be affecting the course member's actual counselling work. Others may believe that this is an area unrelated to the course member's counselling work and should be taken elsewhere, perhaps into personal therapy. In either case all supervisors would also be expected to encourage the course member to address his difficulties directly back in the course. In similar fashion, if a course member voiced a difficulty about his supervisor in one of the training groups, he would be encouraged to address it directly with the supervisor. In both these instances we have further examples of the person-centred responsibility dynamic at work – encouraging the course member to address issues in the relationships where they belong. If supervisors are inclined to permit the trainee counsellor to use supervision time to talk about difficulties on the course they need to be strict in limiting that attention. Box 6.2 presents a supervisor's experience on this matter.

Box 6.2

An Incompetent Supervisor

I realise now that when I started supervising trainee counsellors I was so insecure about the supervision role that, rather than keeping it focused on client work, I just went with anything the supervisee wanted to talk about. In the person-centred approach it is easy to hide our incompetence behind the person-centred notion that the client/supervisee/trainee dictates the process. Inevitably my supervision would drift into personal therapy unless the supervisee kept the boundary. In the main, supervisees would spend a lot of time talking about what was happening to them on the course. With embarrassment, I remember writing to the course to complain that they needed to increase the criterion for supervision time because it was insufficient to meet needs! What needs? Whose needs?

As well as creating a provision for confidential individual supervision a training course will also offer *group supervision* as part of the training. Usually this training group supervision does not offer sufficient supervisory cover for the course member, but works well in conjunction with individual supervision. While the individual supervision is primarily concerned with the ongoing support of the trainee counsellor in relation to his client work, the supervision group is designed to help him to integrate the theory of the course with the practice of his counselling. These supervision groups are usually facilitated by core staff of the course and the relationship offered is not one which includes confidentiality. In fact, it is extremely important that individual members of staff do *not* promise confidentiality with course members. The staff need to be regarded as a team whose members will share information about individual course members. That discussion of the progress of course members is part of keeping in touch with the development of the trainee on the course. A trainer puts herself in an utterly untenable position if she offers a confidential relationship with a course member. Before long she discovers that she is keeping 'secrets' from her colleagues and engaging in a 'special relationship' with the course member (see Chapter 4). The alternative is that the staff creates a 'confidentiality net' whereby the course member can be assured that any disclosures are held to be confidential within the staff team. In practice this way of working is experienced by course members as offering additional 'support', but it is important that they know of the notion of the 'confidentiality net' from the outset of the course.

Some courses include peer group supervision, that is, group supervision without the staff facilitator. This is not simply a means of saving staff time, but a conscious strategy to encourage autonomy. A form of peer group supervision is practised in the University of East Anglia training where the groups have a staff facilitator for the first eight weeks but only for alternate meetings thereafter.

The combination of confidential individual supervision and group supervision meets the range of supervisory needs required by the course member, although the counselling agency in which the course member is practising may offer a third form of supervision usually called 'managerial' supervision, designed to ensure the course member is working in ways which are compatible with the organisation.

The Distinctiveness of Person-Centred Supervision

Counselling agencies are sometimes nervous about their counsellors 'taking clients' to external supervisors and supervision groups. Quite rightly, the agencies want to ensure the protection of both the anonymity and the confidentiality of their clients. They will know that professional counsellor trainers and supervisors will also regard confidentiality and anonymity as of paramount importance. Any counsellor taking her work with a client to supervision would not use the full name of the client and, indeed, would change the Christian name if that could be identified. Also, factual material which might identify the client would be omitted. Despite these cautions which are built into supervision within the profession, counselling agencies are still correct to be nervous about 'client material' being taken to outside supervision. Historically, much of what has passed for supervision within the profession has been thinly disguised 'case discussion'. Some years ago I remember sitting through a session of 'group supervision' in an agency and found that it amounted to little more than the counsellor 'presenting' the client by means of a long speech of biographical detail about this client plus what the client had been saying during sessions. To this was added the counsellor's interpretations of the client and prognosis for the client's future development. In the short time which was available for group discussion 'of this client', group members, now working with third hand information, proceeded to engage in the equivalent of the game of Cluedo to guess about this client's personality dynamics and make their own prognoses. It seemed to me that everyone could leave the session feeling very satisfied with their own cleverness and the support they had offered. I did wonder if anything which had transpired had anything at all to do with the client's reality. Perhaps all that had happened was that the new 'game' of 'case discussion' had been played.

Supervision of the above form, in the complete absence of the client, is of questionable value. In the person-centred approach we hold to the discipline that no judgements can be made of the client or of the counsellor's behaviour in relation to the client on the basis of second-hand information, that is, information relayed by the counsellor. This position emphasises the importance of audio-tape supervision described in the next section, but it also lays a disciplined foundation to individual and group supervision in which the client is not represented. In person-centred supervision, instead of the counsellor 'bringing the client' to supervision, the counsellor brings *herself*. With the focus on the counsellor rather than the client, the kinds of questions which are raised in person-centred supervision might be drawn from the 20 that follow:

- How do I (the counsellor) behave in relation to this client?
- What do I feel in relation to this client?
- What do I think when I work with this client?
- What goes on 'underneath' for me?
- What parts of myself am I using with this client?
- Am I 'changing' (using different parts of me) in relation to this client?
- What parts of myself am I not using in relation to this client?
- What is the nature of my empathy with this client?
- Are there any blocks to my empathy with this client?
- How is my warmth with this client?
- Is my warmth different with this client than with others?
- Do I have any tendency towards 'conditionality' with this client?
- In what ways am I being incongruent with this client?
- Am I feeling any problems in relation to my contract with this client?
- Am I experiencing any 'boundary' problems with this client?
- What am I learning in relationship with this client?
- What are my assumptions about how the client is experiencing me?
- How am I checking on the client's experiencing?
- What is my judgement of this client's locus of evaluation?

● How is my judgement of the client's locus of evaluation affecting my communication with the client?

The reader will notice that only the nineteenth of these 20 questions is about the client. The extent to which the client's locus of evaluation is externalised or internalised is the only client variable which will mediate the person-centred counsellor's communication. As explained elsewhere (Mearns, 1994d), when working with a client whose locus of evaluation is profoundly externalised, the counsellor must take care with her communication lest she introduce conceptualisations into the client's symbolisation. All the other questions represent entries in the counsellor's 'focusing on the therapeutic relationship' (Mearns and Thorne, 1988, ch. 3). None of the work of supervision is based on biographical material about the client. With this different approach taken to counselling supervision within the person-centred approach agencies might feel reassured with respect to the issues of confidentiality and anonymity. In every sense of the term, the counsellor is *not* bringing the client to supervision but she is bringing *herself*.

Audiotape Supervision

In the previous section I emphasised that much of the supervision within the person-centred approach is concerned to work on the development of the counsellor rather than endeavour to work with client material indirectly. However, this does not mean that the person-centred approach rejects the client from supervision. On the contrary, the person-centred approach merely rejects the *indirect* nature of client material which is filtered through the counsellor. Considerable emphasis is placed on working, within supervision, with material that comes *directly* from the counselling relationship. The most practical way to obtain this direct material is by means of the counsellor audiotaping her sessions and working with the audiotape in supervision. The case for audiotape supervision is laid out elsewhere (Dryden et al., 1995; Mearns, 1995). Central to the issue of using audiotapes of actual counselling sessions is the question of client consent. The resistance within the profession to audiotaping gathers around the notion of client consent and the degree to which that consent can ever be properly 'informed'. While that question of informed consent has to be properly addressed, it can also be excessively misused by counsellors scurrying to find a bunker to protect them from the challenge of their work being viewed. I hope that the issue of audiotape supervision does not become entombed by a profession which misuses ethical concerns to protect itself from challenge. Let us remember, if we are taking an ethical perspective, that audiotape supervision is probably the only means we have to check upon the ethical nature of the counsellor's work.

My considerable experience of audiotape supervision, as a counsellor and a supervisor, convinces me that it is one of the best means, not only of supervision, but of training. I firmly believe that training needs could be *entirely* met through audiotape supervision, given the right structure. In that regard I imagine a group of eight course members and one senior trainer basing their entire work of the week on the presentation, by each course member, of a one-hour tape of his current work. Each one-hour tape would take at least two hours in presentation and analysis. I believe that a skilled trainer could use this considerable amount of practical counselling work to draw out the full spectrum of counselling theory. I also imagine that a group working in that kind of way would engage the range of personal development objectives of a counselling training course. In fact, this model would represent a highly creative and consistently person-centred approach to counsellor training.

In audiotape supervision the client is represented by his own words. Certainly, there are various non-verbal cues which were available to the counsellor but are not available to the supervisor in the audiotape, but there is enough representation of the client to begin a supervision process which looks directly at the counsellor's relating with the client. Some examples of this were quoted in an earlier work focusing on audiotape supervision (Mearns, 1995).

> It is remarkable to see the issues which audiotape supervision can raise, compared to conventional supervision with the client absent. Some recent examples the writer has encountered include:
>
> (i) More sense was made of a client who had been described by her counsellor as 'unresponsive' when an audiotape revealed the nervous tendency of the trainee counsellor to leave wholly inappropriate silences. Silence can be a powerful facilitator when the client is reaching the edge of her or his awareness, but when she or he has asked the counsellor a direct question the counsellor's silence is likely to be confusing at best and alienating at worst.
>
> (ii) After a number of sessions in which the supervisee described a particular client as 'highly dependent and manipulating', the only way to get closer to a wider reality was to switch to audiotape supervision. This quickly showed that the client's requests of the counsellor and her affect in relation to the counsellor were quite

appropriate, but that the counsellor's responses were more to do with his own fear of dependency than anything coming from the client.

(iii) The counsellor held a presumption, denied by the client, that the client had experienced early sexual abuse. Although this presumption seemed to be largely based on the counsellor's experience of other clients, she [the counsellor] found it difficult not to let it influence her responses to the client. A switch to audiotape supervision revealed the selective way in which the counsellor was drawing inferences from her client's statements and helped the counsellor to become less imposing with respect to her presumption.

(iv) In indirect supervision, with the client missing, no difficulty had been reported regarding the counsellor's sexuality. Yet the counsellor became concerned about indirect feedback emanating from an earlier client. A switch to audiotape supervision showed more of the quality of the counsellor's interactions with clients than could ever have been communicated through indirect supervision. Painfully, the supervisor helped the counsellor to realise that ways of being which he considered as emanating from his spirituality might be experienced by some clients as his sexuality. (p. 426)

The case for audiotape supervision as a normal part of the supervision of professional counsellors is strong. My experience is that supervisees who have explored audiotape work have largely found it to be of more benefit than most other aspects of their training once they have overcome their fear. When we consider the counsellor in training, the case for audiotape supervision as a routine element of the course is even stronger. There can be no other profession which would consider accrediting new members without their work ever having been witnessed by their trainers.

The 'Assessment' of Clients

A final issue which brings together the areas of counselling experience and supervision is the question of whether clients should be 'assessed' prior to their allocation to trainee counsellors. The whole question of client 'assessment' runs entirely counter to person-centred theory and fits those approaches to counselling which more closely align to the diagnostic 'medical model'. Within the person-centred domain the question of assessment is ridiculous: the assessor would have to make a judgement not only about the client but on the relational dimensions between the client and the counsellor.

In the University of Strathclyde courses we have had to face this issue of client assessment. The University runs a free public

Counselling Clinic which connects the enormous need there is in the community for a free counselling service with the resource the University Counselling Unit has in its mature counselling course members. As providers of a counselling service and trainers of the counsellors involved we faced the question of whether the prospective client should be 'assessed' prior to allocation to counsellors. While we were aware that such assessment existed in other places, we considered that it was a procedure of questionable validity. That assumption was indirectly supported by the fact that there is no research evidence to support either the validity or the reliability of client assessment procedures. During the past four years of our public Counselling Clinic we have not operated a system of client assessment. Instead, we have committed the enormous resources which would have gone into client assessment to the support of the trainee counsellors engaged in the service. Our experience is that very few of the clients using our service present extreme difficulties to our trainee counsellors. This may partly be due to the fact that the course members engaged in our public counselling service have already surpassed the most demanding criteria of voluntary agencies as far as training is concerned. Also, it reflects a strength of the person-centred approach in its de-emphasis of the pathology of the client and its added emphasis on the strength of the therapeutic relationship between counsellor and client.

An important facet of this 'non-assessment' approach to our public Counselling Clinic is how we handle the extreme case. Over the past four years there have probably been six clients who represented particular difficulty for the counsellors involved. In these cases we have offered the resource which might otherwise have been put into client assessment towards further support of the counsellor. The counsellor knows that, in the last analysis, they can choose *not* to work with a client. In fact, their choice has consistently been towards continuing the therapeutic relationship which they have already established. In these extreme cases we have offered additional supervisory support either supplied from one of our core tutors or financed by us through extra provision from the course member's individual supervisor. Essentially, the provision we are making is to support the trainee counsellor in her work rather than to take the work away from the trainee counsellor. Our decision on that emphasis emanated from concern for the client. For a start, we abhorred the procedure whereby a client would have to present his story to a counselling 'assessor' who would not be working with him in the future but would be making a decision on the appropriateness of his involvement with

the public counselling service. The trainee counsellor, if sufficiently supported through supervision, can cope with considerable demands as far as clients are concerned. Our most extreme
situation in this regard found one of our trainee counsellors, a
mature and experienced counsellor from the voluntary sector,
working with *two* particularly difficult clients. The course member
had the option to drop one or both of these clients but chose to
continue with both. Our response was to offer her extra free
supervision which amounted to two hours' supervision for every
client contact hour. This describes a particularly person-centred
response to a problem: instead of dismissing the client we
invested more resources in support of the counsellor to continue
her work with the client.

The person-centred approach has a considerable amount to
offer the profession on the issue of counselling experience supported by supervision. While the profession, particularly in its
increasing tendency towards institutionalisation, would emphasise issues such as client assessment for work with trainee counsellors, the person-centred approach continues to question the
validity of such assessment and to offer an alternative way of
protecting the client and the counsellor. My hope is that the
profession does not become so institutionalised that it must
inhibit work with people in order to protect itself against the
extreme case.

Early in this chapter the counselling profession was praised for
its expansive, 'counsellor-related' approach to supervision. Now
our book moves on to consider another great strength of the
counselling profession – its emphasis on personal development.

7
Personal Development during Training

The Personal Development Demands for Working at Relational Depth

To set the scene for this chapter on personal development I need to review some of the ideas presented in Chapter 2. In that chapter I explored the issues involved in working at relational depth with clients in person-centred counselling. In contrasting this with counselling work which merely demanded *surface relational competencies*, I pointed to the profound personal development demands required for working at relational depth. The free-flowing congruence of the worker is a pre-requisite to meeting the client at relational depth. To achieve that freedom with congruence demands that the trainee counsellor forgoes the security of *portrayal*. There is a natural tendency for course members, early in training, to endeavour to portray therapeutic conditions such as empathy and unconditional positive regard. In an intensive and extensive training course the trainee will find that she cannot meet clients or fellow course members at relational depth through mere portrayal but that the development of congruent functioning poses many challenges to her personal development. Congruent functioning requires a *stillness* and *fearlessness* within the person of the counsellor. Achieving that personal stillness and fearlessness requires that the course member first becomes *aware* of the fears, then comes to *understand* the fears and third, begins to *experiment* with increasingly fearless relating.

Adequate personal development in counselling training requires all three of these steps: awareness, understanding and experimentation with Self. Merely becoming *aware* of the existence of one's fears does not create fearlessness. However, if that awareness moves on to *understanding* then some of the fear may diminish. What also tends to happen at this stage of understanding is that the course member becomes aware that not all her fears have a live basis in the present – many are '*ghosts*' from the past – she is actually not fearful in that area but because it has been held behind closed doors for so long, she has not noticed her own development. The third step of *experimentation with Self* might come as a natural consequence of awareness and understanding. Clients in counselling will sometimes but not always go through that later phase of experimentation. However, a training course is not counselling and the course member places extra demands on herself to move as fully as she can during the training period. To this end the trainee counsellor does not stop at awareness and understanding but actively experiments with her growing fearlessness. This is a crucial stage because the course member will inevitably find that her long-held fears have exaggerated their own existence. Hopefully she finds that when she dares to relate congruently with others the sky does not fall down and the Self is not destroyed; she may instead begin to experience the joys of intimacy borne of meeting the other at relational depth.

The challenge then for training courses is to create learning contexts where the course member can move through all three stages of awareness, understanding and experimentation with Self, in relation to a range of long-held fears and ghosts of fears (Mearns, 1996b). The process begins before the trainees even come together, with the admissions policy of the course.

Admission of Students to Counsellor Training

Course admission procedures represent an important first step in achieving the personal development dimension within training (Mearns, 1996a). Conditions on the course must be created which will serve two main objectives.

1 *To create a structure where course members can forge a trusting environment for intensive personal development work.* The need to create the best possible context for the development of trust is the major reason why intensive person-centred counsellor training courses *maintain the integrity of the student cohort.* While it may be administratively and financially convenient for institutions to operate systems of APL and APEL, allowing students to enter the training at different points depending on previous work, that is so destructive of the integrity of the training cohort that it is inappropriate for person-centred training. Similarly, a modular approach to training, if that means a constantly changing cohort with students opting into and out of modules at different times, would be inappropriate for a course that attempted to tackle

personal development at depth. My emphasis on maintaining the integrity of the student cohort and cautioning against university systems of APL and modularisation is shared by Hazel Johns (1996):

> The need for and valuing of such [*personal development*] work has strengthened the rationale for course groups of a reasonable size – despite pressures for income generation – and for those groups to be coherent and stable over the duration of the course. Movement towards modularisation, APL and APEL (accreditation of prior learning and prior experiential learning) may threaten this pattern of provision and could dramatically dilute the effectiveness of personal development work in higher education and commercial contexts. (p. 29)

2 *To ensure, as far as possible, the rejection at admission of applicants whose personal development is insufficiently advanced for the particularly challenging development contexts in training.* In Chapter 5, I pointed to the importance of course members being 'at a point of readiness' to embrace the personal development dimension of the training. One aspect of the applicant's readiness is the degree of *fear*. Sometimes counsellor training attracts applicants who are too highly fearful. Where the fear is too high, therapy is a better learning context than training. Admitting such applicants to counsellor training results in danger to them and also considerable course time devoted to the exercise of their defences without much progress being made.

In terms of person-centred theory there are two main personality dynamics which might underly this fear and make the experience of training too difficult. Firstly, there is the person whose *locus of evaluation* is simply too *externalised*. A degree of externalisation should be expected but if that is too extreme the fear will be too high. The danger for this prospective course member is that she will have such a powerful need to use others as the locus for her evaluation that she will find it extremely difficult to move beyond the stage of portrayal to experiment with congruence. If she stays within portrayal she can be fairly sure that she can win the approval of others for apparent displays of empathy and unconditional positive regard. On a training course which did not challenge the course member to considerable depth of personal development this course member might well be successful because her portrayal is sufficient. The danger for her, and for her clients, would be if she extended her work into a full-time professional capacity where she could not survive on portrayal.

A second personality dynamic which is difficult to spot in selection is the applicant who has an *excessive need to hold on to her self-concept as it is.* This person cannot risk the possibility of feedback which deviates from her self-concept. The reality is that this personality dynamic is so difficult to spot at selection that the person often proceeds on to the training. In the early stages of the course she appears as a highly motivated course member trying very hard, perhaps too hard, 'to get things right'. As the challenges to her incongruence in relating mount, this person is in genuine despair because she simply cannot 'get it right'. The position becomes extremely fearful for her because the more she is challenged the more she needs to defend her brittle self-concept – it is a matter of survival. There is also considerable sadness for all concerned because this is a person whose desire for intimacy is as enormous as her fear of it. She will quite genuinely want to be a good counsellor and a good course member but at this stage of her personal development the challenges of training are too great.

The reader who is familiar with the conventional language of psychopathology will recognise that the personality dynamics I have been tracing above might broadly correspond to the labels of excessively 'neurotic' and 'borderline'. Elke Lambers offers an introduction to articulation between these terms and the language of person-centred personality theory (Lambers, 1994a, c).

The Personal Development Curriculum

Thus far I have focused on the processes of awareness, understanding and experimentation with Self which would be encouraged in the personal development dimensions of training. It might be useful to highlight some of the elements which comprise the personal development curriculum. Obviously, the only way to approach such a curriculum is in an individualised fashion – the list of personal development aims which follows would not apply to every course member. Each person would have her own profile of needs drawn from this list and others which are not included. Indeed, a useful self-appraisal exercise for course members towards the end of their course is to endeavour to construct their personal development needs profile for themselves and explore how it has evolved in relation to the tripartite processes of awareness, understanding and experimentation with Self.

As an example of the personal development curriculum there follows a list of 25 specific aims relating to the course member's development in regard to her Self-structure, Self in relation, Self as counsellor and Self as learner. These are detailed in Dryden et al. (1995, pp. 98–9).

Self-structure

1 awareness of introjected beliefs about Self and how these influence self-concept and behaviour;
2 awareness of personal processes of 'dissonance reduction' and how these are involved in the 'social construction of reality';
3 understanding how social and personality dynamics have influenced the development of Self;
4 understanding the 'conditions of worth' which operated in own early development and how these continue to influence self-concept, personal development and work with clients;
5 identification of the stages of movement through personal transitional experiences;
6 development of a sufficiently strong sense of personal identity to resist being drawn into the client's pathology;
7 the achievement of a significant degree of 'self-acceptance'.

Self in relation

1 awareness of introjected beliefs about others and how these influence person perception and behaviour;
2 awareness of enduring patterns in own behaviour within inter-personal relations and the needs and fears upon which these patterns are based;
3 awareness of the assumptions, introjections, needs and fears upon which personal prejudices are based;
4 reduction or control over the influences of personal prejudices;
5 awareness of the way in which own sexuality is expressed within personal and professional relationships;
6 understanding of personal (as distinct from psychological) theories of human behaviour;
7 challenging of the dimensions of Self that inhibit the achievement of mutuality in therapeutic relationships.

Self as counsellor

1 awareness of the ways in which personal prejudices influence judgement and behaviour in the counselling setting;

2   awareness of 'blocks' inhibiting personal development with respect to expression of the 'therapeutic conditions' of empathy, unconditional positive regard and congruence;
3   understanding of the dynamics of Self which create vulnerability to 'over-involvement';
4   understanding of the dynamics of Self which create vulnerability to 'under-involvement';
5   awareness of the projections which own behaviour is inclined to encourage in clients and questioning of the motivation underpinning those behaviours.

Self as learner

1   the ability to develop personal learning goals;
2   a disposition to examine critically and systematically personal understanding, attitudes and skills;
3   a confidence to tolerate and learn from the uncertainty which may stem from having assumptions and attitudes challenged;
4   a disposition of openness to experience as it relates to the Self, and an acceptance of responsibility for own behaviour and own learning;
5   the ability to use the products of consultation with others as a part of the process of self-appraisal;
6   the capacity to appraise Self openly and accurately.

Exploring each of these 25 personal development aims would constitute a dissertation in itself. My aim in this chapter is simply to indicate both the breadth and depth of a typical personal development curriculum. While these aims derive from person-centred personality theory, many would find a home within other therapeutic approaches, perhaps in a different language. It is also worth noting that the fourth category, *Self as learner*, has wider relevance than simply helping the course member to make full use of the training opportunities. Each of the six aims traces an internalising of the locus of evaluation and a movement towards the counsellor developing as a reflective practitioner.

When these aims are presented, as above, in abstracted academic form, it is easy to lose sight of how fundamental any one of them may be to the existence of a course member. The phenomenological reality is that any one of these areas may harbour enormous fears for an individual trainee – fears about what she does not know about that aspect of herself and also fears about what she does know.

Training Approaches to Personal Development

When devising training approaches relevant to the personal development curriculum, three criteria need to be taken into consideration.

1 Each course member will portray a different pattern of needs with respect to these personal development aims – therefore the course must create learning structures which are highly *individualised*.
2 Personal development 'learning' is intimately tied to the self-concept and change is not easily achieved. The learning structures must offer numerous and varied opportunities to *visit* and *revisit* the issues involved.
3 Learning structures must be created which allow the course member to relate to the personal development curriculum at all three levels – *awareness*, *understanding* and *experimentation with Self*.

Courses cope with these criteria by adopting a multi-method approach to personal development. Some of the methods employed are discussed in the sections that follow.

Specific Workshops and Exercises

Workshops on areas such as 'abuse', 'inner child', 'sexuality', 'social power', 'spirituality' and 'cultural issues' will have a dual value within the course in that they are useful in helping to understand the range of human experience which will be reflected among clients but there will also be personal development value for the course member looking at herself in relation to these areas.

Specific exercises may also be used to assist the course member's reflection on Self to develop awareness and perhaps elements of early understanding. For example, the exercise of 'personality mapping' is one such example. It takes a minimum of three hours but can usefully fill a six-hour day. The methodology is similar to that of 'concept mapping', with the course member invited to use whatever materials are available (pens, crayons, 'post-it' labels and large sheets of paper) to represent all the elements of her personality as it is known to her. Hence the course member might begin by depicting some of her abilities and major dimensions of Self. She might go on to explore central themes within her personality and values which connect different areas. Perhaps there are parts of her personality which she separates off, parts which are only partially known and others of which she has only a hazy sense. Much can be made of depicting the power of introjections and earlier conditions of worth. She might find imaginative ways of exploring and depicting her self-protective strategies (defence mechanisms). Some areas of her map may contain 'secrets' which need to be protected by the 'post-it' labels. Sometimes the 'post-it' labels will be left so that they can be lifted to display what lies beneath, if that is the mapper's choice – others may be firmly sealed down with tape. After constructing the map the second phase of the exercise is to explore it with a partner. The act of talking it out with another person is, in itself, a powerful experience and can give rise to new insights.

Expansion of Life Experience

Even at the beginning of counsellor training, course members often testify to the salience of life experience events in advancing their personal development to date. There is no reason why that process should stop during counsellor training. This is well described by Dryden et al. (1995):

> . . . the student would be encouraged, supported and helped to monitor efforts they might be making, for example, to become more familiar with different sub-cultures; to put themselves into contact with an otherwise feared group; or actively to experiment with alternative ways of relating in an effort to break inappropriate or inadequate habits. The personal development group is often the focus for encouraging, supporting and monitoring the trainee's extension of their life experience and the power of such experimentation influences not only the individual student but also the other people in the group. It can be very moving, for example, to listen to a trainee who, having identified racist attitudes within herself, actively puts herself into the situation of working in a voluntary information and counselling service within a predominantly Pakistani community or the trainee who bravely contracted himself into 20 weekly sessions in a men's group because he had a fear of men. (p. 105)

Personal Therapy

Many training courses require on-going personal therapy during training despite the fact that there is no clear relationship between personal therapy and counsellor performance (Aveline, 1990; Bergin and Garfield, 1994). Traditions vary widely in their outlook upon personal therapy during training, with psychodynamic training usually requiring it of every course member but the person-centred approach preferring therapy to be a matter of personal choice (Mearns, 1994c). All trainers would agree, however, that it is important to refer course members to personal therapy if the fear they are encountering is too great to be held by the other course structures. Typically, the personal therapy is removed from the care of the course, with no dialogue between personal therapists and course trainers.

Training Therapy

One of the problems with personal therapy as a part of training is that it can too easily become a direction of referral for trainers where they refer difficult issues for the course member more in hope than in expectation and receive little in the way of feedback. Another problem with personal therapy is that the course member will, understandably, take those issues which are most salient for her and will not necessarily present the personal development issues which have been raised by the course. One solution to these problems is *training therapy* where the therapy is seen as an integral part of the training rather than an add-on. There is logic in firmly integrating the therapy because the personal development issues which it is addressing have enormous significance to the training course as well as the course member.

In training therapy there is a regular dialogue involving course tutor, course member and training therapist where all three discuss:

1   The issues which have been referred from the training course to the training therapy.
2   The further understanding which has been achieved through the training therapy.
3   The aspects of 'experimentation with Self' which the course member may develop back in the training.

Training therapy offers a powerful approach to personal development since it integrates high degrees of both containment and challenge. Unfortunately, research into training therapy has been totally curtailed during recent years by the discouragement in codes of ethics of the close association between trainers and therapists (BAC, 1996a). It would be possible for a specific case to be made for the exploration of training therapy but too often codes of ethics are taken as a list of prohibitions rather than as a series of challenging questions.

Personal Development Groups

The personal development group endeavours to help course members to become aware of salient personal development issues, to gain some understanding of those issues and to create a sufficiently safe yet also public context in which the course member may experiment with aspects of her developing Self.

This typical way of working for a personal development group is well illustrated in Dryden et al. (1995).

> The personal development group . . . is also a vibrant context for identifying personal development needs. If an atmosphere of trust and spirit of encounter can be developed in the group, the members can help each other identify needs which might otherwise have been blind spots. Thus, personal development group members may help each other at all stages of negotiating a personal development issue as depicted in the diagram below and in the example which follows.

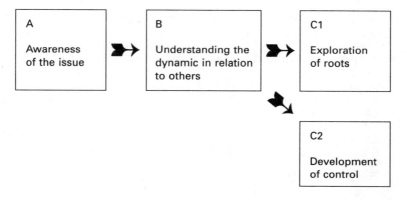

EXAMPLE

Nobody in the personal development group doubted John's attentiveness and caring for clients. Furthermore, he was generally regarded as being more knowledgeable about counselling than anyone else in the group. Yet there was a quality about John which had made it difficult for others to feel really close to him. In a way, it seemed that he was almost too competent. It was only after some months of meeting in the group that one member voiced what others had sensed but not in such a fully-formed fashion. She observed that for a long time she had deferred to him and that that deferring was not so much a response to *what* he said but the *way* he said it and his general demeanour. The way she experienced him was as 'behaving in a very powerful way'. Her clarity helped others to voice their own experiences. One person said that she had felt exactly the same but had presumed that it was her own tendency to feel inferior which was the source of the difficulty. It was difficult for John to hear this because he genuinely felt that he was warm and open to these people and in no way wanted to be experienced as 'powerful'. In a crossover between his personal development group and his supervision group, he began to look at how he behaved in the counselling relationship. Sure enough, when he asked others to listen to audio tapes of his work they confirmed that if they had been the client they might have felt considerably inferior to his rather commanding persona. The supervision group was able to help him to monitor his way of relating to clients through later tapes and back in the personal development group John explored the disjunction between his outward behaviour and his inner feeling, dipping into the roots in his earlier life (stage C1) and also actively experimenting with different ways of being in relation to others in the group (stage C2).

This example represents a fairly typical use of the personal development group and also the interaction between personal development and supervision. The personal development group is one of many groupings in the training course which, if the right spirit of encounter is established, can help members to become aware of personal development issues (stage A) and understand the interpersonal dynamics relating to those issues (stage B). Thereafter, the group can help the members to explore the roots of the issue (stage C1) as well as developing other ways of being (stage C2). Had John been in on-going training therapy that would also have been a useful place to refer further exploration of the roots. However, it is relevant to note that while individual therapy is a good place for exploring issues already identified, it may not be as powerful as groups for actually identifying the problem. John had spent one and a half years in prior therapy without this issue ever being identified. (pp. 102–3)

There is an increasing trend on training courses to displace the facilitation of personal development groups to external rather than core staff. The rationale for this is that it may be difficult for course members to be open in personal development groups if the facilitator is also a tutor-assessor. My own view on this is that it is extremely dangerous to divest personal development to the periphery of a person-centred counsellor training course. Personal development is core to the endeavour and it is vital that core staff can communicate and assist course members in that regard. If the dual role of assessment creates problems then it is incumbent on the staff to find ways of solving the assessment problem rather than diminishing their training responsibility. Certainly, on person-centred training, the dimension of personal development is so central that it is inconceivable to divest it to peripheral staff. This question of the staffing of personal development groups is well discussed by Hazel Johns (1996, pp. 125–6).

Large Group Working

It may seem paradoxical to suggest that working within the whole course group of perhaps 30 or 40 members plus staff can be a powerful means of advancing personal development. Probably the person-centred approach is the only one which has explored this phenomenon through the interest first expressed in large group phenomena by Carl Rogers (Bowen et al., 1980). The unstructured large group is a difficult learning context to predict and to contain (see Chapter 10). That lack of containment and predictability also represents its power as far as raising personal development issues and providing a context for Self-experimentation are concerned. Even when people are not directly involved in a present interaction within the large group they might find that that interaction challenges many of their assumptions or reflects their own fears. One example was the angry outburst between two course members which brought a third to terror and tears. In her phenomenal world an angry confrontation such as she had witnessed should end in psychological annihilation and yet the two principals seemed both clearer and more trusting of each other after the confrontation. Many months later in the large group the third member was seen to confront another in anger. She was experimenting with Self, having become aware of her fear and grown to understand its familial basis.

Hazel Johns (1996) is understandably sceptical about the use of the large group in counsellor training, believing that the same learning potential is present in small groups with greater safety. However, it is the *fact* that small groups are much more easily normed and thereby contained which makes them qualitatively different from large groups which can touch parts of the Self unreached by other methods.

An error which has crept into training is the presumption that, because a large group has functioned well in one context, then it should be brought into every training course. The unstructured large group requires certain conditions for it to function in a congruent fashion. Usually the training course needs to be fairly lengthy and also intense. These ingredients tend to bring with them a strong commitment to the process on the part of the membership of the course and a willingness to address difficult issues rather than bury them. Even with the right conditions it can take some time for course members to become convinced about the veracity of unstructured large group working. Indeed, for some, the challenge of such a public arena is so great that it can take a long time to begin to experiment with Self in that context.

Yet, such is the power of the arena that even small experiments can reap large rewards, as reported by one participant:

> It was a relatively small thing to do – to empathise with someone else across the large group. And yet, I got a huge amount out of it. To actually hear myself speak and finish my sentences was amazing – I was no longer paralysed by the fear of what other people would think of me.

I have dipped briefly into large group working to establish its relevance particularly to the 'experimentation with Self' stage of personal development. Chapter 10 will give a more systematic and detailed consideration of large group working in person-centred counselling training.

In this section I have endeavoured to say a little on the main approaches taken to personal development. There are many other approaches possible, for example, *training group therapy* relaxes the tension which the personal development group tries to hold with respect to therapeutic working and shifts the emphasis from the group as a place which raises personal development issues to one where the course member can also work on the issues which have been raised.

Comparing and Contrasting the Approaches

For the sake of encouraging dialogue on the comparison and contrasting of these different approaches I have prepared a table (Table 7.1) which presents my views on the relative power of each approach to raise personal development issues, to work on these

Table 7.1   *Approaches to personal development: power rankings (out of 10)*

Method	Raising issues	Working on issues	Experimenting with developing self
Workshops/exercises	5	1	2
Expansion of life experience	5	5	8
Personal therapy	1	5	2
Training therapy	8	10	2
Personal development groups	8	3	5
Large group working	8	2	8
Training group therapy	5	10	5

issues and to provide a context for experimenting with the developing Self.

I emphasise that there is no empirical justification for the entries in the table – they simply represent my comparisons as a prompt for consideration. While the ratings for *workshops/exercises* are relatively low, it needs to be noted that these serve other functions within training, most particularly in helping people to think about different client groups, problems and the like. The ratings for *expansion of life experience* are quite high. Personally, I believe that this is indeed the strongest approach because it puts the person into extremely challenging life situations which she has consciously chosen for the difficult issues they raise. To continue to exist in that situation will require her to work on the issues it raises and the whole process is one of experimenting with her developing Self. I give fairly low ratings for *personal therapy* because my own consistent experience as a trainer is that personal therapy is a poor place for raising issues, a reasonable context for working on them but not nearly as vibrant as a group context for experimenting with the developing Self. These low ratings are not meant to be critical of therapy, simply the presumption that personal therapy meets training needs. I believe that *training therapy* is a considerable improvement because the therapeutic work is more focused on needs which are associated with personal development relevant to the training. *Personal development groups* are particularly potent places for raising issues and also provide a good context for experimenting with Self. However, because they hold the tension away from therapeutic work, they provide only limited opportunities for working on the issues. The ratings I give for *large group working* undoubtedly reflect my considerable personal bias in finding this to be a vibrant context for raising issues and experimenting with Self. However, I am also aware that the large group can arouse so much fear as to be ineffective for some participants during the early part of their training. I believe that *training group therapy* is an extraordinarily potent personal development approach across all categories. However, it is expensive in time because to offer space for additional working on the issues raised means that two or three times the amount of space normally given to personal development groups is required.

The reality is that while comparison of these approaches is an aid to our thinking about them, they all have value and different emphases. Each training course dovetails approaches to obtain the mix and balance which is important for its purposes.

The Impact of Personal Development on Other Relational Living

Probably the most widespread problem with personal development is felt in the course member's other close relationships. Training course staff usually warn applicants at interview, endeavouring to explain the fact that the fairly rapid personal development on the course may have an impact on the participant's relationship with her partner. At this point in the interview some applicants smile in a knowing fashion – they have been on courses involving personal development before. Other applicants look back and wonder what on earth you are talking about, because this is, after all, simply a course and why should it affect her relationship with her partner?

Sometimes the problem is created by the combination of the *speed* of the course member's personal development during the training and the strong *emotional support* she is given by the other course members. That combination stabilises the personal development gains and may further speed up the process, even creating a 'greenhouse' effect. Within the course member's primary partnership a widening disparity develops in regard to the speed of personal development. The problem may be exacerbated if the course member becomes dissatisfied with her relatively incongruent existence at home while she is able to relate so congruently on the course. Once they become aware of congruent relating, people are generally shocked to see the extent which relationships in 'real life' are constructed upon incongruence. I am fascinated by the way people correlate congruence with 'unreality' and talk about the 'real world' which is substantially based upon incongruence. Perhaps my fascination stems from the fact that my adolescence was in the 1960s.

While trainers will be aware of this inherent problem in personal development, there is relatively little they can do beyond helping course members to consider their own actions. The problem can be thoroughly desperate for the course member who surely does not want to threaten her primary relationship but also feels that she cannot reverse her development.

Personal development is like that – it is possible to go forwards and sometimes we can pause for a while, but it is impossible to go backwards.

8
Skill Development

Some person-centred specialists will wonder how an entire chapter can be devoted to 'skill development' within the approach. Certainly the approach is not centred in skill development but in the congruence of the counsellor as emphasised in the previous chapter. Nevertheless, person-centred counselling is a skilful activity, albeit that its skills are grounded in the practitioner's personal development.

Reductionistic and Holistic Conceptions of Skill Development

Counselling approaches vary in their conception of skill development. Some hold to a *reductionistic* emphasis whereby skilful behaviour is subdivided into smaller units of discrete skills. Training exercises are then developed for each discrete skill with feedback and assessment available to the course member. Once discrete skills are practised and developed they can then be built upon each other once more to create integrated skilful behaviour.

Other approaches hold to a *holistic* emphasis whereby skilful behaviour is recognised but there is a reluctance to seek to break it into smaller units lest the integrated quality be lost. The view taken here is that the whole is more than the sum of its parts and cannot be assembled from those parts. Another presumption within this emphasis is that the skilful behaviour is inextricably tied to the personal development of the counsellor and to try to separate specific skills would be to encourage incongruence. 'Skills training' proceeds, but in a holistic fashion. Rather than discrete skills being practised, the emphasis is on conducting whole interviews or parts of interviews and monitoring the experience of those involved as well as the development the counsellor is making.

It is probably fair to say that no counselling approach is exclusively reductionistic or holistic in its emphasis. However, approaches vary considerably in their leanings towards the reductionistic or the holistic. For example, Egan's Skilled Helper approach leans heavily towards the reductionistic while Psychodynamic and Person-Centred counselling favour the holistic.

Carl Rogers always maintained a holistic conception of skill development but his encouragement of research, particularly research of a reductionistic character, inevitably created products which could be viewed in a reductionistic fashion. Truax and Carkhuff (1967) and Carkhuff (1969) fruitfully employed a fairly reductionistic perspective to the core conditions and offered much by way of operational definition of these conditions, though that work has not survived into present day training methodology which is more holistic in character.

Although person-centred trainers might favour a holistic orientation in relation to skill development it is important to realise that most course members would be arriving with reductionist expectations. Such expectations are largely spawned by prior education which is almost exclusively established on reductionistic principles regardless of the subject under study. Also, in the early stages, course members may crave a reductionistic framework because of the greater sense of security which it provides. If things can be subdivided, defined and understood the task appears to become so much easier, as one course member reflected:

> At the start I wanted the training to be by numbers . . . 1 . . . 2 . . . 3 . . . 4 . . . a step by step guide as to 'how to do person-centred therapy'. It was incredibly frustrating that the staff wouldn't cooperate in my fantasy.

In the following section we shall see how it is important for trainers to appreciate the entry point for course members in training and to endeavour to meet the course member half-way. However, it is also relevant to note the extent to which counselling training can prostitute itself to fit into a spurious reductionistic expectation. The best example of this in Britain is the previous government's exercise in promoting National Vocational Qualifications (NVQs) and Scottish Vocational Qualifications (SVQs) which endeavour to define appropriate counselling training solely in terms of a reductionistic framework already criticised on theoretical grounds (Johns, 1996; Goss and Mearns, 1997a, b). One of the amazing features of this attempt to reduce counselling training to a simplistic competency-based assessment, previously shown to be inadequate within the social work domain, is the fact that it has been supported, thus far, by the British Association for Counselling (BAC). This support may reflect the closeness of BAC to the voluntary counselling sector and its distance from professional counsellor trainers who have recognised the NVQ (SVQ) initiative for its shallowness. Probably the epitaph for the inevitably failing NVQ (SVQ) initiative is that it has been an astonishing waste of around 50,000 hours of the time of expert counsellors – time which could have been put to much better use for humanity than to serve the political ends of government.

Two Examples of Skills Sessions

It is possible to begin a person-centred counselling training course by meeting course members' expectations half-way. In this regard, one of the best areas is the skilful behaviour which we call empathy.

The Empathy Lab

I was first introduced to the empathy lab by Dr Charles Devonshire some 23 years ago but it doubtless has a history before that time. The lab is not preceeded by any lectures or discussion of empathy. Instead, the empathy lab is used as a means by which the course members explore the phenomenon of empathy for themselves and begin to derive their own theory. Box 8.1 reproduces the basic instructions for the empathy lab and Box 8.2, the 'Reflections Sheet', provides a facility for helping course members to consider their experience and their learning about empathy. That process of reflection continues in whatever time is given after the exercise to report back to the whole training group. This procedure of taking learning from a small intimate setting such as the triad to discuss it in the large group illustrates to course members, early in their training, that it is possible to work with our experiencing in another setting without divulging privileged or confidential material disclosed by the speaker. That experience will be useful when the course members are introduced to the notion of counselling supervision whereby the emphasis, in person-centred work, is on the counsellor bringing herself and her experiencing to the supervision setting rather than focusing on indirect discussion about the client.

Much of the theory of empathy can be derived when the experiences of the various triads in the empathy lab are 'pooled' in the large group. Even the importance of congruence allied to empathy can become explicit, as illustrated in the following quotes from course members on a recent empathy lab:

Box 8.1

The Empathy Lab

DEFINITION
'Empathy is the ability to understand how the other person feels in his or her world – empathy *is not* the ability to assume how *you* would feel in the other person's situation, nor your knowledge of how other people have felt in that situation.'

TIME
3 hours

STEPS
1 Divide into threes, *as far as possible, getting together with people you don't know so well* (empathy is more difficult with a close friend) – scatter to find a quiet space anywhere in the room.
2 Take up the roles of:
  A 'Speaker'
  B 'Listener'
  C 'Observer'
3 The *Speaker* speaks for no more than 30 minutes, with the *Listener* trying to understand and checking his/her understanding. Don't let it drift into a 'discussion'.
4 Then the *Speaker, Listener* and *Observer* have 20 minutes to complete the 'Reflections' sheet, discuss their observations about the process, and identify what has been learned/experienced about empathy.
5 Switch roles, with the *Speaker* becoming the *Observer*, the *Observer* becoming the *Listener*, the *Listener* becoming the *Speaker*. Repeat steps (3) and (4).
6 Switch roles for the final time so that everyone has had the experience of every role.
7 Put your findings on the question 'What has been learned/experienced about empathy?' on to a flip chart for display to the whole course. Be prepared to speak on each of your findings (30 minutes).
8 Return to the main group at exactly the appointed time prepared to report on what you have learned/experienced about empathy.

THE ROLES
The *Speaker* is asked to speak on '*Something important to me*'. This could be 'An important point in my life'; 'A difficult transition I experienced'; 'A difficulty I have at work, home, etc.'; anything which the speaker judges to be *important* to herself or himself.

Box 8.1 continued

Since the intention is not to *force* you, as the Speaker, to be personal if you do not wish, the option is open for the Speaker to identify with someone they have met and role-play that person speaking on the subject: 'Something important to me'.

The *Listener* is trying to do two things:

1 To *understand what* the Speaker is saying and the feelings she, or he, is experiencing.
2 To check and to *communicate* this understanding.

One important point to note is that listening is an *active* process. It is not simply sitting silently absorbing, it requires '*checking out*' your understanding. The process of 'checking out' ensures that you do understand and it also *communicates* that understanding or at least your *struggle* to understand which can be supportive enough for the other person.

The *Observer* is there principally to help the Speaker and the Listener, after the dialogue, to analyse the experience. To do this well the Observer will find it necessary to take notes unobtrusively during the dialogue. A secondary role is to help everyone to keep approximately to the 30/20 minute schedule. If the listening process becomes 'stuck' the Observer should help the Speaker and Listener to talk about that and what could be causing it, before moving on.

Box 8.2
Reflections on the Empathy Lab

1 How did the speaker feel at the beginning? Did those feelings change, and if so, how?

2 How did the speaker feel about each of the people he/she was talking about?

3 How did the speaker show his/her feelings?

4 How did *you* feel, and what sort of things went through your mind while you were listening? (Listener)
How do you think the Listener felt? (Speaker and Observer)

5 What have you learned or experienced about 'empathy' through this exercise?

6 If you have participated in a shorter empathy exercise in the past were there any differences in this longer experience?

- When I lost my 'self-consciousness' and just concentrated on being *with* the speaker, I was surprised at the quality of my empathy.
- My listener tried to do all the right things, but I was a bit uncomfortable – like it felt artificial – I didn't know if she was *really* interested in me.

A three-hour empathy lab followed by considerable discussion is a fairly normal length for a counsellor training course. It allows a full half-hour in which the Listener can become focused on the Speaker. However, in other situations where the training is designed to introduce workers from other professions to counselling skills, it is possible to adjust the timings to create exercises of any length. I have even used a 30-minute variant of the exercise as a means of introducing empathy to a conference of managers.

Focusing

When the behaviour of person-centred counsellors is observed, one of the things they are often doing is, by a variety of means, inviting the client to 'focus' – to come closer to the edge of his awareness and experience whatever new feelings or sensations are present at that edge. Person-centred trainers vary in the way they work with a phenomenon such as focusing. Some would not introduce it *per se* but would work with the phenomenon as a normal part of the counsellor's empathy and the client's response to that empathy. Other trainers would intentionally introduce the notion of focusing and even illustrate some of the ways in which it was manifested in counselling interviews. For example, some of these are illustrated in Mearns (1994j, pp. 84–8):

- The word-for-word reflection.
- Reflection of the client's feeling or sensation using a 'handle word'.
- Adding an emphasis with a questioning tone.
- Slowing the pace of response to the client.
- Using 'touch' to invite the client to focus.
- Silence as means of helping the client to focus.

In introducing the course member to these different specific behaviours the person-centred trainer is coming closer to a reductionistic approach. If the trainer went on to take each of these in turn and school the course members in the relevant behaviours then the approach would indeed be one of reductionism. It is more likely that the person-centred trainer would stop the reductionism at the point of illustrating these different behaviours, using that illustration as a means of showing course members how wide a counsellor's repertoire can be. One course member illustrated that kind of learning:

> I had absolutely no idea that *silence* could be so facilitative. Silence hadn't been part of my style at all – probably because I was always so nervous, I filled every gap there was. It was quite new for me to consider that silence could be important in the *space* it left for the client.

Having introduced focusing in its various forms into the language of the course, the person-centred trainers would now be concerned not with schooling the course member on these individual behaviours, but with observing the course member's own practice and pointing out examples of focusing invitations which were arising naturally through the counsellor's empathy. When course members have this opportunity to see each other's work they find they are introduced to a variety of personal styles as far as focusing interventions are concerned. In that way the course member may begin, gently, to experiment with broadening his repertoire while taking care not to take on too much at once lest he loses congruence. As discussed in the previous chapter, this gradual experimentation with self has a reflexive relationship with the course member's ongoing personal development.

Skilful Behaviour: Outside In or Inside Out?

In 1988, Brian Thorne and I expressed the view that the development of the counsellor's empathy was a matter of helping her to *release her empathic sensitivity* (Mearns and Thorne, 1988, pp. 52–8). Our view, which has become strengthened in the nine years which have followed, was that empathy, like most of the relationship skills within the person-centred approach, is developed from the 'inside out' rather than from the 'outside in'. When I first learned to turn a nut clockwise and thereby engage the bolt, the skill I had acquired was from the outside in: nothing in my previous knowledge would have told me that the nut should turn clockwise. However, in many of the human relating skills of person-centred counselling we have an enormous prior knowledge and experience through the hundreds of thousands of sophisticated human interactions in which we have previously participated. Colloquially we use the word 'sensitivity' to denote that body of knowledge and experience. The training task then becomes one of helping the course member to release that sensitivity in relationship with the client.

This 'inside out' conception of skill development is a central and a distinguishing feature of the person-centred approach. It explains why skill development is inextricably tied to the counsellor's developing congruence. When the counsellor becomes fuller and freer in his response then the skilful behaviour born of vast prior relational experience can emerge. The training emphasis then is on helping the course member to disassemble the various blocks to his congruent relating. That is partially achieved through the personal development work outlined in the previous chapter in tandem with helping the counsellor to monitor and reflect upon his actual counselling experience (Chapter 6).

The Skills Curriculum

In this section I want to list areas of skilful behaviour within person-centred counselling. The separation of these skill areas is a questionable exercise because they overlap with each other and integrate so fully with dimensions of personal development that little can be done meaningfully with them as discrete areas. Yet, it is also important from the point of view of communication that person-centred trainers define the areas of their attention.

Even at this level of definition each of these skill areas may be said to include a constellation of sub-skills. From the point of view of communication and debate it would be interesting to develop to that level of analysis although such a reductionistic approach would offer no significant assistance to the training exercise.

Most of the skill areas listed below are self-explanatory to the reader who has studied the previous books *Person-Centred Counselling in Action* (Mearns and Thorne, 1988) and *Developing Person-Centred Counselling* (Mearns, 1994a) plus the earlier chapters of the present book. This list is by no means comprehensive but is offered as a first step in defining the person-centred skills curriculum. These skill areas are presented in no particular order.

- Releasing empathic sensitivity.
- Responding in a range of ways that assist the client's focusing.
- Releasing a widening portfolio of ways of communicating warmth.

- Releasing congruent responsiveness.
- Communicating clearly and openly.
- Addressing difficult issues, even underlying issues, directly.
- Expressing confusion where that persists.
- Challenging the client in ways that encourage the client's congruent response.
- Developing ways of tapping the client's experience of the process and the relationship.
- Maintaining empathy across a range of 'difficult' clients.
- Experiencing a consistent congruent non-judgemental attitude across a range of clients.
- Establishing psychological 'contact' with clients who are 'difficult to reach'.
- Establishing psychological 'contact' with different parts of the client's Self (where such boundaries have already been symbolised by the client).
- Relating unself-consciously with the client.
- Achieving 'stillness' to meet the client.
- Entering the client's world with willingness, confidence and non-invasive respect.
- Comprehending and responding to a range of client 'personal languages' (Mearns and Thorne, 1988, pp. 64–5).
- Focusing on Self to identify personal issues that may be projected into the client material.
- Remembering important matters of *fact* about the client.
- Remembering key personality dynamics, conditions of worth, introjections, discovered denials and other constituents of the client's self-structure.
- Remembering precisely the *words* used by the client to describe aspects of his self-structure and elements of his experience.
- Remembering the *changes* and development in nomenclature used by the client to denote aspects of his self-structure and experiences.
- Becoming aware of the degree of externalisation or internalisation of the client's locus of evaluation.
- Developing an ability to stay close to the client's expression where relevant (for example, in the case of a client whose locus of evaluation is highly externalised).

Essentially these are 'inside out' skills though some, particularly those connected with remembering, can be furthered by disciplined attention.

Counselling 'Practice' Sessions

As well as the monitoring of actual counselling practice which will take place within individual and group supervision, person-centred counselling training courses will include 'practice' opportunities where course members are offering themselves to each other as 'clients'. These practice sessions are not focused on individual counselling 'skills' as might happen in more reductionistic training. Instead, the trainee counsellor is faced with the task of responding to the client as though they were in a counselling relationship. These practice sessions may be more challenging than real counselling experience, particularly since there is an emphasis on videotaping or audiotaping the work so that it can be reviewed in supervision.

The briefing for practice sessions is crucial, and usually involves fairly extensive notes such as those which follow for the different *roles* in practice sessions and the *range of possibilities* for the sessions.

Briefing Notes on the Roles in Practice Sessions

On being the 'client'

- Perhaps sometimes you can just be 'yourself' rather than trying to portray someone else. If you are being yourself, be aware of the limitations of the practice situation when picking something to talk about. It is *your* responsibility to look after yourself in training.
- If you are portraying someone else, don't think of it as 'role-playing', i.e. don't adopt a position and stick rigidly to it ('I am going to be the aggressive client no matter what the counsellor does'). It is better to consider the whole person into whose shoes you are going to step, and then simply think of the first behaviour you are going to show ('I am going to look very angrily at him when I walk into the room – that anger will be stemming from the feeling I've had all week that we aren't making any progress). Thereafter, as the person you are being, you are able to move with whatever is happening. This way of approaching a role allows the counsellor's behaviour to have the possibility of making an observable impact on the client.
- Just before starting the session it is useful to take a few moments by yourself to relax into the situation, whether you are portraying another person or yourself.

On being the 'counsellor'.

- Remember that practice sessions are much more difficult than the real thing. If your 'client' is playing himself then it's not so bad, but if he is portraying another person then it can be more difficult because of the apparent artificiality. Remember also, that people sometimes *start* by role-playing but then slip into a part of their Self – so don't *presume* it will be unreal.

- Remember also that the purpose of simulation is to explore aspects of counselling in a context where feedback is possible – it is not at all concerned with judging your performance.

- In that spirit of exploration you may choose to investigate some of the factors that are involved in working in particular counselling contexts, or with clients presenting particular problems, or perhaps you are considering specific counselling issues like empathy or congruence. If you are exploring particular skills then it is often a good idea not to take on too much at once.

- It may be tempting to get your 'client' to portray a particular person – perhaps that client with whom you had difficulty last week. This seldom works, because your colleague in training cannot mimic a particular person in your life well enough. However, she can take on a general theme and help you to explore working with that. That is to say, she cannot help you to explore work with one particular 'alienated' client whom you've met, but she can play her own version of alienation to help you to consider the issues which may be involved.

- When setting-up the portrayal of a client don't expect your 'client' to remember too much factual material.

- Fight your way through difficulties in the practice session – don't take the easy option of calling a halt. If you are encountering difficulties, these are often the same kinds of difficulties as happen in the real situation and it can be a valuable experience to struggle with ways to get through them.

- Almost always the counselling context will be *your* territory. In these cases, take some time before the start of the practice session to set out the physical context using whatever furniture is available.

- Take a few moments before the start of the session to become centred.

On being the observer

- In some sessions there may be observers and in others, not.
- If you are the observer keep right out of the counselling work.

Move as far away physically as you can while still being able to hear and see what happens. No matter how frustrating it may be, *don't interfere*! You may be absolutely sure that something important is being missed and you could do it so much better, but in practice we are not concerned with a 'good' performance, rather with using the practice to explore aspects of counselling. Graveyards are littered with observers who interrupted to 'double' the counsellor!

- Observation is a serious task and will usually require the taking of very detailed notes of your observations.
- It is also important to report on *all* of these notes – don't fudge your feedback!
- One of the advantages of having an observer is that she might be more aware than the other people of instances where the 'client' or 'counsellor' has got 'stuck in his role'. It may be that the client has been portraying an emotion and has got stuck with that even after the practice session, or perhaps the client has uncovered elements of his own past which stay with him when the counselling is over. Another form of stuckness is where the 'client' and 'counsellor' have developed a pattern to their communication which persists after the session is over. Sometimes these forms of role-stuckness, particularly when the people aren't aware of them, can be quite disturbing afterwards. Hence, if the observer senses the possibility of any such forms of stuckness, it is her responsibility to the others to help them to talk about it and in that way to 'de-role'.

Briefing Notes on a Range of Possibilities for Practice Sessions

Obviously it is a ridiculous task to try to map out what is essentially an infinite range of possibilities. However, in portraying any situation the 'client' might consider questions like: 'am I just going to be myself, here and now?'; 'in what setting is the counselling taking place?'; 'what is the predominant present experience which is concerning me, and are there any past experiences which are particularly relevant?'; 'at what stage are the counsellor and I in the therapeutic process, and what issues in the relationship predominate at this time?'

Here are some possibilities under these four headings:

'Here and now'
Probably the most powerful practice experiences in training come when the 'client' is just being himself at that time – perhaps airing

an issue of concern for him in his present life and relationship, or even beginning by reflecting on his current experience in training. If you are choosing something from the training make sure that it does not involve the 'counsellor' or any observers. One of the few times I have ever stopped a practice session was when the 'client' chose to address his feelings on the 'abusiveness of another course member' who was, in fact, the 'counsellor'! That kind of thing is not fair.

Although practice sessions are usually relatively limited in time, it is surprising how often the 'client' actually gains some satisfaction from them. Also, of course, the obvious reality of the situation makes it easier for the counsellor at the beginning. One important thing to note when audiotaping or videotaping practice sessions when the 'client' is playing himself is that he must have editorial control over the audiotape or videotape, perhaps choosing to rub it at the end or allowing it to stay in the counsellor's portfolio with conditions on its use. A great many training tapes are obtained in this way, but their continued use must always be with the agreement of the 'client'.

Possible counselling settings

- Private practice (at home or office).
- Counselling in a Voluntary Organisation.
- Counselling a patient in hospital.
- Counselling in the client's home.
- Counselling in the school.
- Counselling in a 'drop-in' centre.
- Counselling in a prison.
- Counselling in a health centre.
- Counselling in the University clinic.

Various predominating client experiences

- Depression (general): 'I don't think I've ever been happy.'
- Depression (transitional): 'Since Johnny died I've been going down and down.'
- Low self-esteem: 'I'm a worthless person.'
- An existential crisis: 'I don't know who I really am.'
- Anger: 'I'm so angry I could kill him.'
- Fear: 'I'm scared of everything.'
- Anxiety: 'It's the little things which seem to get to me nowadays.'

Issues in the therapeutic process
Sometimes it feels difficult to explore, in practice sessions, issues which concern the relationship between counsellor and client, particularly those which develop after considerable contact. Certainly we can't recapitulate the development of a long-term therapeutic relationship, but some of the issues within the therapeutic process can begin to be explored in practice, for example:

- various possibilities for the 'beginnings' of therapeutic contact;
- the client challenging the counsellor;
- various forms of 'stuckness' in the therapeutic relationship;
- where the client has strong negative feelings towards the counsellor (and vice versa);
- where the client has strong positive feelings towards the counsellor (and vice versa);
- where the client has doubts about the counsellor's acceptance or congruence;
- where a measure of dependency has evolved;
- various possibilities for 'endings'.

Reflection and Feedback in Practice Sessions

An important part of the practice session is the reflection which follows. Emphasis is equally placed on the observations of the 'counsellor', the 'client' and the 'observers'. Usually the 'counsellor' can give a good, detailed, assessment of the session though trainee counsellors tend to be more conscious of what they consider to be their 'faults' than is the 'client'. Eliciting considerable detail on the experience of the 'client' is a useful discipline because it repeatedly reminds the 'counsellor' that her presumptions on the client's experience are usually incomplete and frequently inaccurate. That is a cornerstone of person-centred training: being wary of presumptions about the client's experiencing. Box 8.3 offers a partial structure for reflection – this can be particularly useful if observers are not present to structure the reflection session.

Course members are usually more sensitive to the feedback given by *staff* during these practice sessions. This is a perfect, early opportunity for staff to model a person-centred way of relating with the course member by giving feedback which is detailed and as complete as possible. In this feedback the trainer has the opportunity to reinforce the idea that the course member is not expected to be an expert counsellor at the beginning of training

Box 8.3
Ten Questions to Aid Reflection on Practice Sessions

Practice sessions try to get close to the real counselling situation in order to explore some of the key issues involved for us as counsellors. Observers, if they are frank in their observations, can help the 'counsellor' and 'client' in such explorations since they have been able to stand back from what has been happening. However, in the absence of observers, the following questions might provide the basis of a framework for reflecting upon sessions immediately they are ended.

1 (Client) What feelings does the person playing the client have now?
2 (Counsellor) What feelings does the person playing the counsellor have now?
3 (Client) Were there any moments when you felt particularly well *heard* during the session? Explore these together.
4 (Counsellor) What things made it easy or difficult for you to listen to this client?
5 (Client) What non-verbal behaviours of the counsellor were you aware of in the session?
6 (Client) Did you feel unconditionally accepted by this counsellor or were there any doubts?
7 (Counsellor) Did you have any difficulties in valuing this client?
8 (Client) Did the counsellor seem perfectly authentic all the time or were there instances when you sensed that she might not be being congruent? Our sensing of incongruence is often surprisingly accurate, so explore possible instances fully with the counsellor.
9 (Counsellor and client) As well as having many skills in common, we all develop our own personal *style* as counsellors. What aspects of the counsellor's personal style were in evidence in this session and in what ways did this help or hinder?

and, also, to establish a norm in these sessions that as much can be learned by 'missing' the client as by 'connecting' with him. It can be a hard task for the trainer to form that norm of freedom of expression because years of prior formal and informal education may have established in the course member a powerful fear of being judged.

Another aim of the trainer in these feedback sessions is to reinforce the notion of 'personal style', emphasising that person-centred counsellors will vary considerably in the way they relate with clients. The trainer is trying to establish the principle that the aim for the course member is to hold on to who they are as a person and develop that Self into the counselling relationship rather than try to 'model' the behaviour of other counsellors. The trainer might emphasise that individual variability by repeatedly reminding the course members that there is no single 'good' way to conduct the counselling session – different counsellors might respond in widely varying fashions and yet all might lead to a successful outcome. The notion that there are '500 roads to success' in any one counselling interview is one which can be empowering for course members and might remind them not to seek to throw away the persons they are.

As well as receiving feedback immediately following the practice session, the videotapes or audiotapes can subsequently be used in group supervision, providing that use has been part of the initial contract with the 'client'. This is a particularly useful exercise because it helps course members to learn how to use the supervision group even in that period of early training before actual counselling practice begins. Also, taking these 'practice' tapes to supervision should establish the principle of audiotape supervision which was so firmly emphasised in Chapter 6.

'Stages' in Skill Development

Although trainee counsellors vary one from another, when viewing a course membership as a whole there are three discernible 'stages' in the release of skilful behaviour, from 'paralysis' through 'portrayal' to 'congruence'.

Paralysis

In Chapter 2, I made reference to Clarkson and Gilbert's useful depiction of the course member moving through stages of unconscious incompetence, conscious incompetence and conscious competence to unconscious competence (Clarkson and Gilbert, 1991). The tag of 'incompetence' is too strong, but the beauty of this construction is its observation that many course members find the early part of their training painful in the awareness which it creates. As mentioned earlier in this chapter, trainee counsellors, more than their clients, tend to be aware of things they are doing which they consider to be 'wrong'. Despite the fact that the trainers will have been trying to establish a healthy non-judgemental climate of exploration, the previous educational programming of the course member will be encouraging him to emphasise the negative. Prior to this increase in consciousness about his skills, or the lack of them, the counsellor's sessions with clients might have 'flowed' quite well. However, now the counsellor has moved from unconscious incompetence to conscious incompetence, and a *paralysis* may set in (Mearns, 1994i). In its mild form, paralysis leads the trainee counsellor towards 'auditing and editing' his interventions with clients. His increased consciousness about his counselling activity leads him to question what he might or might not say. In a more extreme form the paralysis might mean that the counsellor cannot respond to the client because he can see the danger of a 'mistake' in *everything* he might say. This represents the kind of break-up of skilful behaviour which not only has parallels in other relational living but even in psycho-motor skills. In an earlier book I describe this 'paralysis' (Mearns, 1994i):

> Responses are censored if they might sound too strident, impatient, demanding, interpretative, judgemental, trivialising, cold, superficial or too directive!
>
> With every possible response being monitored and judged critically in this way it is not surprising that the trainee counsellor falls into response paralysis: there appears to be no way of responding because every response might violate some guideline or other. Indeed, the supreme 'Catch 22' is that by over-monitoring these responses the trainee feels that she has denied herself the possibility of being spontaneously congruent, so even a response which passed the earlier monitoring procedure might now be deemed 'wrong'. The trainee might further tie herself in knots by questioning the *motives* underlying her responses to clients. When faced with the attitudinal demands of the therapeutic conditions it is both natural and common for self-doubt to rear its paralysing head. (p. 26)

The trainers can help with paralysis by emphasising the opposite norm of simply being oneself when practising counselling and allowing oneself to make 'mistakes'. The trainer might also invite the course member to be realistic rather than perfect (Mearns, 1994u) – after all, if the course member could produce superior person-centred counselling sessions at the very beginning of training, then the trainer might be in danger of losing her job! Most of all, the trainer can offer enormous support to the course member in the genuine care which she offers as the course member fights his own fear of failure.

Portrayal

The development of conscious competence waxes as the experience of conscious incompetence gradually wanes. Indeed, the pain
of conscious incompetence may push the course member to grasp
any elements of conscious competence which present themselves.
Hence, the course member, quite understandably, tries to take
skills 'outside in' rather than 'inside out'. As he understands more
about person-centred skills the trainee tries to *portray* these skills
and he may even become skilful in that portrayal as observed by
the following two course members:

- 'When I look back on earlier tapes of me working, I am
  deceptively good – I say and do a lot of the right things. But
  when I look into my eyes on the video screen I can see that I
  am not there. I am thinking what to say next – but I'm not
  there – I'm not "present".'
- 'My problem was that I was *good* at portrayal – I could fool
  most people, including myself, so I kept it going for ages. Then
  it all blew up in one session with a client who said he felt cold
  because my warmth wasn't real.'

The movement from portrayal of skills to congruent working rests
on the associated personal development described in the previous
chapter. There is no way of achieving that movement by focusing
solely at a 'skills' level.

Congruence

As the course member's personal development and growing
congruence allow him to reach beyond portrayal he enters that
much sought after state of unconscious competence where he can
work creatively and fluidly with whatever the client brings. At
earlier points in his development he might have been fearful with
each new client or practice situation, unsure whether he could
offer conditions which would encourage a fruitful therapeutic
relationship. As conscious competence develops that fear dis-
sipates and offering the appropriate conditions appears perfectly
natural and congruent. At that stage of development the counsellor has managed to release his congruent relating. The client still
has a choice of whether or not to respond but the counsellor is
offering a consistently encouraging environment.

In her detailed self-appraisal statement at the end of training
one counsellor described her experience in relation to this third
stage of skill development:

'I know I have become more skilful in my client work. But I am not sure how it has happened. I haven't imitated other people (except early on!) and the books don't tell you how to respond to the individual client. When I listen to tapes of my current working I hear me saying things and using sensitivities which must have been buried inside me all the time.'

9
Understanding Theory

Carl Rogers had a great love of theory. He relished the many occasions during the last 20 years of his life when his valued friend and colleague, Maria Bowen, would take up his challenge to theoretical discussion. Carl knew that Maria was an intellectual match for him and that the debate which would ensue could create new learning. It seems at first to be a strange paradox that the therapeutic approach which he developed has not, in the main, attracted a great number of people who have a similar strong interest in the development of theory.

However, this theory deficit in the person-centred approach really only relates to about a 20-year period from the mid-1960s to the mid-1980s during which time the popularisation of the approach was taking place. During the 20 years prior to that time the approach was firmly embedded in theory and empirical research. Indeed, the theoretical stability of the approach continues to owe much to academics originating in that era, people such as Eugene Gendlin, Nat Raskin, Jules Seeman, Fred Zimring, Goff Barrett-Lennard, John Shlien and Jerry Bozarth, to name but a few. However, the enormous popularisation of the approach in the mid-1960s in America brought to it a high proportion of people who valued it as a philosophy for living more than a theory for therapy. Also, most of the crucial discoveries of the approach themselves operated against a core valuing of the promulgation of theory. It was not the practitioner's theoretical sophistication which correlated with effective performance, rather, it was the congruent presence of highly personal qualities that made a difference to clients. A third factor contributing to the reduced emphasis on theory during the popularisation period was Carl Rogers' own movement away from the university sector from which he had become increasingly alienated. There were few theoreticians in the approach spawned by that popularisation period. Certainly, John K. Wood is an exception and Maria Bowen would have been had her life not been cut short before she produced the book she always wanted to write.

The theoretical development of the approach in Britain also suffered from the popularisation phase. Many of those who were attracted to the approach and even those who offered training in it were not schooled in the detail of theory, because it was not the theory which had attracted them. The result was a considerable theory deficit in British person-centred training courses until the mid-to-late 1980s when specialist training courses developed. Too often trainers, prior to that time, would describe their courses as 'person-centred' while they themselves had little knowledge of the theory beyond a superficial understanding of the therapeutic conditions. Often that theory deficit in the trainers was masked by a highly student-centred approach taken to learning, whereby course members would be expected to derive the curriculum in ways which flowed from their own needs and wants. Seldom does a need for theory attain prominence in such circumstances where it has to compete for space against the compelling attractions of personal and inter-personal explorations. Indeed, a norm even developed whereby the course member who immersed too fully in theory might be accused of being 'defensive' in relation to personal and inter-personal exploration.

Fortunately, over the past ten years, a better balance is being achieved with respect to the prominence of theoretical exploration within the approach. Specialist training courses realise that they have an obligation to the course member at least to introduce her to the body of theory within the approach so that she can make her own choices thereafter. Also, trainers on modern specialist person-centred courses have themselves been trained at depth and are familiar with the body of theoretical knowledge. Furthermore, there has been a steady growth of contributions to the development of person-centred theory in the past ten years since Carl Rogers' death. Perhaps it is inevitable that when an approach is so identified with one great man, there is a tendency for others to be a trifle inhibited in the theoretical offerings they make. Certainly, the number of contributions since Carl's death has been marked and, interestingly, most have arisen outside the USA.

Implicit and Explicit Theory

Having set the historic context for the development of theory within the approach, an important early task in this chapter is to explore the nature of 'theory'. There is a common misapprehension that theory is something which we take in from outside of ourselves – that we read books and take in the 'theory' of others. However, the amount of theory which we take in from outside of ourselves is minuscule compared to what we generate from within. We are using our own personal, and usually *implicit*, theories all the time. Personal, implicit theories are ones which we cannot consciously articulate, a fact that probably makes them more powerful in the command they have over us. Our implicit theories may have been derived from our actual experience in the world or they may be unedited introjections given to us as ready-made ways of judging the world. Our personal *explicit* theory, on the other hand, is that body of theory which we have consciously articulated. The explicit theory which informs our judgements will include constructions that formerly were implicit theories before we became aware of them. Our body of personal explicit theory will also include some theory which we have consciously taken in from the outside – theory which originated in the thinking of other people but of which we have become consciously informed through our study.

Box 9.1 illustrates the influence of implicit theory on a counsellor's working. Perhaps a warning needs to be placed on the extract in Box 9.1. While this counsellor was fairly experienced, she was not professionally trained, as is evident from her poor practice.

An important part of the 'theory' work of a course is helping the course members to become aware of their implicit theory. Numerous aspects of a training course contribute to helping the implicit become explicit, notably the supervision groups, the personal development groups and even some aspects of the large group working. In these varied settings the course member becomes aware of the assumptions, and even the fairly involved theoretical constructions by which she is making sense of the behaviour of others, not to mention making sense of herself.

As well as helping the course member to make her implicit theories explicit, the training course is also concerned with inviting her to consider the theoretical contributions of others and thereby expand her repertoire of explicit theory. It is on this point that the course member might experience a sense of 'resistance'. For example, it is extremely difficult and cognitively or even existentially threatening, to open ourselves to a body of theory which conflicts with our deeply held personal theories. We do not so much evaluate externally derived theory in terms of how well the theoretical constructs fit together and lend themselves to testing, rather, we evaluate theory in terms of the degree to which it agrees with our existing personal theories and then seek to justify our criticism by means of theoretical analysis. One of the best accounts of this phenomenon of how humans make scientific theory fit their prejudices continues to be Polanyi (1958). Even

Box 9.1

The Influence of Implicit Theory

A considerable amount of implicit theory 'informs' the judgements we make and even the way in which we construe reality. In the extract which follows, a counsellor recounts to her supervisor an experience with a client 'X':

> I had a powerful, spiritual experience of empathy in my last session with 'X'. As she was talking about how bad her relationship was and how much she needed to 'get out' I suddenly felt an acute pain in my belly. It came so suddenly that it just had to be in relation to what she was saying. I realised that my body was feeling her emotional pain, physically. She was 'confined' and needed to 'get out' of her relationship. She needed her 'Child' to be born. I told her about my powerful feeling of empathy . . . She didn't really respond – I think I went in too powerfully with my empathy – I think she wasn't ready to 'come out' yet.

Although this counsellor may not think that she is applying theory to her work, there are at least seven theoretical propositions embedded in her statement:

1 This pain was 'empathy'.
2 It involved 'spirituality'.
3 My body translated her emotional pain into my physical pain.
4 'X' needs to get out of her relationship.
5 'X's' 'Child' needs freedom.
6 She didn't respond because she wasn't ready to 'come out'.
7 I am right about all these judgements.

externally derived theory which does *not* conflict with our self-concept can be difficult to stomach. Inevitably the language used by the external theorist will not be in line with our own internal language or, perhaps, there is a sense by which we feel ourselves diminished when we find our own internal embryonic elements of theory more eloquently worked and expressed by another.

It is no wonder that the prospect of a meal of theory can create an indigestion. There are important psychological reasons why we should be wary of theory which comes in from the outside. No matter how the theory curriculum is introduced it represents potential dissonance with our own implicit and explicit personal theories. Hence, it is not surprising that, when left with a free choice of curriculum, counsellors in training tend to choose small meals of only those parts of theory which are thoroughly consonant with their existing personal theories. Interestingly, we find in advanced training for supervisors that there is a strong inclination among those more developed practitioners to seek out extra work on theory (Lambers, 1997). Perhaps at that level of development the 'self-concept' and 'self-concept as practitioner' are more soundly developed and can face the potential dissonance of external theory with greater confidence.

A Theory Curriculum for Person-Centred Training

From this point onwards in the chapter I shall be using the term 'theory' to denote *explicit* theory derived from *outside* the learner.

Training courses may find it useful to discriminate between core and extension theory. Courses might expect trainees to study specific elements of the *'core'* theory but regard *'extension'* theory as a matter of interest and choice. Hence, one of the things which 'extension' theory might include is information on other theories of therapy. It is useful to learn about other approaches in order to aid communication with other workers and also to understand the special emphases made by one's preferred approach. In this regard, courses might expect members to become informed about other approaches, but would be likely to leave the choice of the other approaches to the individual.

Other 'extension' material might include 'problem-centred' counselling approaches focusing on specific client difficulties or studies of work with special client groups. For example, counselling for depression (Gilbert, 1992); for anxiety problems (Hallam, 1992); for post-traumatic stress disorder (Scott and Stradling, 1992); counselling for survivors of childhood sexual abuse (Draucker, 1992); for people on prescribed drugs (Hammersley, 1995); for the bereaved (Worden, 1988); for older clients (Knight, 1986); for gay, lesbian and bisexual clients (Davies and Neal, 1996); and with the culturally different (Sue and Sue, 1990; Lago with Thompson, 1996). The person-centred approach demands that the counsellor grounds her working in the individuality of the client in front of her rather than designing that working around a specific 'problem' or stereotype of a client group. For example, the person-centred counsellor would seek to work with the *person* who was depressed rather than to work with the problem of depression. Similarly, the person-centred counsellor would be seeking to meet and work with the individual client who happened to be gay rather than working with the client in a special way because he was gay. Hence, theory on problem-centred working and working specific to client groups would not be regarded as 'core' in person-centred training but would be encouraged as extension work offering perspective on that conception of working and also information about specific problems or client groups that may or may not prove relevant in respect of the individual client.

Other 'extension' theory might include *derivatives* of the person-centred approach or developments from the approach, for example, the application of the approach in working with intergroup tension (Rogers, 1975); the application to research methodology (Mearns and McLeod, 1984); the fascinating and highly successful work of contributors such as Gendlin in respect of focusing (Gendlin, 1981, 1984, 1996), Gordon in relation to parent effectiveness training (Gordon, 1975), as well as Greenberg and Rice in the process-experiential approach (Greenberg, Rice and Elliott, 1993). These are just a few examples of elements of 'extension' theory – many more might be considered.

There is a massive amount of theory within the person-centred approach. We shall list and reference only some of it in this section but even the core curriculum which follows offers far too much to be contained within a single first-level training course. Readers who are prone to 'theory indigestion' might want to skip to the following section – the 'meal' of theory which follows will be here for future reference.

General Work on Person-Centred Counselling

Five of Rogers' books were related to his theory of therapy and underlying personality theory. The roots are already evident in his first book, *The Clinical Treatment of the Problem Child* (Rogers, 1939), becoming more explicit in *Counseling and Psychotherapy* (Rogers, 1942a), reaching fruition in a theoretical sense with *Client-Centered Therapy* (Rogers, 1951), attaining widespread public recognition through his best-selling book *On Becoming a Person* (Rogers, 1961a) and gaining continued attention through the series of papers presented in *A Way of Being* (Rogers, 1980a).

Course members may also be directed towards three papers which are of critical importance to the development of the theory at a general level (Rogers, 1959, 1986; Rogers and Sanford, 1989). Particularly important is the first of these, frequently referred to as the 'Koch' paper; it gives important developments of the Personality Theory subsequent to 1951.

After Rogers' death, his first biographer, Howard Kirschenbaum (Kirschenbaum, 1979), and his long-term friend and secretary, Valerie Land Henderson, produced two excellent readers which afford the student easy access to some of Rogers' most important papers and dialogues (Kirschenbaum and Henderson, 1989a, b).

Moving away from Rogers' own work, we find two important books produced by workers seeking to develop and broaden the approach. These works are useful in considering the boundaries of person-centred counselling (Wexler and Rice, 1974; Boy and Pine, 1982).

A wealth of material is available in three major readers produced for the 1970s, 1980s and 1990s. In total these books offer the student 1,946 pages of papers from key theorists and practitioners across 30 years of the approach. For different reasons, trainers and course members can find it difficult to access these massive works. Lietaer, Rombauts and Van Balen (1990) was published by the University of Leuven Press in Belgium and can still be obtained directly from that source. Levant and Shlien (1984) is a beautifully produced book which suffered at the time of publication from an overseas pricing policy that made it virtually inaccessible in Europe, except to libraries. The introduction of a paperback edition came too late to help its uptake. Though difficult to obtain for reasons of its age, probably the best of these three readers is the first, Hart and Tomlinson (1970). Even the experienced person-centred theorist can gain a considerable amount by re-reading some of the rich papers contained in this early text.

The shifting of the centre of gravity for theoretical work to Europe during the past 15 years has led to the production of six important books coming from workers in Holland, Flemish-speaking Belgium and Britain (Lietaer, van Praag and Swildens, 1984; Van Balen, Leijssen and Lietaer, 1986; Mearns and Thorne, 1988; Swildens, de Haas, Lietaer and Van Balen, 1991; Mearns, 1994a; Lietaer and Van Kalmthout, 1995).

The pace of theoretical work is such that the trainer needs to be aware of forthcoming works of a generic nature in the approach. For example, David Rennie's new book, which will be published by Sage in 1998, offers a fresh and invigorating look at the approach and its boundaries set in the context of many years' research (Rennie, forthcoming). In another forthcoming Sage book, Brian Thorne and Elke Lambers begin what will be the important step of integrating theoretical and practical work in the approach from different European countries. As far as I am concerned, the most important theoretical work to enter the arena for many years is another forthcoming Sage text, offered by Goff

Barrett-Lennard. Having read drafts of a number of chapters in this large book I am convinced that it comes closer than any other to offering a definitive account of the development of theory and practice within the approach throughout its history (Barrett-Lennard, forthcoming). Finally in the 'forthcoming' section is the recent decision by Brian Thorne and myself to replace *Person-Centred Counselling in Action* (1988) with a new book on the approach to be published in Autumn 1999 (Mearns and Thorne, forthcoming).

Personality Theory

The two most fundamental statements by Rogers on the underlying personality theory to the approach are offered in *Client-Centered Therapy* (Rogers, 1951, pp. 481–533) and the aforementioned 'Koch' paper (Rogers, 1959). Students need to be alerted to the fact that Rogers' theory of personality was unfinished. I mean this not in the pedantic sense that any theory may be said to be 'unfinished'. In fact, Rogers was refining and developing his personality theory up to about 1963. In a paper for the Nebraska Symposium on Motivation (Rogers, 1963) he was still sharpening his understanding of the place of consciousness in the rifts which could develop between the Self as it is actualised and the underlying actualising tendency. If we extrapolated the direction of development of his theory it might have led to dangerous territory such as the essentially 'psychotic' nature of what we call normal living and consciousness. Rogers and Laing were much closer in theory than they ever managed in relationship. However, that continued development of his personality theory did not take place, for other directions soon developed, like the 'Wisconsin Study' (Rogers et al., 1967), the dramatic popularisation of the approach in the 1960s, and his later extrapolation of his theories into the sociological arena.

Other papers are available on specific aspects of the theory, such as its phenomenological base (Rogers, 1978a), its approach to values (Rogers, 1964), its concept of the person (Rogers, 1957b, c; Seeman, 1984), the actualising tendency (Rogers, 1963), the generalisation of the actualising tendency to the 'formative tendency' (Rogers, 1978b), the 'locus of evaluation' (Raskin, 1952; Mearns, 1994d) and the social implications of Rogers' theory (Rogers, 1960; Hawtin and Moore, forthcoming). Fundamental to a consideration of the personality theory is the Rogers–Skinner debate published in *Science* (Rogers and Skinner, 1956). In the context of their journal debate these two eminent theoreticians push each other to explore the philosophies and values underlying their theories.

The nature and the process of personality change within the theory is examined in numerous papers throughout the development of the approach from the early 'process scale' work of Rogers through to Barrett-Lennard's careful look at the process of client change and including Mearns' consideration of the dynamics of self-concept change (Rogers, 1961b; Tomlinson and Hart, 1962; Gendlin, 1970a; Van Balen, 1991; Barrett-Lennard, 1992; Mearns, 1992a, 1996d; Van Kalmthout, forthcoming).

Brian Thorne's biography of Rogers (Thorne, 1992) offers an excellent chapter on his theory (pp. 24–43) and a fairly recent book by Tony Merry devoted to the broad approach rather than simply the therapy, offers interesting, accurate and insightful material on the personality theory (Merry, 1995).

Theory of Therapy – General Work

Therapeutic approaches need to offer both an underlying theory of personality and also a working theory of therapy. Approaches vary considerably on the attention given to these two theoretical underpinnings. For example, Gestalt and Transactional Analysis offer intriguing and meaningful theories of personality, but relatively little in terms of a theory of therapy. The broad psychodynamic approach offers unbelievable riches in terms of personality theory, even sub-dividing into an array of emphases, while at the same time presenting an internally rigorous, if not externally validated, theory of therapy.

The person-centred approach offers more in terms of underlying personality theory than is commonly presumed but the attention given in theory and research to the theory of therapy is much more fully developed. Essentially, the curriculum on the theory of therapy includes not only this 'general' section but also the following sections on the therapeutic relationship, the therapeutic process and context, and special applications of the therapeutic approach. Firstly, the present section considers the range of general work on the theory of therapy.

Rogers' development of the theory of therapy is largely presented in *Counseling and Psychotherapy, Client-Centered Therapy* and *On Becoming a Person* (Rogers, 1942a, 1951, 1961a). It is intriguing, however, to detect the roots of his theory of therapy already present in his first book, which he published at 37 years of age (Rogers, 1939); and through that book it is possible to look back even further to some of the roots of the theory of therapy in the work of Jessie Taft (1933).

Of critical importance to the research and development of the theory of therapy was the purely technological invention of the tape recorder and its use in recording therapy sessions for analysis (Rogers, 1942b). It is interesting to note that even up to the present day the person-centred approach embraces the use of tape recorded work for research as well as reflection and supervision (Mearns, 1995) as the least intrusive method of capturing the client's reality. It is the use of the tape recording facility which has allowed the considerable research into the therapeutic relationship and the therapeutic process, as detailed in later sections of this chapter.

There have been many contributions to the theory of therapy since those which were documented in Rogers' early books. Some papers which are specially worthy of note in this regard include Rogers (1980b), Bozarth and Temaner-Brodley (1986), Combs (1986b), Natiello (1987), Combs (1989), Sims (1989), Seeman (1994), Bozarth (1995), Zimring (1995), Hutterer, Pawlowsky, Semid and Stipsits (1996) and Deleu and Van Werde (forthcoming).

Two aspects of the general theory of therapy which are particularly distinctive are its non-directive essence and the aim within the therapy to work with the client at existential depth. The non-directive essence is considered in several papers, including Shlien and Zimring (1970), Cain (1989a), Cain (1990), Grant (1990), Lambers (1993) and Lietaer (forthcoming). The existential dimension of the therapy is considered in Tiedemann and Krips (1991), Daly and Mearns (1993), Mearns (1996c) and Mearns (1996d).

The Therapeutic Relationship

There is a massive amount of research and writing into the therapeutic relationship in person-centred counselling. I shall try to systematise it slightly by creating two sub-sections, the first exploring work on the 'therapeutic conditions' and the second looking at other dimensions of the therapeutic relationship.

The therapeutic conditions

Once again, the early work is best described in *Client-Centered Therapy* (Rogers, 1951) and, most particularly, *On Becoming a Person* (Rogers, 1961a), but perhaps the most quoted work on the therapeutic conditions is Rogers' 1957 paper, 'The necessary and sufficient conditions of therapeutic personality change' (Rogers,

1957a), where his proposition that the therapeutic conditions were both 'necessary' and also 'sufficient' forced the attention of the psychotherapeutic world.

The research accompanying the development of the theory of therapy in regard to the therapeutic conditions is too vast to summarise in this tour of the highlights of theoretical work but certain publications are particularly worthy of note. Goff Barrett-Lennard is important in the development of person-centred theory in the present day (Barrett-Lennard, forthcoming), but 35 years ago he was also an important researcher in the field. In his research published in 1962 he showed a sophistication of design and a willingness to engage the client experience which contributed greatly to the verification of the theory (Barrett-Lennard, 1962). Other works of special note include Mullen and Abeles (1972), Truax and Carkhuff (1967) and Patterson (1984). The Truax and Carkhuff book can be difficult to obtain but worth the search for the trainer because it summarises all the research to that time and also shows how the approach, having entered the domain of research verification, pitched wildly into the world of logical positivism whereby the therapeutic conditions were so *'reduced'* for the convenience of research that they ran the danger of losing their meaning.

In more modern times the *holistic* nature of the therapeutic conditions has been re-emphasised in books such as that of Mearns and Thorne (1988, chs 2–5). In these more recent years there has been a considerable amount of work, much of it emanating from outside America, exploring the conditions in some detail (Lago, 1979; Lietaer, 1984; Watson, 1984; Lietaer, 1991; Mearns, 1993a; Tudor and Worral, 1994; Mearns, 1994f, g, h, k; Grafanaki and McLeod, 1995; Bozarth, 1996; Wilkins, 1997).

Of all the therapeutic conditions, *empathy* has been most fully documented, perhaps because it was more easily researched than the other conditions. The aforementioned work by Truax and Carkhuff (1967) gives an account of the early research and Rogers (1980c) offers a further, detailed account of the research investigations into empathy. Once more, there is a considerable amount of more recent work, much of which comes from Europe and Australia (Bozarth, 1984; Barrett-Lennard, 1988a; Vanaerschot, 1990; Vanaerschot and Van Balen, 1991; Thorne, 1991a; Barrett-Lennard, 1993; Bohart and Rosenbaum, 1995; McLeod, 1995; Barrett-Lennard, 1997; Binder, forthcoming). Trainers might consider introducing the student to some of the literature on *focusing*. While focusing can be seen as an entirely separate discipline to person-centred counselling, it can also be regarded as a means of helping the client to empathise with himself and its principles can easily be integrated into the person-centred practitioner's work. An introduction to the area of focusing can be obtained from Gendlin (1981), Gendlin (1984), Mearns and Thorne (1988), Mearns (1994j) and Gendlin (1996).

No one has successfully proposed therapeutic conditions additional to the six outlined in Rogers (1957a), but in recent years Mearns and Thorne have been introducing terms such as 'intimacy', 'mutuality' and 'presence' as relational consequences of the existence of high degrees of the therapeutic conditions (Mearns and Thorne, 1988; Thorne, 1991b; Mearns, 1994k). Brian Thorne has probably come closest to proposing a new condition with his paper 'The quality of tenderness' (1991c), though it might be argued that this too represents a high degree of existing therapeutic conditions. Brian Thorne also offers his paper 'Beyond the core conditions' (1987), in which he made the first presentation of his highly controversial work with the client 'Sally'. It is surprising that there has been no debate in the journals concerning this work, which some would consider to be a supreme example of the counsellor's commitment to embody the therapeutic conditions and which others might view as unethical. The absence of theoretical debate on this very controversial case makes it difficult for trainers and course members. I remember a lively three-hour session where Brian Thorne responded to students' challenges on that work. Through that medium it became possible to see the work in sufficient detail that it could be fully understood and accepted, but I was conscious that we had the special opportunity of dialogue with the author which offered much more than the written word.

Other aspects of the therapeutic relationship

The therapeutic conditions are so prominent in the literature and research of the approach that it is easy to begin to see them as defining the therapeutic relationship in its entirety. If Rogers' (1957a) thesis on the necessary and sufficient nature of the conditions is accepted then we might argue that all we need to do is to attend to those conditions. However, there are other features to the therapeutic relationship which, while they may not determine therapeutic effectiveness as predictably as the conditions, colour and inform the relationship. Some interesting, general work on other aspects of the therapeutic relationship can be obtained from Friedman (1985), Rennie (1985), Van Balen (1990), Mearns (1994l) and Natiello (1994). Mearns also considers some specific aspects of the therapeutic relationship, including the *power dynamic* (Mearns, 1992c, m) and the issue of *over-involvement* (Mearns, 1992b).

In recent years attention has been drawn to some aspects of the *unspoken relationship* between counsellor and client, considering the fact that even although the person-centred counselling relationship might be characterised by its openness and intimacy, still much of the experiencing of the counsellor and the client about each other may remain unspoken (Mearns, 1991a; Cohen, 1994; Ford, 1994; Mearns, 1994n, o).

The concept of *transference* is not of integral importance to the person-centred theory of therapy where the aim is to meet at a deeper relational level than the transferential. However, since it is so prominent in other approaches, it is relevant that transference has been addressed in the theoretical literature within person-centred counselling. Van Balen (1984) offers an exploration of the literature on transference within the approach up to that date but John Shlien stimulated considerable later debate with his provocative 1984 paper, reproduced again in 1987, 'A countertheory of transference', challenging the way the notion of transference is used in psychodynamic work. The stimulus of his challenge led to a number of responses, including Fischer (1987), Maddi (1987), Seeman (1987) and Kahn (1987).

The Therapeutic Process and the
Therapeutic Context

The key early work on therapeutic process is offered in Rogers' paper 'A process conception of psychotherapy' (Rogers, 1961a, pp. 125–59). This paper is so rich in observation that it may be re-read at different points in the counsellor's career to yield new insights each time. The early work in therapeutic process looked more at the client's process than the process of the therapist or of their working relationship. Apart from the work of Rogers himself, one of the most closely observed analyses of process is offered by Barrett-Lennard (1988b, 1990), while Greenberg, Rice and Elliott (1993) offer a form of process in which the therapist plays a stronger mediating role.

In considering therapeutic process, Mearns integrates elements of his background in social psychology to focus on the trinity of the client's process, the counsellor's process and the process of their relationship. This is illustrated in his paper, 'The dance of psychotherapy' (Mearns, 1994t) and in work on therapeutic *stuck-*

ness (Mearns and Thorne, 1988; Mearns, 1991b, 1993c, 1994p; and also Verlackt, 1995).

Recent work on other dimensions of therapeutic process includes an examination of *confrontation* within the process (Tscheulin, 1990; Mearns, 1994q), the *ending* phase of counselling (Mearns, 1993b) and consideration of the process of *brief* person-centred counselling (Eymael, 1984; Thorne, 1994). It is likely that there will be much more investigation of the process of brief person-centred counselling, as early studies of its impact suggest that strong results may arise from only five or six sessions (Gordon, 1996) and that the gains from this brief work are maintained at three-month and six-month follow-ups (Goss and Mearns, 1997b).

There is no large body of theory and research on the *therapeutic context*, else it would have deserved a separate section in its own right. However, it does seem reasonable to suggest that the therapeutic context could be a critical variable as the vehicle for the therapeutic conditions. Perhaps one of the major areas of neglect in the Wisconsin study (Rogers et al., 1967) was the relatively scant attention given to the variable of therapeutic context. Early work on this variable includes Mearns (1992d) and Mearns (1994r).

Special Applications of Person-Centred Counselling

The person-centred approach, in its emphasis on locating the work within the individuality of the client, would not be concerned with prescribing specific theory for work with particular client problems or groups. For example, the person-centred approach would regard as irrelevant the task of creating a special way of working with alcoholics, with those who have experienced trauma or with people who have been sexually abused. The generically trained person-centred specialist would be expected to relate with the individuals rather than with the problem. Yet, there are client populations and counselling contexts which lie outwith the normal boundaries of working with adult clients who can maintain psychological contact, for example, work with young children, couple/family counselling and work with clients who have difficulty in maintaining the first therapeutic condition of psychological contact.

Examples of theory on working with young children includes Axline (1971), Ginsberg (1984) and Santen (1991). The area of couple and family therapy has also received attention as a specialist application. Some work was presented in a 1989 Symposium in *Person-Centered Review*: for example: Anderson (1989a, b), Bozarth and Shanks (1989), Cain (1989c), Gaylin (1989), O'Leary (1989) and Warner (1989). The three main readers within the approach have each contained some work on couple/family therapy, including Raskin and Van der Veen (1970), Barrett-Lennard (1984), Guerney (1984), Levant (1984), Esser and Schneider (1990), Gaylin (1990) and Rombauts and Devriendt (1990). Other, fairly recent work includes Blackie (1989), Sabbe (1991), Mearns (1994s), Colin (1995) and Gaylin (1996). The most important forthcoming book is Charlie O'Leary's provisionally titled *Family Therapy and the Person-Centred Approach*, to be published by Sage in 1998.

One of the most exciting developments in person-centred theory as well as practice over the past 15 years is the development of *client-centred pre-therapy*. Pre-therapy is designed as a way of working with clients who have difficulty in maintaining the first therapeutic condition, that of psychological contact. This may be a client who is otherwise diagnosed psychotic or with profound learning difficulties, or it may be a client who does not suffer such a chronic disability but has moments of 'losing contact'. Much of the writing in this area has come from the founder of the work, Garry Prouty, and his European colleague, Dion Van Werde. The main book is *Theoretical Evolutions in Person-Centered/ Experiential Therapy: Applications to Schizophrenic and Retarded Psychoses* (Prouty, 1994). This book is extremely rich in theoretical concepts and well written, but the price set by its European distributor means that it remains relatively inaccessible. It is to be hoped that Garry Prouty publishes more on his creative and theoretically sound system of working. Other papers under his authorship which are available include Prouty and Kubiak (1988), Prouty and Pietrazak (1988), Prouty and Cronval (1989) and Prouty (1990). Dion Van Werde's writing on pre-therapy includes Van Werde (1990, 1994a, b).

Supervision

The theory on person-centred supervision is sparse. A probable reason for this is that supervision is simply not such a central endeavour in the USA and most parts of the world, compared to Britain where there is a life-long requirement for professional supervision regardless of the experience of the counsellor. In the USA supervision is mainly regarded as a requirement during training or early development. Nevertheless, Patterson (1964,

1983) provides us with two interesting papers, while Maria Bowen (1986) looked at personality differences in relation to person-centred supervision. More recent papers on person-centred supervision explore some of the critical issues involved (Mearns, 1991c), and a challenge to the profession on the use of client material in supervision (Mearns, 1995).

Person-Centred Psychopathology

As mentioned earlier, person-centred counselling does not prescribe specific treatments for different diagnostic categories. Indeed, for many years the approach forsook the clinical terms of psychiatry and clinical psychology, believing that the diagnostic language diminished the persons it endeavoured to describe. The person-centred approach does not require the diagnostic language of psychiatry – it is perfectly possible to work effectively by adopting an ideographic rather than a normative approach to disorder – understanding the specific conflicts of the individual client rather than accommodating his individuality to a broader category. Despite the practical and philosophical consistency of avoiding clinical language, the main effect of standing apart from the language of the mental health field was that the approach became dangerously marginalised in that important arena. Carl Rogers and his colleagues may have been justified in practical and theoretical terms, but, while they achieved huge popularisation, the mental health field did not follow their lead. More recently, person-centred psychologists have sought to articulate with the language of mental health, not to adopt a diagnostic treatment system but to aid communication with other mental health workers and enable the student of the person-centred approach to understand that different language so that she could work ideographically within mental health settings. In the theoretical work referenced below the reader will note the absence of historical references to person-centred psychopathology but the considerable attention which it has received, particularly in continental Europe, since 1986.

Contributions to a *general* view of person-centred psychopathology include Swildens (1986), Van Kalmthout and Pelgrim (1990), Lambers (1991) and Swildens (1991). The specific issue of person-centred *psychodiagnosis* has been addressed by Boy and Pine (1986), Boy (1989) and Cain (1989b) while other writers have looked at the issue of working with *difficult client populations*, not specific to particular diagnostic categories, such as Margaret

Warner's excellent paper on 'Fragile Process' (1991) and other work by Fusek (1991) and Hundersmarck (1995).

Various writers have attempted to articulate person-centred concepts with specific clinical categories, for example, Elke Lambers gives a person-centred perspective on the *neurotic* client (1994a), *personality disorder* (1994b), *borderline personality disorder* (1994c) and *psychosis* (1994d). Other writers offer work on *multiple personality* (Roy, 1991), *borderline* (Kroll, 1988; Bohart, 1990; Swildens, 1990; Van de Veire, 1995) and on *psychosis* (Rogers et al., 1967; Gendlin, 1970b, 1990; Teusch, 1990).

Client Experiences

One of the strange paradoxes in person-centred counselling is how relatively little material there is on the client's experience. Certainly, some of the best early research emphasised the importance of measuring the client's view with respect to the establishment of the therapeutic conditions (for example, Barrett-Lennard, 1962), but very little research and theory starts with the client's experience of the process. For an approach which describes itself as 'client-centred', virtually all the establishment of theory has been 'counsellor-centred'. Carl Rogers was himself aware of this deficiency and in a letter written a month before his death he warmly welcomed the then forthcoming book entitled *Experiences of Counselling in Action* (Mearns and Dryden, 1989). This book at least divided itself equally between theory derived from the experiences of counsellors and theory derived from clients.

Certainly, the most important researcher in this area of the client's experience is David Rennie, who has published considerable research and theory (for example, Rennie, 1987, 1990) but whose forthcoming book promises to be particularly interesting on the subject (Rennie, forthcoming).

Other contributions to the client's experience include the early research of Lipkin (1948, 1954) as well as later work from Van der Veen (1970), Lietaer and Neirinck (1986) and Cain (1989b).

Criticism

There is virtually no criticism of Rogers' theory of therapy – most of the criticism which exists relates to his theory of personality. This lack of criticism certainly does not imply that the theory of therapy is beyond criticism but it may reflect the fact that it is extremely difficult to make informed criticism of a therapeutic approach unless one understands that approach fully. It is rare that therapy critics take the time to invest themselves in an approach to the extent which is required to make informed criticism. For example, Mason's criticism is as vehement as it is ill-informed (Mason, 1989). Mason may have offered informed criticism of the approach in which he was schooled, but it is too much to expect that he can offer effective criticism of an approach in which he has no training. A more interesting criticism is that of Bill Coulson (Kirschenbaum, 1991). Coulson's criticism is not that the theory of therapy is flawed but that it is to be questioned morally and ideologically. In other words, his problem with the approach is not that it is ineffective but that it influences people in ways which he considers inappropriate. I have not met Bill Coulson since 1972, at which time he was one of the foremost trainers in the approach. It would be interesting to hear his criticism in more detail because it is certainly based on an informed position.

There is more criticism on the theory of personality underlying the approach. Brian Thorne presents an excellent summary of this criticism as well as offering some 'rebuttals' in his biography of Rogers (Thorne, 1992). Probably the best sources of critical debate on the personality theory can be found in the Rogers–Skinner debate (Rogers and Skinner, 1956). The two adversaries are such skilled theoreticians coming from quite different value-bases that the basic principles of Rogers' personality theory cannot fail to come into question. A wonderful training device is to divide a course membership in two and invite each half to study and argue the position of Rogers and Skinner. In order to help to balance pre-existing prejudices, it is useful to invite both 'teams' also to read Skinner's famous book, *Walden II* (Skinner, 1948) and, perhaps, *Beyond Freedom and Dignity* (Skinner, 1971).

Other critical papers which are also paraphrased in Thorne's biography include Buber and Rogers (1960), Vitz (1977), Van Belle (1980), May (1982) and Nye (1986).

This section has simply tried to provide a selection of prior and current work which might inform the theory curriculum for person-centred training. Yet, although it has been selective, there are well in excess of 200 referenced works. With a pre-existing body of theory such as this, it becomes necessary for the person-centred training course to help course members to consider the uses they might make of theory.

Using Theory

Person-centred counselling is highly scientific in its approach to the use of theory. There is no attempt to use theory to predict the behaviour of an individual client. However, theory can be used by the person-centred counsellor to begin to understand the client's experience as reported by the client. The theory will not give a detailed understanding – only empathy can do that. However, theory can help the counsellor to feel more secure and thereby to stay open to receiving fully the client's experience. Box 9.2 introduces theory in relation to work with the client Lorraine.

This theoretical analysis leans partially on Rogers' 1951 statement of his 'Nineteen Propositions' (Rogers, 1951) comprising the basis of his personality theory, but also on his more evolved (1959) re-formulation of his personality theory in which he introduces the notion of the conflict between self-actualisation and the actualising tendency (Rogers, 1959).

The person-centred counsellor working with Lorraine would take great care not to misuse the theory. She would not use the theory to *predict* anything concerning the client, nor would she use the theory to try to *influence* the client. The theory exists to help the counsellor to formulate a tentative and hypothetical understanding of the client which will be sufficient to help the counsellor to stay open to the client's experience and thereby to work at relational depth with the client. For the counsellor to begin to use the theory to make predictions, for example, to presume that this is a 'positive' conflict going on within the client in the sense that the actualising tendency appears to have a stronger voice than previously, would be to miss Lorraine in her present experiencing. There is nothing 'positive' for Lorraine in her current experiencing.

At the start of this section I suggested that the person-centred approach to the use of theory was particularly 'scientific' – this requires explanation. The nature of psychological theory is such that it is most inefficient when used predictively. Psychological theory is constructed on the basis of statistical significancies: tendencies of behaviour across a range of people. If 60% of a population behaved in a fashion which followed the prediction of a theory and 40% did not, then that theory would achieve considerable statistical significance. However, in counselling we are working with an individual client. If we endeavour to predict the behaviour or experience of that individual client on the basis of the theory we would be wrong four times out of ten. A

Box 9.2

Lorraine: The Value of Theory

Lorraine was bleeding when she came to her third counselling session. She had cut herself exactly 50 times – once for every year of her life.

As a senior member of the 'First Division' of civil servants she had reached higher than most other women in the history of the Service. She had even managed to achieve that height without sacrificing her need to have a family. Yet, in the safety of therapy, she revealed her despair. She is a 'prisoner' of a part of her Self which could find success despite, or was it 'because of', the oppression of her childhood. She knew from early childhood that she had to get her 'First' from Oxford. Had she been the desired male child, it would have been Balliol or even Trinity, but Somerville, or even Hilda's would have to do – at least that was the way it was in 1965. Now, her life was a conflict of what she had achieved and the fact that she had never been 'free'. Even her children, and this caused her greatest distress, were elements in her construction of a 'successful Self'.

To a counsellor without the support of a coherent theory underpinning her work, Lorraine might have represented a confusing, distressing and even a somewhat frightening encounter – a client depicting a picture of unquestionable social and professional success yet manifesting profound distress including chronic and acute self-mutilation. However, the counsellor who is schooled in person-centred personality theory can use the basic building blocks of the theory, conditions of worth, self-actualisation and the actualising tendency, to understand the kind of dynamics which may be operating in Lorraine's development to date. Briefly, Lorraine appeared to describe a pattern of oppressive 'conditions of worth', possibly conditions of worth which could, by definition, *never* be met (if she had to be the male child). Even under the oppression of such conditions of worth, the Self still endeavours both to *maintain* itself within the parameters of these conditions and also to make the best job it can of *developing* within such dreadful circumstances (under the influence of the actualising tendency). Hence, the process of self-actualisation takes place whereby the person may actually succeed very well while staying within the strict parameters of her fundamental conditions of worth. Hence, Lorraine sensed that her success was not 'despite' but '*because of*' the oppression of her childhood. However, although the Self actualises itself the best way it can under such oppressive conditions of worth, it is almost inevitably creating a conflict (at least for the future) between that Self-as-it-is-actualised and the actualising tendency – the motivational force in the direction of growth. At this present stage in her life it may be that Lorraine is experiencing that conflict between the Self, actualised in terms of the pre-existing conditions of worth, struggling to hold on as the actualising tendency questions the meaningfulness of living life that way.

much more accurate and efficient way to proceed is to enter the phenomenal experience of the client to work with him as an individual rather than as a probability factor.

So, the value of theory to the person-centred counsellor is in the interim and fairly general understanding which it may offer, sufficient not to predict the behaviour of the client but enough to afford the counsellor a degree of security and understanding to help her to engage the client more fully.

The 'Teaching' of Theory

Person-centred trainers can give themselves a hard time over the question of how course members might be introduced to theory. Broadly speaking, there are three positions adopted by trainers. All three positions have value and trainers might make their choices of the balance they wish to achieve among them.

1   *Be entirely 'student-centred' with respect to theory learning*   Theory is well 'caught' when it is perceived as relevant to needs. An entirely student-centred approach would not introduce theory to course members nor make demands on their learning of theory, but would respond to specific needs with relevant sections of theory. For example, when a course member is feeling thoroughly 'stuck' in the therapeutic process with a client they might meaningfully be referred to some theory on 'stuckness' (Mearns, 1994p). Or, perhaps the course member is working in a psychiatric setting and needs to communicate with colleagues in the dominant language of psychopathology. This student might enthusiastically read Elke Lambers' introduction to the articulation of psychiatric language and person-centred theory (Lambers, 1994a, b, c, d). At any other time, if the course member was directed to study these elements of theory regarding 'stuckness' and person-centred psychopathology, the amount learned might be much smaller, and the pain considerably greater!

2   *Introduce the 'field' of theory to the student*   Some trainers will judge that the whole useful field of theory will not necessarily arise in terms of the needs experienced by the course member during the training year and that trainers have some responsibility at least to introduce the course member to the range of the theory during training so that the course member will have some awareness of where to look when specific needs arise at a later point. This position was described in the 'individualisa-

tion of the curriculum' in Chapter 3. This second position with respect to the teaching of theory seeks to introduce course members to the range of theory without presuming that this theory will have an immediate relevance for the course member or that she will be able to apply it in her current working. The aim in this approach is to create 'markers' for course members to which they can return at times of later relevance. Hence, students might be introduced to Barrett-Lennard's excellent paper on therapeutic process (Barrett-Lennard, 1990); Garry Prouty's pioneering work in 'client-centred pre-therapy' (Prouty, 1994); or Dave Mearns' efforts to tease out some of theory of the 'unspoken relationship' (Mearns, 1994n, o). Theoretical areas such as these three examples might be introduced even though the course member does not have experience of lengthy therapeutic processes with clients, was not working with clients for whom a pre-therapy approach was relevant or for whom the unspoken relationship had not yet become an issue in practical counselling work. Yet, having been introduced to the theory on areas such as these, that theory is more easily accessed at a later time of felt need.

3 *Make theoretical demands on the student* It is difficult to imagine a specialist person-centred counsellor who is to be a professional representative of the approach within the counselling community, a potential supervisor and perhaps a future trainer who has not struggled with Carl Rogers' 'Nineteen Propositions' (Rogers, 1951) or studied the famous 'Koch' paper to clarify the conflict between self-actualisation and the actualising tendency (Rogers, 1959). In other words, trainers might take the view that certain elements of theory are simply so fundamental to the approach that, even although they are not reflected in current needs, they should be studied at depth rather than simply introduced. If that decision is taken, to make explicit demands on students with respect to theory learning, the trainer can still use her skill and understanding of person-centred theory to facilitate the learning process. For example, an 'engagement pathway' could be constructed by which students relate to a compulsory element of theory in a variety of ways over a period of time. There might be five elements to such an engagement pathway:

- The element might be introduced by means of a *lecture* or *paper*. The success of the lecture (if it is of high quality) is to stimulate interest in the area – the lecture is not an efficient means of learning on its own.

- *Private study* is essential on most aspects of theory which is new to the course member. However, once again, private study on its own is not particularly efficient.
- The *'study group'*, represents a potentially nutritious learning environment whereby course members, working in small leaderless groups of about four or five members, share their understandings of the area under study, helping each other with illustrative examples and experiences. The study group offers a distinct improvement over private study though each supplements the other.
- *Bring the language of the theory element into the course.* Once a new element of theory is introduced, the whole core staff can make an effort to illustrate relevance to that theory element within supervision groups, personal development groups and any other parts of the training. If staff are diligent on this matter it can make a big difference in 'grounding' the theory within the ongoing experience of the course members. This requires the trainers to stay abreast of the theory elements which they are each introducing.
- The *'assignment'* can be a powerful way to consolidate learning on important elements of theory. The course member has to engage fully with the theory element in order to present her learning in an assignment. In Chapter 3, where assessment was considered, there was further guidance on how a dialogue may be maintained even after the submitting of the assignment. That dialogue may further develop the course member's understanding of the theory element.

Person-centred counselling trainers vary widely in their preferences across these three main training strategies. At one extreme an entirely student-centred approach may be taken to learning. As discussed in Chapter 1, this extreme approach would be relevant if the training frame was large enough to contain it. However, the realities usually are that only a limited time is available for the actual training course and we could not have confidence that a huge amount of the body of theory would come to needs-relevance for the course member during that relatively short period. If the notion of a longer 'training period' evolves in the profession, then a larger 'frame' would result, thus improving the conditions for a more student-centred, needs-based approach. The fact that course members return after some further years' experience to undertake supervision training with a hunger for theory, suggests that this wider training period is a useful notion.

At the other extreme, trainers might set a highly prescriptive schedule of theory learning, tested by assignment. The argument of these trainers is that they have a responsibility to the course member, not to mention the clients and future colleagues of the course member, to ensure that the trainee is schooled in the theory of the approach.

For my part, I tend to be suspicious about extreme positions. While the emphasis on a detailed and extensive compulsory theory curriculum might represent an arguable case, I have also seen trainers who hide behind that overloading on theory because of their own discomfort with the personal development dimensions of counsellor training. Similarly, while the entirely student-centred approach may be coherently argued, I have also seen trainers hide behind that to avoid exposing their own lack of sophistication with respect to theory. My own view is that all three of these pathways have a considerable amount to offer and that, rather than narrow ourselves as trainers, we might usefully engage different methodologies with respect to the various elements within the theory curriculum. Perhaps we might stay close to our model by also considering our students' views on the matter.

Developing Theory

Training courses may even go beyond the acquisition of previously researched theory towards developing their own theory by means of research workshops and student theses. Indeed, this was the basis of much of the formative research in the person-centred approach during the 1950s and 1960s. Theory development at that time was underpinned by the work of aspiring doctoral students, for example Goff Barrett-Lennard (1962).

In Britain we find the interesting situation of two different emphases within counsellor training. On the one hand we have Masters courses which include an important element of student research through the thesis but, because there is only so much time available, spend less time on some of the other important demands of training. Diploma courses on the other hand devote their 400–450 contact hours more to those elements of the training which are necessary to underpin the day-to-day counselling work of the student. On Diploma courses the idea of student research is valued, but other training needs are regarded as more imperative. Interestingly, the Diploma courses have more easily been able to meet the criteria of Course Accreditation with the British Association for Counselling than have Masters courses because of the huge amount of resource which Masters courses have to subtract from non-research elements.

While it would be entirely inappropriate for training standards to be dropped with respect to the core elements of training (Dryden et al., 1995; BAC, 1996c), the profession perhaps needs to find some way of addressing the development of theory as an integral, albeit additional dimension of training. Perhaps if we further develop the notion of the 'training period' as extending a few years beyond basic training, the matter of engaging trainee counsellors in the task of developing theory might find a place to play its part. Certainly, the person-centred approach needs to pay attention to this dimension of articulating the development of theory with the training, for that was the firm basis on which it was founded in Chicago in the 1950s.

One of the areas where the approach could develop considerable theory is in the working of the unstructured large group. Large group working, explored in the next chapter, is a peculiar animal which is special to the person-centred approach. Other approaches decry it but the person-centred world still holds on to this untameable animal – perhaps *because* it is untameable?

10
The Large Group Meeting

When the Governor came in and saw the scene after the stabbing he ordered the prisoners to be locked up in their cells immediately. But Big Malky [a screw] stepped in and said 'That's not the way we do things here – we'll have a Community Meeting.'

(Boyle, 1994)

In Jimmy Boyle's account of the time following the stabbing of one prisoner by another in Barlinnie Prison's 'Special Unit', the prisoners and screws responded to a potentially destructive crisis by investing in the 'Community Meeting', which had become possibly their only source of hope.

In counselling training, course members are often equivocal at best about community meeting time. For the course members the community meeting may represent a confusing experience for the very fact that it is unstructured. For the prisoner, Jimmy Boyle, and also for the late Malcolm McKenzie, the community meeting offered a slender hope – it was a free meeting which carried the possibility, or was it the illusion, of freedom. When you are a prisoner or a screw both locked into an oppressive system the open communication of a community meeting represents a frightening freedom. When you are a representative of the repressive moral authority the open communication of persons across authority boundaries represents the most dreadful threat, which is why Barlinnie's Special Unit was closed down in 1994.

The Structure of the Large Group Meeting in Counselling Training

The large group meeting, sometimes called the 'community meeting', may contain anything from 20 to 40 people and is comprised of all the course members and some or all of the core staff. The meetings are unstructured in the sense that there is no agenda except that which is raised by the participants. On a one-year full-time training course there are likely to be one or two meetings per week, lasting between one and two hours. Part-time training may opt for a small amount of community time each day or a larger amount every two weeks and perhaps longer meetings more occasionally. These large group meetings are generally slower to evolve in part-time training than on full-time courses, perhaps because they are seen to be more *central* to the day-to-day existence for full-time trainees. One of the few disadvantages of part-time training is that it is difficult to be so fully immersed in the process when only engaging it one day in seven. Trainers need to gauge the centrality of the course to the lives of the course members before they decide to invest time in the unstructured large group meeting – the large group meeting will simply not work if it does not receive a fairly large investment from the course members and, in turn, the course members cannot be expected to make that large investment in an unstructured event with unpredictable outcome if the conditions are not right for them.

It can be important that course members feel they have the freedom to decide to increase or decrease the time devoted to large group meetings. Indeed, it is important that course members know that the course community as a whole can decide to stop large group meetings if that is the general wish. As described in an example later in this chapter, having the freedom to dispense with community meetings can even be an important step in engaging with them.

The Functions of the Large Group Meeting

Eight functions of large group meetings in person-centred counselling training are identified below though, of course, these will often overlap or combine.

Sharing Information

The large group meeting offers a good opportunity for communication with all course members and representatives of the staff present. Information can be shared about the day to day running of the course and also current issues within the profession.

Making Communal Decisions

A person-centred course seeks to achieve its training *functions* while being open to modifying training *structures* in accordance with the ideas and contributions within the course community. Typically, a course staff would begin the process by offering certain structures based on experience with previous courses. However, thereafter, it is within the power of the whole course community to alter those structures in order to meet individual needs more effectively. The large group meeting is one of the few places where the whole course can communicate on possible changes to the course programme or structure.

Raising Course Issues

The large group meeting time also represents an opportunity for individual course members to bring to a wider forum issues concerning the course that have been raised in smaller formal or informal groups. This can be extremely important for the 'health' of the course in that it provides an opportunity for issues to be addressed quickly and also directly rather than disappearing into undercurrents of unspoken disquiet. So, for example, course members or staff members might raise questions regarding the participation of members of the course community or about the resources being provided for the course or about satisfaction or dissatisfaction with any elements of the working programme. It is important to note that the community meeting time merely represents an *opportunity* for these issues to be raised more publicly and directly; it is entirely a matter for individual decision as to whether they are brought to the community or not. In courses where the norm develops to keep such challenges away from open disclosure there is a tendency for disquiet to feed on itself and magnify.

Raising Personal Issues

On a counselling training course there are many places where people can raise personal issues and the large group is one of these. The personal issues that people bring to the large group are not different from those taken, for instance, to the personal development group. Perhaps the issue is raised because its time has come and this opportunity presents itself, like the 23-year-old course member who voiced her frustration and despair that 'It is so difficult always to be working with people who are older than me – I see some of them look me up and down as though they are thinking "What can this young lass offer me?"' At other times the large group may be chosen for the major forum which it offers for considering personal issues which are particularly serious, like the course member who had reached, until then, an unspoken degree of self-doubt expressed in his statement 'I need to say this – although it is the most scary thing for me – I think I just can't do this – for ten years I have looked forward to becoming a counsellor – and now I just don't think that I can make it.'

Sometimes people fear the large group because there are so many people present that they cannot trust they will be understood by everyone. Sometimes it is that very size and diversity of the group which lends some hope – that perhaps I will be understood by someone.

Working with Conflict

The large group setting presents the opportunity for community members, including staff, to address relational issues between them. Often these are issues reflecting an increasing understanding and feeling of intimacy but, also, the possibility is afforded to deal directly with issues of conflict. The large group creates a powerful context for dealing with conflict in that the very size of the group offers the likelihood of support even for extreme positions. In any matter of conflict the concern of the staff is that the large group might work towards an increasing *clarification* of the issues involved. It is a mistake to seek *resolution* of conflict because that can put undue pressure on one or both of the parties to come to an artificial solution. It is one thing to ask the parties to clarify their position but quite another to demand that one or both changes that position. Paradoxically, the de-emphasis of working towards resolution can mean that it is easier to obtain. A footnote on this issue for trainers is that it is vital to ensure that a minimum of two core staff are present at community meetings in case one of them is involved in a direct conflict with a course member. In that event the other trainer, as well as members of the course, can help both parties to explore what lies under the conflict for all parties.

Box 10.1 describes a particularly difficult conflict raised by the course member Andrea in relation to another trainee, John. The whole experience was difficult for *all* concerned. It was difficult for Andrea to raise the issue and it was difficult for John to hear and respond to it. It was also difficult for the others present because the question of 'abuse' is always painful. However, since the issue was raised there was at least the chance to work towards

Box 10.1

Conflict in Caring

When he came into the community meeting that morning John had no idea that his world was in danger of falling apart. For Andrea, on the other hand, the community meeting represented not a beginning, but a possible ending to what for her had been a painful process. From two weeks earlier she had felt uncomfortable in the extreme with the attention which John had paid to her during and following a practice counselling session. She struggled with whether the problem was that she was being both super-sensitive and insensitive in feeling uncomfortable with John's attention on her. On the one hand he had offered her an unquestionable quality of attention and understanding but why had he also offered her a caress at the end of their session? Andrea had accepted his offer and felt bad thereafter. Rather than blame herself or try to bury her discontent she took the braver decision of confronting John. She chose the community meeting as the place to raise her discontent for two reasons. Firstly, it offered a large arena in which both parties might be supported and also she feared that John might slip out of her challenge in any more private setting.

John heard Andrea's confrontation in that community meeting. He felt an enormous warmth when Andrea said that she genuinely felt John's caring towards her but he felt quite sick when she described the fact that she had felt 'abused' by him. He describes his feelings best in his own words:

I felt devastated – I had no idea this was coming. At first I felt that *everyone* was against me. I retreated into my very familiar self-protective shell. That shell gives off a really hard image – a 'hurt and hard' image. As I was giving off that image I remembered hoping like hell that just one person would see the 'hurt' part, although I knew that most would see the 'hard' bit. I got a lot of forceful feedback from women on the course on my hard image – one mentioned how it reinforced her own feelings of being abused. Eventually I heard other voices – someone saying that he was scared – that it could have been him. Another person said that she did what I had done, often – she added that it was only men who were accused of abuse. Another woman said that it did not matter that I had not intended to abuse, it was the *effect* which was important. Another woman said that that was nonsense. *I* said that I genuinely felt that I had not been abusing, but that I could see the result and that I could learn from that. Someone asked me if I was saying that to try to stop things. I heard my voice saying '*Yes*'. That was the first moment in the confrontation where I was being congruent. I think that changed things for me and, instead of just defending myself, I actually laid myself naked to the community. After a fairly lengthy silence where I realised that everyone was waiting for me to speak I was amazed to find myself talking

---

Box 10.1 continued

about how I had felt about Andrea during that session two weeks earlier. I spoke about how I had felt incredibly warm and loving towards her. I heard myself saying that these feelings were fully involved in my caress. I also said that I could see how this was 'abuse', not because of the feelings I had experienced but because I had expressed them covertly in my caress.

---

its clarification. If it had stayed hidden it would have been cancerous in the life of the group and it would have lost the opportunity for the learning it created for many members, not only the principals.

Keeping Track of Realities

Reality is 'socially constructed'. In any social system the members come to share understanding and agree a working 'reality'. Within person-centred training there is an ever-present challenge to us to build congruence into our relations and thereby into our reality. One of the consequences of this is that course members tend to become aware of the realities that have developed in their social systems outside the course and how most of these are based on a collective collusion of incongruence. Paradoxically the reality outside the course often begins to be referred to as 'the real world' in contrast to the apparent unreality on the course. That the 'real world' runs on norms around incongruence can be a shocking discovery, although perfectly understandable in terms of the social psychological need of human beings to build predictability and presumed safety into social relating. The large group meeting offers a forum to consider and keep track of the whole issue of realities both inside and outside the course. Box 10.2 describes one course member's desperate struggle with realities.

'Coming Out'

The notion of 'coming out' in relation to previously hidden parts of the Self was explained in some detail in Chapter 3 where the community meeting was described as that most public of arenas for the purpose. In this section it is sufficient for us to present a

---

Box 10.2

I hate you. I hate me

I come here three days a week and I live one reality, then I go home for four days and live another. But they are opposites – and they are tearing me apart. I hate you. But I am one of you, so I hate me. You are showing me all the falsity in my life. I have tried to reject you but I keep coming back. You show me a world where people really 'meet' each other. I join in that world and I can actually do it. But I have built my life on *not meeting*. My reality outside here is that I *don't* 'meet' people. You have shown me that reality. I hate you. I hate me.

---

couple of examples of course members using the meeting for this purpose.

- 'For weeks now my personal development group has been helping me to become more responsive. In all groups, particularly this large group, I hide in silence behind the pretence that it takes me longer to respond than other people. I just wanted to announce my defences to you all so that I couldn't hide behind them so much from now on.'
- 'It's really important for me to be open about me – and this is the most scary place for me to do that. I have felt a *fraud* for most of this course. I came on this course only wanting the qualification – I never really felt that I needed the training. That wasn't true of course – it was a way for me to defend against the fear I had about personal work.'

Experimenting with Congruence

The notion of using the community meeting as a place to experiment with developing congruence is discussed in Chapter 7 of this book and also in Section 11 of *Developing Person-Centred Counselling* (Mearns, 1994b). Examples of this use of the community meeting often come late in the life of the course. I remember a particular male course member who had confided privately on the incredible difficulty which he had in showing his loving, caring side. In late community meetings of that course I could see him experimenting, sometimes in a clumsy fashion, with trying to find words and ways to express the caring he genuinely felt towards colleagues. Some of those colleagues knew the significance of this man's contributions while others were a little confused but also respectful of his fitful communication.

Sometimes course members can best show their own striving towards congruence in their own words:

- 'I've been struggling with *not wanting to be seen* – so I am just going to say anything I feel or think in this group and see what happens.'
- 'I am totally confused. For a few weeks now, I've just been being *me* – all my judgementalism I have let spill out rather than hiding it – and yet you haven't crucified me. As I say this I am more scared than I have ever been in my life. I am really showing you *me* as I meet myself.'

I have a personal rule that I do not use illustrations from work with current clients or course members. In offering Box 10.3 I am breaking that rule because I was so moved to read this part of the course member's account of her struggle with congruence in the arena offered by the large group. As I reproduce her words, I am aware that I do not know where she will go with this in the last half of her course.

Box 10.3

Struggling with the Community Meeting: Struggling with my Congruence

I find myself, each time the community meets, struggling to 'find the right time' or 'find the courage' or to find the 'appropriate' words to express myself in a way which is acceptable to the group. And yet, I know that what I have to say is relevant to me, and is relevant to my development, and that it is also relevant to the community as a whole, in as much as I am part of that community. I know that not contributing to the group as a result of my fear, is unbearably frustrating. I am coming to understand that although I may find it difficult not to second-guess the reaction of the group, and although it is comfortable for me to feel liked and accepted, I cannot afford to do this at the expense of being true to myself. I want to learn how to communicate honestly and openly with people – in whatever situation. There are many associated fears for me in this: I am afraid I might not be able to trust myself to respond to people with honesty and without defensiveness; I am afraid that I can't trust my own reactions, and I am afraid to face conflicts which arise in the group. I am afraid to stand alone, but also afraid not to! It seems to me that I am on the very edge of this possibility of congruence. I know I must jump, for my own peace of mind, but will I fly, or will I fall (wingless), to the ground and land with a thud? The uncomfortable answer appears to be that I can't know until I take the risk to try.

Large Group Process

Large group process is entirely different from small group process. The source of that difference is that small groups can be *normed* much more easily. This is the reason why small groups can be made to feel much more secure, safe and trusting than the large group. The human being is incredibly skilful, in working co-operatively with a small group of others, to find unspoken ways of creating an environment which is sufficiently predictable to feel secure and also trusting. On the other hand, in a group of 30 or 40 persons, this illusion of safety through norming is not readily achieved. In that sense the large group offers a more cruelly real representation of humanity than any of the smaller training groups. While the smaller groups are important for helping people to begin to explore the parts of themselves which need that secure environment, the large group offers a continuing context in which those discoveries may be tested against a wider and less controllable reality.

The process of a large group is often experienced as strange and perhaps frightening when compared to the small group. For example, there is a reduced feeling of responsibility felt by individuals in a large group. This 'diffusion of responsibility' is well noted in the social psychology of large groups. Hence, a phenomenon of the large group experience is the *vacuum of response* – a person may express something which is very important to him and yet receive virtually no response. Sometimes people refer to this as 'things dropping into a hole in the middle of the group'. In smaller groups that vacuum does not arise because people feel a *responsibility* to respond, whereas that responsibility in the large group is diffused and can disappear. Members tend to blame the structure of the large group for this phenomenon, but really it is simply exposing a dimension of the human being.

Often the 'process' in a large group is *untidy* compared to a small group. Things are rarely processed as completely in a large group as in a small group. This is as much a factor of arithmetic as anything else – a course member may raise an issue on which 30 other people might have something significant to say but there is little possibility of all that being expressed before someone has moved things on.

One of the finest concepts for epitomising the large group was coined 20 years ago by John McLeod. He described the large group, within person-centred training, as a 'moral arena' (McLeod, 1977). This was a wonderful insight into the large group process at a time when that phenomenon was in its infancy. To this day the relevance of that construction applies: the large group is a vibrant and, understandably, fearful arena in which people have the possibility of encountering each other in a fashion that is not made safe by conventions of structure.

Stages in the Development of the Large Group

The very essence of the person-centred approach contradicts any notion that the researcher can predict stages in the development of the person. The same thesis applies at the social psychological level. Yet, I am sufficiently foolhardy as to posit four stages within the development of the large group in person-centred counselling training. As much as anything else these stages are offered heuristically as an encouragement to rejoinder and dispute.

Stage I: Polite Tolerance

Early in the course, members are unsure about how the large group should/could work and relate to it with a somewhat deferential tolerance, presuming that it must exist for a good reason. Some of the course membership will have read published items on large group process but this usually does not make a difference. This phase of polite tolerance can continue until some meaning is experienced for the group in which case it may move on directly to Stage III, but much more common is to experience the uncomfortable and often fairly long-lasting Stage II.

Stage II: Confusion and Disorientation

As mentioned earlier, small groups focused on supervision or personal development can be normed quite easily by the course members. The members come to implicit and even explicit agreements as to how these groups should proceed. The norms established in small groups may be challenged and changed from time to time but while they exist they serve to define, as well as to restrict, what can happen in the group. However, the large group with no pre-defined focus does not offer that safety of limitation. It may seem to be freeing to offer unstructured time but that freedom is so unusual in our social living that it can be confusing and disorienting. People respond differently during this stage in the development of the large group. Members struggle with the problem that there is no way of predicting in advance how an intervention will be received because norms have not been laid down about that kind of thing. In much of our life we may have tiptoed around 'conditions of worth' endeavouring to find the ways in which we should behave in different group contexts in order to win approval, or at least, to avoid disapproval. People respond to the confusion and disorientation of the large group in different ways. Some can push themselves to continue to function despite the confusion and disorientation. They offer elements of their experiencing and they respond to others and in that way encourage the large group process to continue and develop. Some other people do not find it so easy to be visible in this unpredictable context and may be silent for much of the time. Sometimes they struggle to ascribe a meaning to the confusing and disorienting process by, perhaps, defining themselves as different from the others:

- 'I'm just not a "large group" type of person.'
- 'My process moves too slowly for the big group – I find myself lagging behind, thinking about something which is long past.'
- 'I don't like the fact that a lot of what you say doesn't get a response. I'm not going to say something and have it fall into that hole in the middle of the group.'

Another response to the phase of confusion and disorientation in the large group is to become alienated from it or even angry about the structure, the other group members or the staff. Some comments of course members about the large group include:

- 'What a waste of time. I spend most of the meeting staring at a stain in the carpet.'
- 'All I do in community meetings is try to survive them . . . without drawing any attention to myself.'
- 'I don't see why we have large group meetings – much more trust can be built in the small groups.'
- 'My greatest fear in the large group meetings is that someone will say something to me.'
- 'The staff seem to like community meetings but most of the rest of us don't.'

If that alienation felt by course members is offered then it can be responded to and this becomes part of the active process of the group. As the group members begin to find that they have negotiated some difficult feelings, even anger, they may begin to *glimpse the potential* (Stage III) of large group working. However, if the anger or other difficult feelings are not presented in the group but withheld and dissipated elsewhere, then the large group has little opportunity to move on. Indeed, sometimes the large group does not get beyond this second stage of confusion and disorientation because its energy is dissipated outside. Getting stuck in Stage II may be related to the course structure and what the course means in the life of the participants. If the course has a considerable degree of centrality in the life of the members then they will not be satisfied with an enduring policy of avoidance and will begin to address their issues more directly. Another reason for the large group becoming stuck in this second phase is where the staff show an unwillingness or inability either to respond to 'difficult' feelings raised by group members or to be open about similar feelings they may have. There is an old adage in person-centred group working that the group process mirrors the staff process. This contains partial though not complete truth. The staff, through their own fears or incompetence, can *inhibit* the development of a more open process in the large group. However, theirs is not the only responsibility – the staff alone cannot move the process on.

Stage III: Glimpsing the Potential

At different points in what may be a fairly long-lasting Stage II, more and more group members may begin to glimpse the potential of the large group:

- 'I find that I can speak in the large group now even though I can't be sure of how people will respond to me, or even *if* they will respond to me.'
- 'I don't think there is anywhere in the world where you are so *visible* as in the large group. That used to paralyse me, but it does offer a powerful place to show yourself.'
- 'You can't be incongruent here for any length of time – there's bound to be someone who will "call" you on it.'
- 'It's a strange experience in the large group compared to small groups. Because there are so many people and I don't *have to* respond, it's easier for me to become more "centred" – to see what I really am feeling.'
- 'We avoided direct confrontation for a long time but now that we have done it things are a lot freer – it's like I can be much more of myself and even though that is scary, it will work out OK. In a funny way the large group is a lot more *supportive* because we don't avoid difficult things now.'

- 'Yesterday in the large group I learned the most important thing in my life – that expressing my difficult feelings helped me to realise my loving feelings.'

No staged theory of development is ever neat and tidy. The reality of large groups is that there is often a 'looping' between Stages II and III with some glimpses of the potential interspersed with confusion and disorientation. However, as more members of the group make the choice of engaging with the large group and being more open about themselves in relation to others, the group may move into its fourth stage.

Stage IV: Valuing and Working in the Open Process

At this point in the development of the group the members are no longer scared of each other. It has become much easier to be open and spontaneous within the large group. Members can use the large group to experiment with their Selves and develop congruence as described in Chapter 7. The important thing about this stage of the large group process is that the members have achieved that harmonic way of relating while not giving up their individuality as persons. This is a harmony through congruence rather than a harmony through norming. In most other forms of group working, differences and difficulties among the members are avoided by structuring the activity in such a way as only to allow certain forms and directions of communication. The large group, at this stage of its development, has not restricted its communication, in fact it has more and more opened it out. However, because the members have been willing to voice their concerns, their fears, their anxieties, their dislikes, their caring, their warmth and their loving, they are able to be free with each other while not giving up any parts of themselves. While the large group may earlier have been a cold and even fearful place, the course member might be amazed to find that at this stage of its development the group feels like the best 'home' that one could have. It is a home where people are prized for their differences rather than merely liked for their similarities.

At this fourth stage in the development of the large group it usually feels as though there is not enough time to achieve everything which might be tackled in that context. While, earlier in its development, people might have resented the apparently large amount of time 'wasted' on large group working, now the course members might spend whole days in the large group.

The Challenge for the Staff

The large group meetings may include all the core staff or only some. Obviously, it is an ideal for all staff to be present but the economics of higher education have an appropriate part to play, and investing in the participation of four or five staff members will mean reducing the staffing on other parts of the course. As mentioned earlier, it is important, however, not to let the staff representation fall below two, so that there is at least one staff member available to offer the wider perspective if the other is very personally involved.

The staff role in large group working is paradoxical. They are not there to *manage* the process. The whole essence of the large group process is that the course members should feel a freedom to participate in whatever ways they wish. The notion of the staff actively managing a process runs counter to that freedom. However, the challenge for the staff is to struggle to relate *openly* and *congruently* no matter what is happening. This is the same kind of expectation that is placed on the person-centred counsellor in relation to her client – although the process may be very difficult for the client, we do expect the counsellor not to become stuck and incongruent, or at least, we can expect the counsellor to struggle with any stuckness or incongruence which she may be experiencing.

We can translate this responsibility on the staff to relate openly and congruently into a few specific *challenges*.

The Challenge, not only to Respond, but also to Initiate

If the staff are to be open as well as congruent we would expect that it would be natural from time to time for them to 'initiate' new material into the large group. If the staff merely restrict themselves to *responding* to course members then they are too closely mimicking the counselling role rather than that of an active member of the group.

The Challenge to be Transparent

The staff need to be open, not only in what they say, but also in what is lying behind their contributions. If the staff member merely says something like 'I wonder what the silent people are feeling', it can sound too confusing and even mysterious. In just the same fashion as in person-centred counselling, the staff member wants to give information on what is behind her statements, hence, a more appropriate way of relating in the large group would be to say something like 'I'm wondering what is going on for the people who are not saying anything. I guess I'm asking that because I'm a bit fearful – I tend to get a bit frightened and think of the worst when I don't know what's going on.' This kind of intervention, including the *'because'* (see Chapter 4), is now centred in the person of the staff member and allows many more responses: course members may respond to the question of silence or they may respond to the fear of the staff member. In this way of working the staff member is an active participant in the group rather than a shadowy and somewhat mysterious reflector of group process. Students of psychodynamic working will clearly see the difference in this person-centred approach to group work.

The Challenge not to Foreclose on Issues and Processes

One of the dangers is that the staff try to avoid what may be difficult processes and experiences by using their power to stop or re-direct the process. The challenge to the staff is to contribute personally in the direction of 'working in the open process' and certainly not to foreclose on that open process.

The Challenge to Tolerate the Ambiguity of an Unstructured Process

In the educational domain an unstructured process is most unusual. Many of the course members will enter the training with a prior educational experience in which the responsibility for structuring the process has been laid entirely in the hands of the course staff. In the expectations of some course members there will be an ambiguity represented by the staff member who refuses to structure the process.

The Challenge Openly to Encounter Each Other as well as the Course Members

It is perfectly healthy to the process of the large group for staff members to encounter, and to challenge, each other. Such challenges need to be congruent and not manufactured. But it is important that staff do not sit on their differences and keep them for staff meetings. They are asking the course members to share in the responsibility for the working environment, so it is incumbent upon the staff also to share their own process. The staff sharing their differences offers much to the members of the course. It shows that there is no one 'staff reality'; it shows that differences can be honestly held; it shows how challenge and confrontation can be directly expressed; and it shows how clarification, if not necessarily resolution, can be achieved through a commitment to communication.

Reactions of Course Members to the Community Meeting

Throughout this chapter numerous reactions of course members to the community meeting have been presented. Perhaps it is amusing to end the chapter by listing some further descriptors which participants have offered about the community meeting:

- 'One hour of interminable boredom.'
- 'The most alive human relating I have ever experienced.'
- 'Excruciatingly slow and turgid.'
- 'Like being in a group of scared mice.'
- 'Unbelievably exciting.'
- 'Terrifying.'
- 'Incredibly safe.'
- 'Really challenging.'
- 'Too cosy.'

Perhaps the experience of community meetings is best described by the fact that these individual reactions were gathered following the same meeting!

11
Professional Issues

The Professional Issues Curriculum

The term 'professional issues' in counselling encompasses all the matters *around* the counsellor's work with the client. Dryden et al. (1995) describe it thus:

> This curriculum includes everything the counsellor does to make the work possible and to assist in its quality outside the actual skills of the counselling interaction. It encompasses, for instance, attention to the *context* of the work: ensuring the suitability of the work setting, being diligent over attendance and punctuality, and, in general, being responsible *to* the client without taking responsibility *for* the client. (p. 126)

Dryden et al. (1995) offer further clarification of the kinds of issues which would be included in this curriculum:

- selecting and contracting with a supervisor;
- using tape recorders in counselling – practical and ethical issues;
- personal safety and security for the counsellor;
- writing case notes;
- record-keeping, confidentiality and the law;
- writing letters to clients;
- developing a resource network;
- making referrals;
- introduction to the Code of Ethics;
- case studies on ethical decision-making and problem-solving;
- setting up a private practice;
- advertising a counselling service;
- dealing with client fees;
- indemnity insurance;
- setting up a counselling agency;
- the counsellor as change agent within an organisation;
- monitoring and evaluating the competence of the counsellor – including quality assurance and clinical audit;
- evaluation of client work outcomes;
- understanding, interpreting and evaluating research reports;
- individual counsellor accreditation and national registration;

- national and international developments within the field;
- nature and purpose of supervision after training;
- counsellor stress and burn-out;
- opportunities for further training;
- professional development after basic training.

For some of these issues the method of consideration on the course will be by means of a *formal* session. For example, the issue of 'counsellor accreditation and registration' can most efficiently be introduced by means of a special session delivered by someone with expertise in this area. This is an example of the kind of issue which courses feel a responsibility to introduce but it is not one which is usually relevant to the immediate needs of the course members. Some courses are alive to that fact and approach this issue by means of the formal introduction but also offer a free follow-up consultative service for ex-students when they arrive at the point of making an accreditation application.

Professional issues may be better presented if they are woven into the fabric of the course rather than presented in a single session. For example, 'national and international developments within the field', might be approached in an ongoing fashion by continually drawing course members' attention to issues in the current journals and papers presented at conferences. The regular large group meeting offers an easy context for this communication.

Another pathway by which professional issues are approached in training is through the 'informal' curriculum, for example the way professional standards are modelled by the staff in relation to the training, including the diligence of staff on the matter of their own attendance, punctuality and preparation for sessions as well as their thoughtful attention to administration. Modelling a professional approach does not simply mean fulfilling commitments, it may also include matters such as showing course members the importance of taking care of oneself as a professional worker with people. In this respect it is important that trainers are able to say 'No' to those requests from course members which would put the staff member under excessive pressure. As was discussed in Chapter 4, this is an important issue in person-centred training. It is not a matter of the trainer trying to do everything the course member wants – the trainer is a person too, with limits and priorities, and must model the management of her time and personal resources.

I do not propose to go into detail on all the elements of a typical professional issues curriculum. In most of the issues mentioned at the start of the chapter the person-centred approach does not demand a different kind of consideration from other approaches: these are issues which are common to the whole profession, regardless of the specific approach. However, it might be useful to pick one of these areas to show how learning can be approached from a variety of directions. Let us consider the issue of *ethical decision-making*.

A training course will want to introduce the subject of ethical decision-making quite early in the training so that course members are at least introduced to the relevant Code of Ethics and have an opportunity to study it before they are involved in actual counselling with members of the public. This is one of those issues where a person-centred training course endeavouring to operate from an entirely student-centred model might run into difficulty. It is not particularly likely that course members would raise the need to study such a Code at the outset of training unless primed to that by the staff. Yet, the course would generally be regarded as owing a duty of responsibility to the public to introduce course members to such a Code before practice began.

Simply reading a Code of Ethics at the beginning of training is probably one of the most inefficient ways of learning. It is better to help course members to project themselves into ethical situations and then to engage them in the task of ethical decision-making. Box 11.1 illustrates the kind of 'critical incident' around which can be built consideration of ethical issues.

The particular critical incident presented in Box 11.1 can also be used to focus on gender issues in counselling. For example, it is interesting to compare course members' reactions to the incident if the gender of the counsellor and client are reversed. In that circumstance some course members maintain a consistency of judgement but others regard the incident as much more serious if it were a male counsellor and a female client. Indeed, there is a disturbing tendency to regard the female counsellor version with a degree of humour!

As well as creating slots in the formal curriculum for attention to ethical decision-making, this is such an important issue that it would also be woven into the fabric of the course, notably into the supervision groups where course members and trainers could constantly reflect elements of current practice against points on the Code.

There could be circumstances where matters of ethics arise within the informal curriculum, for example in the behaviour of trainers. It is highly relevant for a course to issue course members at the outset with a copy of the Code of Ethics and Practice for

---

Box 11.1

'Malcolm'

You are a female counsellor working in private practice and Malcolm is one of your clients. From the first session it has been clear that he was really *ready* for counselling. Now, after 20 weekly meetings, the difference in him is quite astounding. He was always an attractive man, but lacked belief in himself. Now that the belief is substantially returned he is positively vibrant. You know he still has work to do and will have hurdles to overcome, but even now he is one of your most successful clients. It is appropriate for you to accept much responsibility for the successful process with Malcolm, for you have been able to offer him an intensity of relating and a level of commitment which has been much greater than normal.

However, you are also aware of your response as a woman to Malcolm. Indeed, you have recognised your strong attraction to him from the beginning and have raised that issue regularly in supervision as a precautionary measure. You are aware of the dangers of 'over-involvement' and you are also aware of the beauty and power of your relationship with Malcolm not to mention the undoubtedly positive changes taking place in him.

There are other issues, like his former wife from whom he is in the process of separating, who, from his account, is abusive and discounting towards him. But you have recognised that your feelings are very strong, and you and Malcolm have shared your largely mutual feelings. Your supervisor has repeatedly cautioned on the fact that your personal involvement with Malcolm might abuse your counselling relationship.

You are an experienced counsellor and are aware of the issues and dangers. You are also a woman with needs and feelings. You feel that Malcolm can be responsible for himself. You and Malcolm have been able to talk about everything . . .

What are the ethical issues involved here?

How would you, as the counsellor, handle these ethical issues?

(Be prepared to report back on these questions)

Trainers (BAC, 1996a) as the guideline to their own practice. Furthermore, a person-centred staff might be expected to deal with any ethical issues regarding trainers as openly as possible within the course community, with the caveat that it would be important to respect the needs of individual course members involved.

The Aim of 'Full Involvement' and the Danger of 'Over-involvement'

As mentioned earlier, the professional issues curriculum does not and should not differ from that of the rest of the profession, hence the relative brevity of this chapter. However, one area which can present particular difficulty for trainers and course members alike, is the expectation of the 'full involvement' of the person-centred counsellor with her client. There is a danger that person-centred counsellors, because of their desire to meet the client at a level of full involvement, will be perceived by practitioners of other approaches as being *over-involved*. I remember a most confusing conversation with a counsellor from another approach who was challenging me with considerable anger on the evidence of my over-involvement in published cases. She cited as evidence of my over-involvement my willingness to have clients phone me at home, my visit to a graveyard with a client and a lengthy, ten-hour, session I had had with a suicidal client. To her these represented clear evidence of my over-involvement whereas to person-centred counsellors they might be seen as indicative of commitment. Of course, both conclusions are incompetent because we cannot make a judgement of over-involvement on the basis of simple structural issues. To make a judgement of over-involvement we need to look at the functions which the counsellor's behaviour is serving and the experience of the client. If the counsellor's behaviour is primarily serving the function of meeting her needs rather than the client's then a judgement of over-involvement is properly established. I use the following as a working definition of over-involvement:

- *Over-involvement* occurs where the meeting of the emotional needs of the counsellor attains inappropriate prominence and the client is drawn into, or confirmed into, an inclination to play a complementary role.

The person-centred approach will always be vulnerable to the accusation of over-involvement. It is interesting that within the profession there are few accusations of the opposite, of 'under-involvement'. Sometimes the level of detachment of the counsellor is, to the client, so perverse as to be experienced as abusive (Allen, 1989) and yet the apparently cold, distant counsellor, unaware of and uncaring about the client's experience would seldom be put to ethical challenge.

'Over-involvement' and 'full involvement' are usually un-related dimensions. As a working definition of 'full involvement' I would suggest the following:

● The challenge to *'full involvement'* for the person-centred coun-sellor expects a strong and consistent *commitment* combined with a willingness and ability to work with the client at *relational depth* with the existence of high degrees of the therapeutic conditions which that demands.

Elsewhere I have written on the critical importance of the counsel-lor's *commitment*, as perceived by the client (Mearns, 1992d). The nature of the counsellor's commitment may mean different things for different clients. With most clients it may simply mean that the counsellor is perceived as diligent and consistent in her respons-ibilities to them. With another client it may also mean having extraordinary patience to remain consistent to him over a long and slow process. In another relationship the 'commitment' of the counsellor may mean staying open with the client despite his considerable efforts to reject (for example, 'Paul's' counsellor in Chapter 1). On another occasion the counsellor's contracted com-mitment with the client during major trauma was daily sessions plus the possibility of evening phone calls.

This combination of a willingness to meet at relational depth, and commitment, does not mean that the counsellor is over-involved. It is sloppy thinking to presume that full involvement and over-involvement are on a continuum. The essential differ-ence is that in full-involvement the counsellor is making clear professional decisions bearing in mind her own boundaries as well as those of the client. In over-involvement the counsellor is exceeding her normal boundaries because of the gain she is achieving in terms of other needs. Another, pragmatic, difference between full involvement and over-involvement is that the coun-sellor willingly involves her supervisor to a considerable extent when offering full involvement with the client, but in over-involvement the view of the supervisor tends to be avoided.

Boxes 11.2 and 11.3 offer the counsellor, supervisor and trainer stimulus material in the form of so-called 'symptoms' of over-involvement. These lists are not meant to be authoritative because, as mentioned earlier, a judgement on over-involvement cannot be made on the basis of simple counsellor behaviours. Indeed, the lists are used to stimulate debate and encourage course members to discuss their own experiences. The presence of two different lists of symptoms reflects the fact that different parts of our personality may be over-involved. In labelling these categories I

Box 11.2
'Parent–Child' Over-involvement Symptoms

- The counsellor becomes over-protective towards the client.
- A 'halo effect' appears in the counsellor's reports about the client.
- The counsellor makes promises to the client as to outcome.
- The counsellor begins to assume responsibilities *for* the client.
- The counsellor freely extends the boundaries of the work contract in terms of time, frequency, place of meeting, in an *unsystematic* fashion.
- The counsellor takes on an *advocacy* role for the client in relation to others.
- Thoughts about the client repeatedly 'flood in' to the counsellor's mind.
- The counsellor shows an unusual intensity and quality of feeling when considering the client.
- Some issues concerning the client feel as though they are life or death ones.

Box 11.3
'Child–Child' Over-involvement Symptoms

- 'Collusion' between counsellor and client (against 'outsiders').
- Counsellor shows an increased emotional reactivity in relation to the client (more joy, anger, tears).
- When with the client, the counsellor shows more child-like non-verbal and expressive behaviour.
- More *touching* between client and counsellor.
- 'Confidentiality' may slip into a collusive 'secrecy'.
- 'Distortion of reality' in the counsellor's accounts of the client.
- Counsellor finds it difficult to think about the client in a *detached* way.
- Thoughts about the client repeatedly 'flood in' to the counsellor's mind.
- Counsellor stops raising work with this client in supervision.
- The relationship may involve sexual behaviour.

---

unashamedly borrow the 'Parent' and 'Child' terminology from Transactional Analysis which has provided these beautifully concise ways to conceptualise those phenomenological realities. In working with these stimulus materials the trainer is careful to teach the trainee how to use such ideas to stimulate our *own* evaluation, rather than regard these as evaluations made on us by someone else. This way of working with such materials thus supports the course member's internalising of his locus of evaluation rather than further externalising the locus.

An important consideration for trainers is how to respond to the course member's over-involvement when that occurs. Obviously, we might imagine some dramatically abusive examples which could indicate that the course member is inappropriate to be a counsellor. In my experience such examples are extremely rare among trainee counsellors. Most examples of over-involvement discovered in training depict the course member's struggle with the dynamic of involvement. She is accepting the challenge to be fully involved but those parts of the Self which might become over-involved are only in the process of being discovered and controlled or resolved, as in this example.

Pauline

Pauline, a counsellor in training, identified for herself in the supervision group the fact that she was 'over-involved' with an elderly male client. She realised that she was doing much more for the client than fitted a counselling role. She was being an advocate on his behalf, she was trying to reassure him, and at times she was even bringing him presents. On several occasions each week she would find the thought of him flooding into her mind when she was doing something quite different. The final straw which led to her awareness that this was over-involvement was when she found herself crying as she thought of him.

It is important that Pauline is treated with respect and with caring. It is a natural part of her humanity which has become involved, albeit inappropriately in the counselling role. If we, as trainers, can be gentle with her then we are modelling the notion that she can be gentle with herself. If the trainer's response to such over-involvement is excessively judgemental and punitive there is a grave danger that over-involvement will be driven underground, something which would be extremely dangerous for all concerned: clients, trainees, trainers and also the course.

We must expect course members to make more mistakes with over-involvement, just as with other things. Personally speaking, I would rather have a course member who now and again became over-involved in a non-abusive way than one who stayed so under-involved that she never made psychological contact. It is easier to help a course member to cure a case of mild over-involvement than detachment.

Person-centred trainers and counsellors need to accept the fact that they will be criticised by the practitioners of other approaches who take a structural view of over-involvement and judge the counsellor's behaviour in terms of the detachment of their own approach. The alternative would be to seek to reduce the signs of the counsellor's involvement which would be to destroy some of the most important active therapeutic agents within the work. The equivalent would be to demand of the psychodynamic therapist that she desist from behaving in ways that encourage transference because that is unpleasant for many clients.

The person-centred counsellor has to walk a difficult road in respect of her professionalism. She cannot merely offer *detachment* as evidence of her professionalism as is achieved in many other approaches. Instead, she must run the gauntlet of the prejudices of other workers who would define her most human offerings of commitment, consistency and caring as evidence of her 'over-involvement'. It is not an easy choice.

12
Variations for Counselling Skills Courses

Counselling 'skills' courses are much shorter than professional Diploma level courses. The main difference between the two is that 'skills' courses do not provide the *amount* of training necessary to practise as a counsellor, though the quality of that training will be of just as high a standard. Counselling skills courses may be of any duration from a 15-hour introductory weekend through a short 30-hour module run, perhaps, on the basis of a 3-hour evening session for 10 weeks, up to a full Certificate Course in Counselling Skills, usually of 120 hours duration if it is of university standard. Most of these Certificate courses properly refer to themselves as a qualification in 'counselling skills' though a few still go by the name 'Certificate in Counselling', which is somewhat misleading because it implies that it is a qualification to counsel, which it is not.

In considering the variations between Diploma-length courses and counselling skills courses we shall use the Certificate model as the comparison.

Purposes of Skills Courses

Skills courses attract applicants for two main purposes. First, the skills course may be regarded as an introduction to person-centred counselling by those who may be considering a move towards Diploma-length training. For people who have had little previous counselling experience or training a Certificate in Counselling Skills is an excellent place to begin. It offers an introduction to the basis and basics of counselling with time to practise and also an early experience in doing assignments within the counselling domain. All this experience tends to provide a strong springboard into Diploma level training. Sometimes the Certificate course can be counted as a credit towards a later Diploma. However, this kind of 'credit accumulation' is rare in person-centred training where the predominant view is that the full 400–450 hours of the Diploma are needed with stability in the student cohort because of the extent of personal development work required in Diploma training (Chapter 7).

The second main function of skills courses is to help course members to develop and apply counselling skills to non-counselling settings. This is an extremely important and productive function, with numerous areas of human endeavour potentially able to benefit from the congruent application of person-centred counselling skills, for example, nursing, teaching, social work settings, personnel/welfare work and management to name but a few. There are some areas within these professions which require full counselling training, for example if the hospice nurse or community psychiatric nurse is to engage actual counselling contracts with patients then a Certificate level course is insufficient. For some years in Britain there was considerable danger created by the assumption that the community psychiatric nurse would require only an additional Certificate level course or even a smaller, introductory level training in counselling skills in order to offer counselling. Fortunately, community psychiatric nurses themselves have realised that their psychiatric nursing training does not substitute for counselling training, particularly in regard to the personal development curriculum. More CPNs now seek the full Diploma training in counselling.

Some social work settings require full counselling training, depending again on the nature of the contract between the worker and the client. More often it is the application of counselling skills to social work settings which is of relevance and for that the Certificate level course may offer sufficiency.

Personnel/welfare work may carry a counselling expectation, rendering a Diploma level course necessary. However, if the employee counselling is provided by an external agency then skills training will be more relevant to the interviewing and facilitation role of the worker.

It is difficult to conceive of a counselling role within the professions of teaching and management since these are domains where there is a pre-existing power hierarchy in relation to the 'clients'. This is not to deny the enormous efforts over many years of 'school counsellors', rather, it is to emphasise the difficulty of that position where there is an intrinsic conflict with the 'in loco parentis' role. I doubt whether managers would even consider 'counselling' as part of their role but both they and teachers may recognise that counselling skills can represent an important addition to their repertoire of relational skills.

Later in this chapter an example will illustrate the application of counselling skills in a teaching setting but, for now, Boxes 12.1 and

Box 12.1

Hospital Staff Nurse

The job itself had made me realise the relevance of counselling skills. It would be fair to say that *every* patient we work with is in distress. People are wonderful at handling their distress – the way they use humour, for example, to gain a morsel of strength – jokes from the leg amputee about only needing half-price shoes; patients with hip replacements giving each other ten minutes start in their 'race' to the toilet and even the dying patient joking that 'this was the time to start smoking'! Yet there are many times when the joking falls silent. Sometimes they get frustrated on behalf of each other – they feel each other's distress quite deeply. In their own ways, the patients try to support each other even though they are in distress themselves.

I began to stop rushing past them. In nursing there is always something to do – sometimes that's how we avoid *our* distress . . . by being busy. I began to slow myself down and would spend a little more time with patients.

When I did my counselling skills training I found that it wasn't so much the *amount* of time I spent with the patient, but the *quality* of my contact. If I can respond to where the patient is, emotionally, in this moment then I am offering him a human being to meet him in his distress. If he does not want that, then that's fine – he simply jokes and I joke back. An example is Mr —. He's an old man with a lot of self-respect, but his spinal injury means that he needs special tools and ten minutes to put his knickers on. So, the other day he eventually gave up and went back in bed. I went to him, in private, and all I said was, 'It's hellish hard work, isn't it?' This offered him the opportunity to talk a little, which he did. The thing that was really causing him distress was not his immediate disability but the thought that maybe his wife would have to put his knickers on.

12.2 offer accounts from a hospital staff nurse and a company managing director on the relevance of counselling skills to their work.

Similarities and Differences between Skills and Diploma Courses

As might be expected, there are considerable similarities between a person-centred skills course and its larger relative, the Diploma in Counselling. Both courses explore the 'therapeutic conditions'

Box 12.2

Managing Director

I have found the counselling skills course to be the best management training I have had – and I have had a lot of very expensive
management training. It was a fluke that I found it. Dragged
along to counselling by my wife helped me realise that there
was more in life than my ego. Later, doing the training more out
of a personal interest, I found that it helped me to become more
than one-dimensional in my management of people. I was
careful not to go 'overboard' with it – I hate 'converts' as a
matter of principle! It started by accident, really. I was having a
meeting with a fairly senior member of our middle management. This was to be the first stage in his dismissal because he
wasn't cutting it. For some reason, I know not why, I found
myself *empathising* with him. It was quite genuine – I really
wondered what was going on for this man who had previously
been so reliable and who still had his dignity. To go into detail is
unnecessary, but suffice to say that the interview ended with a
result which was different from what I and 'Personnel' had
envisioned. Indeed, I later found that I had a bit of explaining to
do with 'Personnel'!

and practise 'helping interviews', though these are not necessarily
'counselling' interviews in the skills course.

Inevitably there will be a big difference in the time which can be
given to personal development. Trainers need to be selective in
their personal development curriculum, perhaps focusing on an
area like 'transition' which will have meaning both for the course
members and also those with whom they are working. Hence, a
special emphasis might be placed on course members exploring
their own 'transitions', to gain some understanding of these
dimensions of their Self as well as learning more generally about
the theory of transitions. For example, the course member who is
applying counselling skills in various settings may be limited by
her own development in relation to particular transitions. A case
in point is the new hospice nurse who found a strong internal
resistance when she tried to listen to patients talking about their
life and death. In personal development terms this difficulty was
related to her own incomplete grieving process for a close
relative.

Certificate course staff are attentive to the dimension of personal development in the *learning structures* they create. Usually
they will manage to create structures within the training where a
fair degree of trust can be quickly established to help course

members to make individual personal development gains. Dividing a course into smaller working 'cells', each with its own trainer, is a way of creating what is usually experienced as a 'safer' environment than the *large group*. Indeed, large group working itself tends to be rather difficult on a skills course. This does not have to do with differences in the membership of the course, but is more related to the fact that a lot of time needs to be invested in large group working before an appreciable dividend can be obtained. As was mentioned in Chapter 1, one of the mistakes that trainers can make when moving from one structure of training to another is to presume that the same systems will work in the different structure. Unstructured large group working is one area where there can be such difficulties in transposition.

In the shorter, 'skills' course there will be less work on the purely *counselling* dimensions such as the intricacies of the therapeutic process, long-term therapeutic work, person-centred psychopathology and client-centred pre-therapy. Also, there will be no formal counselling *supervision* although there tends to be considerable support offered to course members in relation to their work beyond the course.

Counselling skills courses are extremely demanding of the trainers in regard to the *application* of the work into a huge variety of quite different settings. In this work the trainer cannot simply rely on her own experience in counselling relationships but must be able conceptually and practically to apply the skills in work contexts which are completely new to her. Very quickly the trainer will have to project herself into this novel context, understanding the kinds of expectations which would be on the course member in that setting and how these might mediate his behaviour. While this is demanding for trainers it also offers a particular opportunity for the person-centred trainer to define the situation as one in which she and the course member *both* have knowledge and skills which they are going to put together in this training venture. The trainer has her considerable experience of counselling skills and the course member has the knowledge and experience of his own profession. This is potentially a superb combination for co-operative working in which the trainee retains the authority from his own expertise. The trainer who does not approach the training relationship with the same equanimity but who presumes her own expertise across the full range of skills applications will not be so likely to embrace the ability of the trainee and may even create a dissatisfied undercurrent.

Something which is not so much a difference between the two kinds of courses but perhaps an accentuation on the shorter course is the fact that course members may be dramatically affected by what could appear to be relatively simple course experiences encouraging them to reflect upon Self and Self in relation to others. This is simply related to the fact that more members of shorter courses will be entirely new to the whole domain. The result can be a lively course which is stimulating for staff, but also demanding. One course member gives us a glimpse of this kind of event:

> A simple, early exercise, invited us to focus on a 'transition' we had experienced. In complete naivety I thought about the death of my husband all those years ago. Suddenly, I was in complete distress. I had thought that his death was a long-gone thing with me. I knew it was sad, but, my God, I had no idea how much of me was still back there. Maybe that is why I had never had another relationship which worked. It took me by surprise. I'm glad the staff were not 'thrown' by it – they were extremely caring. I felt like I had been 'sick' in public and they had quietly mopped it up and sat with me. It didn't put me off the course either, but I am seeing a counsellor – it's amazing that this could have been buried for so long and yet be so near the surface that a simple question could expose it.

Congruence

A tempting mistake for designers of shorter person-centred courses is to presume that there is simply not time to work on the course members' congruence and that this should be laid aside in favour of helping them to behave in ways which *portray* unconditional positive regard and empathy. In fact, the reality is that person-centred counselling skills are simply not effective if they are not experienced as congruent within the worker. Consider the two teacher–pupil dialogues presented below. The pupil, who had a history of using his fists, has automatically been suspended from school following a particularly violent incident in which he put two other pupils into hospital. Although he is going to be suspended pending investigation of this incident, it is the school's policy to offer all suspended pupils a session with a teacher where they may put their own case before they leave the school.

Scenario A

Teacher: So, how do you think you can get out of this one?
[*Silence*]
Teacher: What's your side of the story – I'm here to help you, you know.

Pupil: Oh, yeah!
Teacher: So, what can we do?
Pupil: You can do what you f— like.
Teacher: There's no need for that.
Pupil: Can I go now?
Teacher: Of course, you can go any time you like.
    [*Pupil exits*]

Scenario B

Teacher: OK Paul, first of all I want to say I am pissed off with you
    getting involved with those two again. Right, now that that's out of
    the way, I'm here to get your side of the story. What made you hit
    out?
Pupil: What makes you think *I* hit out?
Teacher: Because the other two guys are in hospital! Look Paul, I am
    curious about what made you do it. OK, I'm frustrated as hell that
    you've got into bother after such a long time, but I'm also surprised
    – it must have been something big to get you to use your fists again
    . . .?
Pupil: They called me a 'black bastard'.

There are a number of ways in which these two teachers differ
in the skills, or the lack of them in the case of Scenario A, which
they are applying. One particular dimension in which they differ
is that the teacher in B is more open and congruent with the pupil.
This means that the pupil knows what the teacher thinks of him.
He knows that, on the surface at least, the teacher is 'pissed off'
but he knows that it is nothing stronger than that. He also knows
that as well as the teacher being frustrated he is also surprised and
curious. In a very short space of time and in quite a straightforward fashion this teacher has made his feelings clear. He is
transparent and the pupil does not need to be suspicious about
what else may lie beneath the surface. In the case of Scenario A it
is not possible to be sure of any of this teacher's feelings, so the
likelihood is that the pupil will treat the teacher with considerable
suspicion and even alienation, responding accordingly.

Certainly, 'congruence' does not have the same, full relevance in
shorter courses as it has in training for person-centred counselling
where the 'therapeutic use of congruence' has its special application in the counselling relationship. In counselling, the counsellor's congruent responses have therapeutic relevance as keen
reflections to the client's process. That is a very important technical function of congruence within the counselling relationship
(Mearns and Thorne, 1988, ch. 5).

However, the human dimension of congruence in providing an
open and transparent picture of our experience of the other

person continues to have relevance in any human contact. Within many realms, including school teaching and youth work, some workers have what can appear to be a brash but very straight-forward way of communicating with young people. Although that may seem to lack sophistication it often gets a reliable response from the young person who values its clarity and straight-forwardness.

Congruence is inextricably involved in meeting another human being at relational depth (see Chapter 2). This also has relevance to the application of counselling skills in non-counselling settings. Even fleeting contacts can be powerful if they are at relational depth. Box 12.3 reproduces an incident which happened in a school classroom. The power of the teacher's intervention was its simplicity in reaching beneath the pupil's fury to touch her in her distress. I had the privilege of witnessing this incident in the classroom and rated it as perhaps one of the most moving examples of 'contact' from one human being to another. Essen-tially, that is what we are trying to achieve in applying person-centred counselling skills to non-counselling settings – to gain from the improved communication afforded by the very human skills which comprise the person-centred approach.

Box 12.3

Judy

Dick, the teacher, was beginning his S4 register class when Judy started to provoke another pupil into quite a serious fight in the classroom. Dick stopped the fight only to find that Judy turned on *him* with a torrent of abuse such as is rarely heard inside school walls. She was screaming her anger and hate at Dick. Dick's reaction was both unusual, and striking. He stepped back rather than forward as if to respect her space and he was silent. The atmosphere was incredibly tense, and after what seemed a long silence Dick responded to Judy with obvious concern in the words: 'What's up Judy?' Judy broke down in tears and she and Dick went into the next room to talk while the class dropped into quiet conversation. Judy disclosed extreme difficulties with her father at home. Some years earlier her father had ended an incestuous relationship with her, but this morning she had found that he had 'started on my little sister'. Judy had come straight from home and had got her feelings mixed up in the classroom. A normal 'disciplinary' reaction to her 'bad behaviour' would not have produced the 'window for disclosure' which Dick's caring had achieved.

The 'Central Dynamics' Applied to Shorter Courses

The *responsibility dynamic* in person-centred training remains un-affected by the length or focus of that training. The trainer retains a consistent professional responsibility *to* the course member regardless of the length of training. Also, there is no argument which would suggest that in shorter training the trainers should accept an element of responsibility *for* the course member. It is simply not relevant to regard members of shorter courses as requiring more nurturing. In fact it is easy to make the mistake of taking more responsibility *for* trainees on shorter courses for the simple reason that it is physically possible for staff to maintain a dependency culture over a shorter length of course while that would represent an impossible weight on a larger training. Where an element of that dependency culture is established on a skills course, that can do disservice to the course members if they move on to a Diploma training with the wrong expectation.

The second 'central dynamic' of person-centred training de-scribed in Chapter 3 is the *development of self-acceptance*. While this could not be an explicit aim on a shorter course because there is simply not the space for the processes which need to be invested, it is quite extraordinary the degree of self-acceptance which may nevertheless develop. Often the reason for this lies in the *readiness* of the participant who may have been preparing to open himself to this training for many years. Also, these courses tend to create very supportive learning climates which can greatly assist personal development. So, although the development of self-acceptance cannot be an explicit aim of shorter training the movement which participants make is inevitably in that direction due to the climate created by staff, the support which participants give each other and the readiness of the participants for such movement.

The third 'central dynamic' of person-centred training is the *individualisation of the curriculum*. Potentially, there is more scope to individualise the curriculum in counselling skills courses because the course member will be applying the work within his own specific environment rather than in the common profession of counselling where there would be more expectations regarding a common curriculum. Furthermore, the practice of dividing the course into smaller 'cells' as mentioned earlier can greatly increase the scope for the individual influencing the curriculum within each of the cells. Again, person-centred trainers working on shorter as well as longer courses would be alive to the contributions of the individual and also the need to make the material meaningful, in the case of shorter courses, to a wide variety of settings.

The fourth 'central dynamic', the *individualisation of assessment*, is important in skills courses because the range of previous experience of assessment will be even more marked than on Diploma courses where participants have usually undergone some prior assessed work in preliminary training. On those assignments which endeavour to relate the work of the course to the practice environment of the participant, the trainer must rely considerably on the participant fitting these assignments meaningfully to his individual work contexts. While assignments may be individualised, summative self-assessment is more difficult to undertake compared to Diploma training where course members have much more time to invest in the consultation process with each other. In addition, the work environment of skills course members is so diverse that it is more difficult for them each to offer feedback on the other's work in that practical context. Nevertheless, continuous self-assessment through the maintaining of a personal journal and completion of an end of course self-assessment statement are relatively easy activities to include in skills training and encourage the kind of self-reflection, not to mention self-assessment, which exercises the course member's locus of evaluation.

Another Application of Counselling Skills Training: Parenting

Only a few participants come on to counselling skills training with the explicit idea of helping them to develop their communication with children and yet many course members leave the training with significant gains in that area. The precedent of applying person-centred counselling skills to parenting is historically established in the highly popularised work of Thomas Gordon whose 'Parent Effectiveness Training' (Gordon, 1975) proved to respond to an enormous need.

The potential for applying person-centred counselling skills to parenting is enormous and merits re-statement in this chapter. Consider the possibilities for parents who are helped to listen to their children; consider the parents who discover the 'conditions of worth' they impose upon their own children; consider the possibility of parents helped to meet their child at relational depth; consider, as well, the importance of parents learning the difference between offering congruent communication with their child and *invading* their child's separate existential world. If person-centred counselling skills training is to help parents, let us do it properly, such that respect for the separateness and individuality of the child is paramount, else we will have created a parental tyranny. I shall close this chapter with an example (Box 12.4) of the application of counselling skills which I have used for years, but never published. It consists of a mother's dialogue with her child – a dialogue in which she epitomises the quality of respect and the non-invasive empathic skills of person-centred counselling.

Box 12.4
Person-Centred Skills in Families

Seven-year-old Peter has been particularly 'grumpy' this evening, and a dispute has led to an early bedtime. After giving him some time to 'come down' after the dispute, his mother visits him. She strokes his head and face as he lies, still with a sullen, detached expression. After some time she speaks.

Mother: Was anything difficult for you today?
  [*Silence*]
Mother: Difficult to say anything . . . is it?
  [*Silence*]
Peter: It's not *fair*!
Mother: What's not fair?
  [*Silence. His mother strokes his arm gently.*]
Mother: Like . . . too many people have been getting on to you?
Peter: Yes [*Sobs a little – then stops.*]
Mother: So we were getting on to you . . . and was someone else as well?
  [*Silence*]
Peter: Miss Hubbard said I was a liar.
Mother: And you feel bad about that.
Peter: I *hate* her [*cries loudly*].
Mother: You hate her and also you look as though you feel . . . sad? about it.
Peter: It feels awful – really awful – I'm not a liar – I just didn't know what to say when she shouted at me. [*Peter explains the whole story.*]

Looking Back and Looking Forward

In its previous twelve chapters this book has reported on the practice of person-centred counselling training and on the thinking underlying that practice. Numerous illustrative examples of the experiences of course members have been presented but, with the exception of Chapter 4, comparatively little direct experience of trainers has been reproduced. In order to improve that balance and as a vehicle to focus upon some present critical issues in training and future possibilities for training, this chapter takes the form of an interview with myself where I address the questions that have been most frequently asked of me in relation to person-centred training. Perhaps this chapter will serve to anticipate and offer a response to some of the questions of the reader.

Can trainers and course members become friends?

The straightforward answer to this is 'Yes, of course'. Much of the opposition and suspicion around friendship between trainer and course member stems from the long-established psychodynamic tradition where considerable transference is developed, not only in the therapeutic relationship, but also in training (albeit unintentionally). Where a high degree of transference is engendered it becomes more difficult to trust the basis on which the friendship is formed because, almost by definition, there is no 'real' relationship present.

Fortunately, the counselling profession is not entirely dominated by the artificial relationship of the psychodynamic tradition. However, the person-centred trainer should not presume that simply because she is not setting out to encourage transference, that none is present. Also, the argument needs to be widened from transference to 'power'. In any trainer–trainee relationship there is a power difference between the two participants. If the appropriate responsibility dynamic has been achieved then the power difference should be much reduced, with each party taking responsibility for themselves in the relationship. However, it is still important that the trainer really attends to the course member's perspective as well as her own and does not too easily presume that the trainee views the relationship with the same equality as does the trainer.

To deny the possibility of friendship within a person-centred relationship would be to exclude major tracts of the humanity of the people involved. However, it is necessary to impose some blanket restrictions without regard to the specific issues and people involved. For example, the trainer would avoid sexual relationships with course members without examining the propriety of that in each specific case but merely as an unswerving rule designed to protect the profession as much as the course member and the trainer. The counselling training fraternity has become stronger on that prohibition than any other area of education. In other university departments such relationships might be frowned upon, and looked on with some suspicion and even questioning, but they would not automatically lead to the expulsion from the profession of the member of staff. Probably this emphasis within counselling training is an extrapolation of the strong prohibition on sexual relationships between counsellors and clients. It is reasonable to expect that all counsellors should live within that blanket prohibition, although it may seem to be less relevant to the training relationship where the course member can be expected to retain her personal power. In this instance it is important that there is no scope for arguing an alternative position for the simple reason that it is usually not the competent and responsible counsellor who argues the alternative, but it is the incompetent practitioner who uses such freedom as licence. Also, although person-centred training encourages its special responsibility dynamic, that does not mean that every course member will exercise it consistently. There is always a danger of unreality. This scenario is sharply focused by the apocryphal and somewhat crude quote from the older trainer who confronted his trainee's expression of affection for him with the challenge 'I wonder how I would appear to you if I wasn't your trainer but we were meeting for the first time at a party. Would I appear so attractive or would I look like an ugly old fart?'

Personally speaking, I have always valued the friendships I formed with members of courses and many of these have lasted long after the training, even although we are seldom in contact. In recent years when I have been doing much less small group work on training courses fewer such friendships have been formed but I do recall with fondness a recent course where I was an active member of the 'men's group' and still feel attached to these men.

What is the greatest *strength* of person-centred training?

I think the greatest strength is its emphasis on personal development work. I also think this is the area which unifies the various professional level person-centred training courses. Although they may vary in a number of ways, there is universal agreement on the centrality of personal development. Also, there would be fairly widespread agreement on the essential features of personal development for person-centred training, with issues such as self-awareness, the taking of responsibility for Self and developing self-acceptance seen as central to the development of the reflective practitioner within the person-centred approach. Courses can vary considerably, particularly in the degree of structure offered to course members, but they are all, essentially, seeking to obtain the same kind of movements on the personal development dimension.

The paradox is that while this is the most important dimension of person-centred training, it is also the most difficult to describe to those who have not experienced it. In recent years the University of Strathclyde has been supporting the development of person-centred counselling training in Croatia and thus far we have had two psychologists from that country undertaking our own training. In both cases they noted the centrality of the personal development dimension and also the fact that they could only understand that dimension once they had participated in the course.

Personal development for person-centred training, with its strong emphasis on simultaneous support and challenge, is powerful both in the way it is experienced and in the impact it has upon the personality. And yet, it is entirely under the control of the individual course member. Both our Croatian visitors mentioned above allowed themselves to engage the personal development dimensions openly. Some other course members, perhaps for the reason of their own fear, may not have been able to be so open and will not have realised the potential of the personal development work until that fear is to some degree diminished.

What is the greatest *weakness* of person-centred training?

Traditionally, the greatest weakness has been the relative lack of emphasis on the learning of person-centred theory. This is something trainers have been addressing in the past few years but historically the approach suffered from a perception that theory was of little value. Paradoxically, this weakness is also reflective of a strength in the approach. The considerable research carried out by Rogers and his colleagues did indeed show that the personal qualities and attitudes of the counsellor were more important than the counsellor's university education and slickness with theory. This emphasised to the profession that training as a counsellor needed to find ways to develop the Self and the Self-in-relation, hence the major 'strength' of the approach, mentioned above. However, this emphasis on the personal and the inter-personal also drew attention away from the detail of Rogers' theory of therapy and his underlying theory of personality. The prospective person-centred counsellor could then feel that she had permission to relegate the learning of theory to the periphery of her development.

Perhaps the worst consequence of this state of affairs was that the person-centred approach became an easy target for those who wanted to attach themselves to an approach which felt intrinsically attractive but which did not make excessive learning demands upon them. I am astonished at the number of people I meet who call themselves 'person-centred counsellors' who have undertaken little or no training and certainly not an intensive Diploma level course. I doubt whether the same number of untrained counsellors would refer to themselves as 'psycho-dynamic' or 'Gestalt' without training in those approaches. It seems that there is a presumption that simply feeling a philosophical bond with the person-centred approach is sufficient qualification to adopt the label.

In 1988, on the first page of the first chapter of the book *Person-Centred Counselling in Action*, my dear friend Brian Thorne and myself suggested that the person-centred approach 'travels light as far as theoretical concepts are concerned'. Perhaps it would be more accurate to say that, historically, many person-centred practitioners have 'travelled light on theoretical concepts' but that the approach itself is rich both in terms of its theory of therapy and also its underlying theory of personality. While the person-centred approach emphasises that its theory of personality, like any psychological theory, cannot efficiently be used to predict the behaviour of an individual client, a sound understanding of the theoretical concepts and processes makes an enormous difference to the coherence, stability and professionalism of the person-centred counsellor. When these qualities in theoretical sophistication are added without diminishing the personal qualities of the practitioner in relation to the client, then we have something very solid indeed.

What holds course members back most in training?

The three things I would mention are not necessarily unrelated. They are fear, a self-esteem which is simply too low, and a difficulty in taking responsibility for Self. Interestingly, all three of these are quite difficult to identify in all but the most intrusive of selection procedures. The problem is complicated by the fact that we would expect a degree of difficulty in relation to each of these: it is a normal part of person-centred counselling training to find movements in the direction of becoming less fearful, showing a gain in self-esteem and taking more responsibility for Self.

The problem with all three is that if the fear is too high, the self-esteem too low or the difficulty with taking responsibility too ingrained, then, at best, the course member may become quite 'stuck' in the training for long periods of time and, at worst, she might find the training experience to be so unpleasant that she has to leave.

It is to the great credit of scores of course members that they have fought through high degrees of fear, severe problems with low self-esteem and profound difficulties in taking responsibility. Indeed, the strong argument against trying to develop selection procedures which would discriminate effectively on these factors is the fact that a number of trainees have struggled through these to become effective counsellors and particularly sensitive supervisors to later course members.

There are many *fears* which can slow a trainee's progress. One of the most common is the *fear of being found out*. I remember that I suffered from this in my early development as a counsellor. Perhaps that is what makes me particularly sympathetic to the course member who feels burdened by such self-doubt, and so excited when such a trainee takes time in the community meeting to declare her fear and thus face her devil. This 'fear of being found out' is unrelated to the course member's actual ability, though the fear itself can diminish the functioning like any self-fulfilling prophecy. The quality of the feeling is encapsulated by the course member who gave permission to reproduce the quotation in Box 13.1

The 'fear of being found out' is partially a fear of being found out *by others* but it usually also includes a fear of being found out

---

Box 13.1

Fear is the Key

Throughout the first term of the course I felt that everyone was looking at me. I would try to put on a competent, confident image but I was sure that most of them could see right through me. I had a lot of investment in this training but it was difficult just to start from scratch – as a 'learner'. The fact was that I had done a lot of counselling before I came on the training – I was expected to be a good counsellor – I expected myself to be a good counsellor. Yet, no one except my clients had ever seen me counsel. So I lived in fear of being 'found out' as a fraud.

Right at the beginning of the course we spent two days in small groups making videotapes of our counselling practice. When I saw this on the timetable I thought of all sorts of reasons to withdraw from the course. I forced myself not to withdraw and I went through the two days, surviving somehow. My rationalisation to myself was that I was lucky that my 'clients' in this exercise had given me an easy time. I think the reality was that I did a fair job with clients during those early stages of training but I still found it difficult in supervision because I wanted to stay hidden. For months I found reasons why I could not submit audiotapes of my client work.

The breakthrough for me came when I decided simply not to hold it any longer. During one community meeting I 'came out'. I told everyone my secret – that I was afraid of being 'found out' as an experienced, but incompetent counsellor. It wasn't only the feedback I received in that meeting which turned the tide for me but the fact that I had dared to 'come out' so publicly.

---

by ourself. Counsellors who are reckoned to be fairly experienced, or who believe themselves to be fairly experienced, can be particularly prone to this fear of what they might see if they openly expose themselves to the mirror provided by others. In extreme cases this fear can block a course member throughout the whole of her training, though the emphasis in recent times on considerable videotaping of practice work and audiotape supervision of real client work makes this less likely than before.

The course member whose *self-esteem is simply too low* can find counselling training to be a painful process. If we are to compare a person with average self-esteem and another with a particularly low self-esteem on a training course, an appropriate metaphor might take us to the race-track to watch a race in which some runners are running on the flat while others are going over hurdles and trying to keep pace. Every new challenge on a counselling training course can feel like a 'hurdle' to the person with low self-esteem, while looking like a 'reasonable challenge' to other course members. And yet, the person-centred approach can achieve so much more in regard to such a trainee than most other training approaches. I remember with continuing distaste an incident many years ago when presenters of another therapeutic approach who had been invited on to our course actually ridiculed one of our course members on behaviour which was associated with her low self-esteem. Certainly that member of our course would never have found a place on that other training approach or, if she had, she would have soon departed. I think it is a strength of the person-centred approach that this person could struggle, but survive and enhance herself, throughout the years of her training course. Also, such a person who has struggled from a position of low self-esteem will not be so challenged to understand her client engaged in the same kind of struggle.

Yet, there are extremes of low self-esteem which simply make it impossible for the course member to engage with the fairly demanding nature of person-centred counselling training. At these extremes it needs to be recognised that a better context for learning is therapy rather than therapy training.

There can be many reasons why a course member finds it difficult *to take responsibility for Self*. Sometimes it is simply a function of the person's earlier experience in educational contexts. The course member simply has to unlearn ways of relating to tutors that put the tutor at the centre of their locus of evaluation. When this is the extent of the problem the difficulty does not usually persist. However, in other instances, the difficulty with taking responsibility for Self entertains a deeper seated pathology. Again, there are as many variants of this as there are human beings, but Box 13.2 illustrates one course member who needed to be a kind of 'victim' of the inadequacy of the course, such was her fear of taking responsibility for her Self.

In fact, the course member cited in Box 13.2 is unusual insofar as she fought through from her position of alienation to engage the training with the kind of energy which is associated with those who have been released from that kind of prison. Other trainees in similar circumstances have gone a different route, as illustrated by the following extract from a trainer's diary:

> Trudy has finally managed to leave the course today. Basically, the course was never right for her. She challenged the course, not on every issue, but on one issue after another. Instead of making an effort to make use of what was being offered, her orientation was more one of 'what is being offered is not good enough for me to make use of it'. This scenario kept re-creating itself with respect to one issue after

Box 13.2
Why don't you take responsibility for me?

I hated you. I hated you all. None of you were doing it 'right'. You were not taking responsibility for me. When you pushed that back to me I hated you even more. How *dare* you! You had confronted me with the fact that I complained about one thing after another. When you confronted me, I *had* you. You had proved that you weren't 'accepting' me. I gave it to you good in that community meeting – I gave it to *all* of you. Then, in a meeting with two of the staff, you suggested that I should go into therapy. Again, I could hit you with your 'lack of acceptance'. In a sense you were my 'prisoners'. There was absolutely nothing which you could do which would not fit my construction that you were charlatans. I spent the first third of the training playing a kind of 'game' in which you could never be 'good enough' and in which I would eventually have to leave the course in righteous indignation.

another, until she had to leave. I remember in the very first week of the course I thought 'She's already trying to find a way in which to leave.' This kind of thing can be damaging to a course because everybody invests so much. In a sense, the person-centred approach is a kind of 'sucker' to this kind of process, simply because we refuse to categorise it, dismiss it and despatch it to personal therapy. Yet, the reality is that no training course can handle this with any confidence because the needs involved are much more powerful than any need to become a counsellor.

When, and how, should trainers terminate a trainee's course?

This is a tough question for the person-centred trainer. A nice 'fudge' is to say that the person-centred trainer cannot make this decision but that it must be left to the course member, who is in the best position to make such a decision. Unfortunately, this presumes that the course member in difficulty will have *awareness* of that difficulty. While this is often the case there still remain exceptions where that awareness is not achieved. Rogers' theory suggests that *under certain conditions* the individual will be able to exhibit a high degree of self-awareness and make decisions which would not only be healthy for herself, but also for those around her. The theory is often misunderstood and taken to suggest that people will *always* exhibit that awareness and make growth-promoting choices for themselves and others. The simple truth is that the training context does not provide the therapeutic conditions in the same degree as a therapeutic relationship so we cannot expect the same kind of therapeutic consequence of enhanced self-awareness and decision-making. Person-centred trainers, therefore, cannot entirely devolve responsibility to the course member and must be prepared to terminate a trainee's course in extreme circumstances.

Having established the ultimate responsibility of the trainer in this regard, it must also be emphasised that on 95% of occasions where a course member is in extreme difficulty, she initiates the question of leaving the training herself. It is only in the minority of instances where it is the trainers or other course members who raise the challenge. Even in this minority circumstance, once the challenge is raised the course member will generally take the challenge seriously and address it fully. Only exceptionally will the course member seek to avoid that challenge and evoke the ultimate responsibility of the trainers.

Hence, the responsibility of trainers in relation to the course member in difficulty is threefold:

- The trainer must not suppress her own *challenge* to the course member nor inhibit appropriate challenge by other members of the course.
- Regardless of whether the challenge has come from the trainer or from other course members, the trainer needs to be prepared to *support* the course member who is facing the challenge. 'Support' in this sense does not mean collusion or any dilution of the challenge that is offered but it means support of the person within the context of the challenge.
- If the trainee should continue to seek to avoid the challenge it is the trainer's responsibility to maintain attention to the issues. Courses will generally have a procedure for continuing to address the issues with course members in this degree of difficulty. Often this would involve the course member in meetings with staff to review the difficulty, look for ways forward, make plans and certainly to establish clarity on the issues involved. It can be useful for the staff to maintain notes from such meetings so that clarity can be maintained.

The truth is that supporting a course member in difficulty, seeking ways to remediate that difficulty, and perhaps eventually ending the process in the termination of the trainee's course is painfully difficult for trainers of any counselling tradition. Usually the course member who is going to present a big difficulty such as this makes herself known fairly early in the training. Perhaps she has a personality which is simply inappropriate for counselling in terms of her lack of ability to empathise or the kind of personality which makes it impossible to make full psychological contact or, even more difficult, a tendency to be abusive. Course members with any of these difficulties require considerable work by staff in exploring and seeking clarification about the difficulties, not to mention offering personal support. Inevitably, numerous opportunities are given to the course member to allow for the possibility of change. The result of this process is that it can, in practice, take a considerable time before the situation is finally faced that the course member simply has not been able to become aware of the extent of her difficulty, and therefore she cannot be left with the decision over her continuation through the course and into the profession. This challenge for the staff is particularly poignant on a self-assessed course where trainers need to address during the training the impossibility of the process of self-assessment for the trainee with this degree of deficiency in self-awareness.

Although the situations I have described are exceptional, the person-centred trainer must not be so absorbed by a naive conception of the approach that she fails to accept responsibility for terminating the training of someone who is dangerous to clients and to the profession.

What excites you most about training?

Two things particularly excite me – working with our students, who are usually willing to take responsibility for themselves and relate easily with me, and seeing the growth of self-acceptance in a course member. The course member who is willing to take responsibility for herself offers the trainer the possibility of a relationship. On the other hand, in the case of a course member who is reluctant to take her own responsibility, the trainer is not so important as a person but is a functionary contracted to provide the required services. It must be said that one of the attractions to this work is that course members are pretty good at taking responsibility for themselves and the difference, when they are compared to students on other university courses, is dramatic in this regard. I find that if the course member is willing to take responsibility for herself then it is less relevant how developed she is as a counsellor at the start of training. She may be fairly new and even naive in relation to the whole world of counselling but can make enormous and fast progress if she has that openness to herself and openness to the other which comes with taking responsibility for Self.

A second really exciting experience as a trainer is to witness the course member making gains with respect to self-acceptance. Often these gains are made late in the training. One response to this could be to wish that they had happened earlier so that the trainee could then have made even more of the opportunities available during the course. However, movements in self-acceptance are so permanent that they have to be valued whenever they take place because the person will be able to make so much more of the opportunities which present themselves even after the training. Box 13.3 gives a course member's account of what was certainly a significant shift in self-acceptance.

Box 13.3

Accepting Myself

Early in the final term of a two-year part-time course, Jan takes time in a community meeting to report on a significant happening in her life:

A huge change happened in me around the time of our residential weekend. A voice kept coming into my head saying 'You can let other people see you, you know'. For a while I kept pushing it away – my reply to it was 'Don't you believe it!' But the voice kept coming back. It reminded me of the film *Field of Dreams* where the voice kept coming into Kevin Costner's head 'Build it and they will come' – it was as eerie as that. Then, in one of the small groups during the weekend I found myself crying. I think the tears were about a whole lot of things and a lot of years but the reasons for them aren't as important as the fact of their existence. I had just let myself 'be' and cried in public. I didn't need to hide any more – I could just be who I was. The joy I felt in those tears was like nothing I have felt before. I didn't even have to make people understand me and people didn't force me to be understandable. I had reached a point where I could simply *be myself* without apology, without explanation, without editing, without role-playing, without manipulating, without the fear of unconsciously manipulating, without monitoring my every utterance, without wondering how I was perceived and without the eternal fear of judgement. For the first time in my life I accepted myself more than I feared other people's judgement.

Are there any personal problems as a trainer which you haven't solved?

Two problems come to mind immediately. They both involve paradoxes and, at this time of writing, I am genuinely stuck with them. Perhaps I am stuck because in both of them two parts of myself are juxtaposed.

One sounds quite simple and yet I have never been able to solve it. My problem is how to respond when a course member asks me a question and it seems as though there may be much more behind the question for the course member. It is not easy to give examples of such questions because they only really have meaning in relation to the personality of the course member and the relationship between us. Nevertheless, I shall try to use a concrete example to illustrate my difficulty. For example, the course member's question 'Why do you work out a timetable for the course?' immediately creates a conflict in my mind. The conflict is between seeing the question as the tip of the iceberg and wanting to explore whatever is behind the person's question. Is it, perhaps, that the course member is dissatisfied with the degree of structuring created by the timetable? Is this an important challenge to our structuring which might lead to the course members exerting more personal power in relation to the structuring of the timetable? Is it that this person is losing out, in terms of meeting her own needs, because of the structuring of our timetable? Part of me would want to dip beneath the course member's question to find what lies beneath because any of the above examples offers an exciting and fruitful exploration.

However, another part of me deplores the presumptuousness of answering a person's question with a question. I remember horrible feelings of being manipulated early in my own learning experience when I was exploring other approaches. I found that my questions were seldom honoured with a straightforward answer but instead the trainer sought to delve into what lay beneath them, and in the process she kept the attention away from herself. Certainly, there was sometimes a sarcasm in my question or even a trap, so the trainer was quite right to be suspicious or to ask what lay underneath. Yet, the feeling of powerlessness as a trainee has stayed with me and now, as a trainer, I find myself always wanting to give a straight answer even to a crooked question. Hence, my response to a question such as the above on the creation of a timetable might totally miss the point of the person's question, though it would always be factually honest. In my response I might explain the reasons for us offering time-tables for each week but also the fact that we welcomed alternatives being proposed in the community meeting. As I am giving an answer such as this I am frequently aware that it is totally missing the process of the trainee. I know that once I have given the answer and it has met with its response, then I will ask the questioner if there is 'anything else'. Yet, I also know that my need to provide a straight answer to a straight question may have led us to miss the moment. This is a true practical paradox for me because I honour equally the importance of dipping beneath the person's question and also the importance of honouring the course member through the answering of her question.

A second unsolved problem for me as a trainer is the question 'Would it improve my relationship with course members if I wasn't so damned responsible?' At many points in this book I have outlined the importance to person-centred trainers of desisting from taking responsibility *for* the course member but to be most assiduous in maintaining their responsibilities *to* the course member. I am particularly fastidious – or perhaps the better term is 'neurotic' – in that regard. If it is my responsibility to do something I almost never fail in that regard and when I do fail I give myself an extremely hard time. My question of myself is 'Can I lighten up?' Might it not improve my relationship with course members if I could become less obsessive about 'being responsible to' them. I think I give my colleagues a hard time in this regard because I find it hard. I am sure that I am highly critical when we slip up in our administration or fail to fulfil promises.

The paradox for me is complete when I remember times in my own development when trainers 'let me down'. They were certainly more expert than I am now in working with the consequences of that. My present response to course members tends to be little more than an abject apology and an effort to do better, whereas I remember my own trainers confronting me with my own expectation that they should be perfect and pushing me to work with all that was connected with that expectation.

Once again, this seems such a simple thing and yet, for me, it remains an enduring paradox. I do feel that it is important to maintain our responsibilities *to* the other person and yet, I am also aware that some delinquency in that regard can bring its own rewards. Maybe I should 'lighten up' and stop trying to be a paragon – people can't relate with paragons!

What do you find *most* difficult in this work?

As I think about this question I find myself taking a deep breath because I know that my greatest difficulty is one which is experienced by many trainers, of any discipline, and one which is not easily solved. My greatest difficulty is dealing with the gulf between the course member's assumptions about me and the reality of me. Within the classical psychodynamic tradition this difficulty is simply labelled 'transference issues' and the responsibility for it is entirely thrown back onto the trainee.

It is too easy for a trainer brought up within the classical psychodynamic tradition merely to defend Self by inferring the pathology of the trainee. The person-centred trainer does not have that easy exit from such conflict. Whenever a course member challenges me as a trainer with questions such as: 'You are behaving irresponsibly'; 'You are not giving me enough support'; 'You are neglectful in your responsibilities'; or 'I experience you as abusive', I cannot simply credit that to the pathology of the course member but I must equally be open to the possibility that the criticism contains truth or, at least, a partial truth. However, the truth is that I have found it difficult to stay as 'open' as this to feedback over 25 years as a trainer. I have kept only a rough count, but I am aware of incidents with 32 different course members where I have been accused of being 'like' their neglectful or abusive father or 'grandfather'. Perhaps a more disturbing feature is that I have been likened to abusive 'Scottish' fathers or grandfathers by a large number of English course members. I think there is a stereotype in England which links 'Scottish males' with abusiveness. Even as I describe these statistics in a fairly dispassionate way I find the pain of it engulfing me. It is extremely difficult as a trainer to respond openly and honestly to what can feel like a too often repeated phenomenon. I can understand my psychodynamic colleagues in resorting to a stereotyped response to this phenomenon.

I have presented this as the 'most difficult' dimension of the work for me. I have faced descriptions of myself which would make even the most insensitive man cry. I have been called an 'abuser' by more people than I can remember. Four people have used the word 'Satan' in relation to me and probably the most frightening of all was the course member who described me as 'the devil incarnate'. I have oft repeated that to people but, somehow, it has never diminished the fear which it has invoked in me.

It would be misleading to exaggerate this difficulty. I can endure it because it is more than balanced by the generosity and also the accuracy of observation from course members. For example, a course member recently challenged me with the observation: 'My sense of you is that you are not *disinterested* in me, but that you have not *taken an interest* in me.' Personally, I found this to be one of the most generous observations I have experienced. The course member was absolutely correct that I had not taken a personal interest in her. However, she was also generous in her understanding that this was not motivated by my 'disinterest' of her. The fact was that I simply did not take it as part of my particular role as a trainer to foster that specific interest. [I need to note at this point that I believe that core person-centred trainers *should* establish a close and personal interest in course members, and that, in our training courses, this is an emphasis of the core trainers, but mine is not a core trainer role.]

So, how do you *respond* to trainees' assumptions about you?

First, when a course member raises any kind of 'difficulty' they have with me I genuinely *value* it. I always remember a former trainee who, six years after our training contact, told me about the bizarre assumptions she had held about me. She had never exposed these assumptions and they had represented a significant 'block' in her training. Ever since that time I find myself placing enormous value on the course member who would present me with her assumptions more immediately. The person who gives me her assumptions more immediately is doing me a great honour. She is permitting me the possibility of response and allowing me a publicly witnessed dialogue. I love it when the person affords me this respect, particularly in a group context where our dialogue can be witnessed and in that way checked for veracity. In those situations I find myself demanding to myself that I be fully congruent in responding, *whatever* that response is. I may be angry or frustrated at the content of the challenge which has been placed and I will express that, but I *also* know that my deep respect for the challenge being framed will come out. In any case, the alternative is unthinkable: the alternative would be to present an incongruent smile, a portrayed warmth or a transferential judgement. Any of these possibilities would actively encourage further 'transference' if that was an active phenomenon and engender it if it were not. Instead, I demand of myself total congruence in response.

My preference is for such confrontations to take place in public. I know that trainers differ on how they like to work with this and that many prefer to deal with it on a one-to-one basis. For my part, I see this issue as a normal part of the training experience and like to work with it, ideally within the large group – for there is much to learn from this, even vicariously. Often one person's process in relation to this kind of material sparks off the process of another. Also, the public context offers a check on the response of both the course member and the trainer and in that way affords *protection* to us both. I am protected from the excesses of the course member's assumptions by the wider reality provided by the course membership who will challenge apparent unrealities. Also, the same wider reality is supportive to the course member on the matter of my response. For example, if I, as the trainer, were to respond in a fashion which 'put down' the trainee, then there would be a likelihood of that being challenged within the large group, whereas it might simply have its controlling and abusive effect if it were happening in a private meeting between myself and the course member.

As a footnote to this discussion I need to confess that I have experience of the alternate role in this kind of confrontation. I remember a meeting I had with Carl Rogers in his home in late 1972. In that meeting he challenged me on how I had been treating him in recent times. I realised that he was right – I had been challenging him and criticising him at every opportunity both in private meetings and in groups. I realised and spoke in that meeting about the fact that he had been such an important person in my life through his writing, to the extent that I had re-directed my career and moved to the other side of the world. In a way, to establish my separateness and my value, I had got into a thing where I had to put him down. Of course, he was used to that, and came out with the suggestion, which is also a book title, that 'When you meet the Buddah, you have to kill the Buddah to meet the person'. For the next 15 years Carl Rogers was a person I could meet as a person.

How might person-centred training develop in the future?

In Britain, at least, over the past ten years there has been an emphasis on the curriculum and processes of what we might call 'initial training'. This emphasis has been understandable because it has been a response to the challenge set by BAC Course Accreditation (BAC, 1996c). It has been a considerable challenge to design person-centred training which is both consistent with the model and also meets external standards for validation.

Now, with that basic foundation in place, it is time to look to the nature and shape of 'post-initial' training for person-centred counsellors. While there was a need for a fair degree of common curriculum, although individualised process, during initial training to ensure that basic training needs for the profession were met, once that is achieved the post-initial curriculum can flow more exclusively from the experienced needs of the graduate.

Two approaches to post-initial training are developing within the person-centred specialism. We might refer to these, for convenience, as the 'open-learning' approach and the 'subject-specific' approach.

The 'open-learning' approach

During initial training, person-centred counsellors become skilled in using open-learning structures such as the various small groups to meet their different learning needs. This developed ability can be exercised during post-initial training by creating similar open-learning structures which graduates can utilise, each in quite different ways. In the Counselling Unit we have noted several developments in this regard; for example, we are currently offering and resourcing a monthly half-day group for the 12 students who deferred from our previous year's courses. The timetable for this group is created by the needs of its members. Often the emphasis will be on group supervision since that in itself affords a student-centred curriculum and makes maximal use of the counsellors' ongoing counselling practice. But the counsellors' needs take the group in many other directions as well, for example, helping each other to complete outstanding assignments, engaging emerging personal development needs and addressing self-assessment reviews.

Even students who have not deferred the award of their Diploma often find the need to organise their ongoing 'open-learning' groups. Sometimes these groups meet only for the first half year following initial training but even that short time offers important support. There can be a considerable 'let down' experience when the graduate suddenly moves from a life full of support on the training course to one which can feel empty of that support immediately following. As might be expected, this is usually more of an issue for those engaged in full-time training. These ongoing 'support' groups may go on for many years. Indeed some of the staff in our Unit are still involved in regular weekend meetings with colleagues from their own initial training courses.

Another open-ended training/support group which we have found ourselves forming in recent times is a group for new supervisors. Distinct from supervision training, this group affords a regular half-day per month for new supervisors to come together without a programme beyond that of sharing their supervision experiences and getting the support from each other as well as the consultancy of a group facilitator.

The 'subject-specific' approach

Some post-initial training initiatives arise from trainers responding to specific and similar needs expressed by a number of graduates. An example of this is the development of *supervision training*. Having successfully completed their own training period and built up a large amount of counselling experience, graduates are asked by others entering the training period to fulfil a supervision role. In recent years a person-centred counselling supervision pedagogy has been evolving with interesting discoveries such as the hunger of graduates for this post-initial training; the willingness on the part of trainee supervisors to take responsibility for their own learning; and the strong motivation on the part of new supervisors to study person-centred theories of therapy and personality. As Carl Rogers often noted, a hunger for theory more often follows experience than precedes it.

Another 'subject-specific' development is the post-initial training offered for counsellors in the *primary care* sector. These courses presume an existing Diploma level generic training but build on that to help the graduate to develop expertise in the demanding sector of primary health care where many professional counselling appointments are now emerging. Another specialist area which should emerge is specific training in *client-centred pre-therapy* for graduates who are working with client populations experiencing profound learning difficulties or psychoses which make the establishment of psychological contact a problem. Other person-centred counsellors not working with such client populations also seek training in pre-therapy because it can offer additional skills in dealing with the normal range of clients who may experience moments of losing contact. Another specialist application for person-centred graduates in the near future is certainly going to be *person-centred family therapy* (including couple therapy). It is perfectly possible for person-centred graduates to work with couples and families following initial training – the generic base is sufficient for the work. However, there is a growing interest in the experience of working with couples and families in a person-centred fashion. This interest will be fed by future publications, for example, O'Leary (forthcoming), and is sure to spawn specialist post-initial training.

These are only some of the post-initial training ventures which have begun to emerge or to be glimpsed. The next ten years should provide as much excitement in the development of the post-initial phase as the past ten years have done for basic training.

Do you forsee any future *crises* for person-centred training?

Possibly the growing institutionalisation of the profession of counselling will present a crisis for the person-centred specialism. By definition, the institutionalisation process runs counter to a person-centred emphasis. The institutionalisation process demands more and more conformity of practices. A small example of this, within Britain, is a recent addition to the guidelines for BAC Course Accreditation detailing how relations between the course, the course member and the placement agency should be conducted (BAC, 1996c). These guidelines much more closely represent the approach of psychodynamic training in requiring the training course to take responsibility *for* the trainee counsellor and to become involved in the relationship between the counsellor and the placement agency. The whole construction cuts across the responsibility dynamic of person-centred training to a degree which makes it virtually untenable. In our case we found a way to leave aside the whole notion of 'placements' rather than contradict the responsibility dynamic in such an important area.

Sometimes it will be possible, as in the above example, to stave off the structures enforced by the institutionalisation of the profession but later challenges may prove impossible. A vital ingredient of the early development of the BAC Course Accreditation Scheme was its applicability to *all* counselling approaches. Courses were required to justify their approaches to training in

Box 13.4

The Difference between 'Functional' and 'Structural' Guidelines

Guidelines for counselling training may be expressed in either a functional or a structural fashion. A functional expression states the objective which needs to be met and requires the course to articulate how that is to be achieved within its own core theoretical model, whereas a structural framing requires *prescribed* solutions to the stated issues. Inevitably, the institutionalisation of any profession tends to result in a gradual slippage from functionalism to structuralism. Here are three examples of functional and structural expressions of training guidelines.

Functional	*Structural*
How does the course address the problem of trainees working with 'difficult' clients?	Courses should build in a system of client 'assessment' to protect trainees from difficult clients.
Does the course effectively address the issue of the trainee's personal maintenance and development during training?	The course should require trainees to be in personal therapy during training.
Is the course's assessment system sufficiently robust to protect the profession?	The course must be tutor-assessed.

terms of their core model. If schemes such as these begin to demand specific *structures* derived from only some approaches, then alternative approaches will either have to stay out of such schemes to maintain an integrity or increasingly compromise to the extent that the various counselling approaches begin to lose their distinctiveness. So long as challenges for training courses are framed *functionally* rather than *structurally* they will encourage development as well as maintaining a professional challenge. However, if the consequence of institutionalisation is to resort to structuralism in order to police a specific demand, then dangers arise. Box 13.4 illustrates three examples of functional and structural articulations of training guidelines.

The functional expression of guidelines allows courses, from any tradition, to find their own answers, knowing that the answers they reach should and will be challenged by other members of the profession. In other words, it is not sufficient to justify solutions simply in terms of them being 'person-centred' – that, in itself, is not a justification. The justification must prove itself either empirically or conceptually to members of the profession as a whole, as that is represented by the professional body. This combination of a functional expression of guidelines allowing diversification of the different approaches with a robust system of challenging within the profession should create optimal conditions both for the growth and the accountability of training. Too often in the past person-centred trainers have focused more on growth than accountability. This has led to the marginalisation and sometimes even the ridiculing of the person-centred specialism in some countries. If person-centred counselling is to achieve its potential then its trainers must not be so 'precious' about the approach that they withdraw it from public accountability.

How are you going to end this book?

The only way to end is to go back to the beginning to find out what the trainee, Alison, has to say at the *end* of her training.

Box 13.5

Alison Re-visited

I don't feel 'finished', but I do feel 'started'. What has happened for me, and many on the course, are deep and significant 'shifts' inside me. I am a less *'scared'* person. Before the course I wouldn't have realised that I was a scared person – but I *was* – and that basic fear underpinned and slightly undermined all my relating. Now that I am less scared within myself I am much more able to 'facilitate' rather than 'direct' people – to help *them* to find *their* strength as I said at the start of the course. It is extraordinary to see how much power is released when we feel a little less scared of who we are.

References

Allen, L. (1989) 'A client's experience of failure', in D. Mearns and W. Dryden (eds), *Experiences of Counselling in Action*. London: Sage. pp. 20–7.

Anderson, W.J. (1989a) 'Family therapy in the client-centered tradition: a legacy in the narrative mode', *Person-Centered Review*, 4(3): 295–307.

Anderson, W.J. (1989b) 'Client/person-centered approaches to couple and family therapy: expanding theory and practice', *Person-Centered Review*, 4(3): 425–7.

Aveline, M. (1990) 'The training and supervision of individual therapists', in W. Dryden (ed.), *Individual Therapy*. Milton Keynes: Open University Press. pp. 313–39.

Axline, V. (1971) *Dibs: In Search of Self*. Harmondsworth, Middlesex: Penguin.

BAC (1996a) *Code of Ethics and Practice for Trainers*. Rugby: British Association for Counselling.

BAC (1996b) *Code of Ethics and Practice for Counsellors*. Rugby: British Association for Counselling.

BAC (1996c) *The Recognition of Counsellor Training Courses*, 3rd edn. Rugby: British Association for Counselling.

Barrett-Lennard, G.T. (1962) 'Dimensions of therapist response as causal factors in therapeutic change', *Psychological Monographs*, 76(43) (Whole No. 562).

Barrett-Lennard, G.T. (1984) 'The world of family relationships: a person-centered systems view', in R.F. Levant and J.M. Shlien (eds), *Client-Centered Therapy and the Person-Centered Approach*. New York: Praeger. pp. 222–42.

Barrett-Lennard, G.T. (1988a) 'Listening', *Person-Centered Review*, 3(4): 410–25.

Barrett-Lennard, G.T. (1988b) 'The pathway of client-centered therapy'. Paper presented to the First International Conference on Client-Centered and Experiential Psychotherapy. Leuven: Belgium.

Barrett-Lennard, G.T. (1990) 'The therapy pathway reformulated', in G. Lietaer, J. Rombauts and R. Van Balen (eds), *Client-Centered and Experiential Psychotherapy in the Nineties*. Leuven: University of Leuven Press. pp. 23–54.

Barrett-Lennard, G.T. (1992) 'A person-centred systemic model of change'. Developed from a paper presented at the Second International Conference on Client-Centred and Experiential Psychotherapy, Stirling, Scotland.

Barrett-Lennard, G.T. (1993) 'The phases and focus of empathy', *British Journal of Medical Psychology*, 66: 3–14.

Barrett-Lennard, G.T. (1997) 'The recovery of empathy – towards others and self', in A.C. Bohart and L.S. Greenberg (eds), *Empathy and Psychotherapy: New Directions to Theory, Research and Practice*. Washington, DC: APA Books.

Barrett-Lennard, G.T. (forthcoming) *Carl Rogers' Helping System: Journey and Substance*. London: Sage.

Bergin, A.E. and Garfield, S.L. (1994) *Handbook of Psychotherapy and Behavior Change*. New York: Wiley.

Binder, U. (forthcoming) 'Empathy and empathy development with psychotic clients', in B. Thorne and E. Lambers (eds), *Person-Centred Therapy: A European Perspective*. London: Sage.

Blackie, S. (1989) 'My experience of counselling couples', in D. Mearns and W. Dryden (eds), *Experiences of Counselling in Action*. London: Sage. pp. 112–24.

Bohart, A.C. (1990) 'A cognitive client-centered perspective on borderline personality development', in G. Lietaer, J. Rombauts and R. Van Balen (eds), *Client-Centered and Experiential Psychotherapy in the Nineties*. Leuven: University of Leuven Press. pp. 599–622.

Bohart, A.C. and Rosenbaum, R. (1995) 'The dance of empathy: empathy, diversity and technical eclecticism', *The Person-Centered Journal*, 2(1): 5–29.

Bowen, M. (1986) 'Personality differences and person-centered supervision', *Person-Centered Review*, 1(3): 291–309.

Bowen, M., Miller, M. Rogers, C. and Wood, J.K. (1980) 'Learning in large groups: their implications for the future', in C. Rogers, *A Way of Being*. Boston: Houghton Mifflin, pp. 316–35.

Boy, A.V. (1989) 'Psychodiagnosis: a person-centered perspective', *Person-Centered Review*, 4(2): 132–51.

Boy, A.V. and Pine, G.J. (1982) *Client-Centered Counseling: A Renewal*. Boston: Allyn and Bacon.

Boy, A.V. and Pine, G.J. (1986) 'Mental health procedures: A continuing client-centered reaction', *Person-Centered Review*, 1(1): 51–61.

Boyle, J. (1994) Personal communication.

Bozarth, J.D. (1984) 'Beyond reflection: emergent modes of empathy', in R.F. Levant and J.M. Shlien (eds), *Client-Centered Therapy and the Person-Centered Approach*. New York: Praeger. pp. 59–75.

Bozarth, J.D. (1995) 'Person-centered therapy: a misunderstood paradigmatic difference?', *The Person-Centered Journal*, 2(2): 12–17.

Bozarth, J.D. (1996) 'A theoretical reconceptualization of the necessary and sufficient conditions for therapeutic personality change', *The Person-Centered Journal*, 3(1): 44–51.

Bozarth, J.D. and Shanks, A. (1989) 'Person-centered family therapy with couples', *Person-Centered Review*, 4(3): 280–94.

Bozarth, J.D. and Temaner-Brodley, B. (1986) 'Client-centered psychotherapy: a statement', *Person-Centered Review*, 1(3): 262–71.

Buber, M. and Rogers, C.R. (1960) 'Dialogue between Martin Buber and Carl Rogers', *Psychologia*, 3: 208–21.

Cain, D.J. (1989a) 'The paradox of non-directiveness in the person-centered approach', *Person-Centered Review*, 4(2): 123–31.

Cain, D.J. (1989b) 'The client's role in diagnosis', *Person-Centered Review*, 4(2): 171–82.

Cain, D.J. (1989c) 'From the individual to the family', *Person-Centered Review*, 4(3): 248–55.

Cain, D.J. (1990) 'Further thoughts about nondirectiveness and client-centered therapy', *Person-Centered Review*, 5(1): 89–99.

Carkhuff, R. (1969) *Helping and Human Relations*. New York: Holt, Rinehart and Winston.

Clarkson, P. and Gilbert, M. (1991) 'The training of counsellor trainers and supervisors', in W. Dryden and B. Thorne (eds), *Training and Supervision for Counselling in Action*. London: Sage. pp. 143–69.

Cohen, J. (1994) 'Empathy toward client perception of therapist intent: evaluating one's person-centeredness', *The Person-Centered Journal*, 1(3): 4–10.

Colin, W. (1995) 'Als cliëntgerichte therapeut werken met ouders en kinderen. Een uitdaging', in G. Lietaer and H. Van Kalmthout (eds), *Praktijkboek Gesprekstherapie*. Utrecht: De Tijdstroom. pp. 258–66.

Combs, A.W. (1986a) 'Person-centered assumptions for counselor education', *Person-Centered Review*, 1(1): 72–82.

Combs, A.W. (1986b). 'On methods, conditions, and goals', *Person-Centered Review*, 1(4): 378–88.

Combs, A.W. (1989) *A Theory of Therapy*. Newbury Park, CA: Sage.

Daly, T. and Mearns, D. (1993) *A person-centred counselling interview*. Training video. Glasgow: Counselling Unit, University of Strathclyde.

Davies, D. and Neal, C. (1996) *Pink Therapy*. Buckingham: Open University Press.

Deleu, C. and Van Werde, D. (forthcoming) 'The relevance of a phenomenological attitude in contact with people with psychotic tendencies', in B. Thorne and E. Lambers (eds), *Person-Centred Therapy: A European Perspective*. London: Sage.

Draucker, C.B. (1992) *Counselling Survivors of Childhood Sexual Abuse*. London: Sage.

Dryden, W. and Thorne, B. (eds) (1991) *Training and Supervision for Counselling in Action*. London: Sage.

Dryden, W., Horton, I. and Mearns, D. (1995) *Issues in Professional Counselling Training*. London: Cassell.

Esser, V. and Schneider, I. (1990) 'Client-centered partnership therapy as relationship therapy', in G. Lietaer, J. Rombauts and R. Van Balen (eds), *Client-Centered and Experiential Psychotherapy in the Nineties*. Leuven: University of Leuven Press. pp. 829–46.

Eymael, J. (1984) 'Strategieën en houdingen van therapeuten in kortdurende clientcentered en gedragstherapieën. Een evaluatie door psychotherapeuten, onafhankelijke beoordelaars en cliënten', in G. Lietaer, P. van Praag and H. Swildens (eds), *Client-Centered Psychotherapie in Beweging*. Leuven/Amersfoort: Acco. pp. 273–302.

Fiedler, F.E. (1978) 'Contingency model and the leadership process', in L. Berkowitz (ed.), *Advances in Experimental Social Psychology*, Volume 11. New York: Academic Press.

Fischer, C.T. (1987) 'Beyond transference', *Person-Centered Review*, 2(2): 157–64.

Ford, J.G. (1994) 'The public expression of private experience: a relatively unexplored dimension of person-centered psychology', *The Person-Centered Journal*, 1(3): 11–17.

Foulkes, S. and Anthony, E. (1957) *Group Psychotherapy*. London: Penguin.

Friedman, M. (1985) *The Healing Dialogue in Psychotherapy*. Northvale, NJ: Jason Aronson Inc.

Fusek, L. (1991) *New Directions in Client-Centered Therapy: Practice with Difficult Client Populations*. Spring Lecture Series, The Chicago Counseling Center, Chicago, IL.

Gaylin, N.L. (1989) 'The necessary and sufficient conditions for change: individual versus family therapy', *Person-Centered Review*, 4(3): 263–79.

Gaylin, N.L. (1990) 'Family-centered therapy', in G. Lietaer, J. Rombauts and R. Van Balen (eds), *Client-Centered and Experiential Psychotherapy in the Nineties*. Leuven: University of Leuven Press. pp. 813–28.

Gaylin, N.L. (1996) 'The self, the family, and psychotherapy', *The Person-Centered Journal*, 3(1): 31–43.

Gendlin, E.T. (1970a) 'A theory of personality change', in J.T. Hart and T.M. Tomlinson (eds), *New Directions in Client-Centered Therapy*. Boston: Houghton Mifflin. pp. 129–73.

Gendlin, E.T. (1970b) 'Research in psychotherapy with schizophrenic patients and the nature of that "illness"', in J.T. Hart and T.M. Tomlinson (eds), *New Directions in Client-Centered Therapy*. Boston: Houghton Mifflin. pp. 280–91.

Gendlin, E.T. (1981) *Focusing*. New York: Bantam Books.

Gendlin, E.T. (1984) 'The client's client: the edge of awareness', in R.F. Levant and J.M. Shlien (eds), *Client-Centered Therapy and the Person-Centered Approach*. New York: Praeger. pp. 76–107.

Gendlin, E.T. (1990) 'Schizophrenia: problems and methods in psychotherapy', in K. Hoeller (ed.), *Readings in Existential Psychology and Psychiatry*. Seattle, WA: Review of Existential Psychology and Psychiatry. pp. 181–92.

Gendlin, E.T. (1996) *Focusing-Oriented Psychotherapy*. New York: Guilford.

Gilbert, P. (1992) *Counselling for Depression*. London: Sage.

Ginsberg, B. (1984) 'Beyond behavior modification: client-centered play therapy with the retarded', *Academic Psychology Bulletin*, 6(3): 321–34.

Gordon, D. (1996) *The Introduction of a Counselling Service into Primary Care in Lanarkshire*. Hamilton, Scotland: Lanarkshire Health Board.

Gordon, T. (1975) *P.E.T. – Parent Effectiveness Training*. New York: Plume Books.

Goss, S. and Mearns, D. (1997a) 'A call for a pluralist epistemological understanding in the assessment and evaluation of counselling', *British Journal of Guidance and Counselling*, 25(2): 189–98.

Goss, S. and Mearns, D. (1997b) 'Applied pluralism in the evaluation of employee counselling', *British Journal of Guidance and Counselling*, 25(3): 327–44.

Grafanaki, S. and McLeod, J. (1995) 'Client and counsellor narrative accounts of congruence during the most helpful and hindering events of an initial counselling session', *Counselling Psychology Quarterly*, 8(4): 311–24.

Grant, B. (1990) 'Principles and instrumental nondirectiveness in person-centered and client-centered therapy', *Person-Centered Review*, 5(1): 77–88.

Green, H. (1967) *I Never Promised You a Rose Garden*. London: Pan.

Greenberg, L.S., Rice, L.N. and Elliott, R. (1993) *Facilitating Emotional Change*. New York: Guilford Press.

Guerney, B.G. Jr (1984) 'Contributions of client-centered therapy to filial, marital and family relationship enhancement therapies', in R.F. Levant and J.M. Shlien (eds), *Client-Centered Therapy and the Person-Centered Approach*. New York: Praeger. pp. 261–77.

Hallam, R. (1992) *Counselling for Anxiety Problems*. London: Sage.

Hammersley, D. (1995) *Counselling People on Prescribed Drugs*. London: Sage.

Hart, J.T. and Tomlinson, T.M. (eds) (1970) *New Directions in Client-Centered Therapy*. Boston: Houghton Mifflin.

Hawtin, S. and Moore, J. (forthcoming) 'Empowerment or collusion – the social context of person-centred therapy', in B. Thorne and E. Lambers (eds), *Person-Centred Therapy: A European Perspective*. London: Sage.

Hundersmarck, A. (1995) '"Lastige" clienten ongeschikt voor cliëntgerichte psychotherapie?', in G. Lietaer and M. Van Kalmthout (eds), *Praktijkboek Gesprekstherapie*. Utrecht: De Tijdstroom. pp. 188–98.

Hutterer, R., Pawlowsky, G., Semid, P.F. and Stipsits, R. (eds) (1996) *Client-Centred* and *Experiential Psychotherapy: A Paradigm in Motion*. Frankfurt am Main: Peter Lang.

Johns, H. (1996) *Personal Development in Counsellor Training*. London: Cassell.

Kahn, E. (1987) 'On the therapeutic value of both the "real" and the "transference" relationship', *Person-Centered Review*, 2(4): 471–5.

Kirschenbaum, H. (1979) *On Becoming Carl Rogers*. New York: Delacorte Press.

Kirschenbaum, H. (1991) 'Denigrating Carl Rogers: William Coulson's last crusade', *Journal of Counseling and Development*, 69: 411–13.

Kirschenbaum, H. and Henderson, V. (1989a) *The Carl Rogers Reader*. Boston: Houghton Mifflin.

Kirschenbaum, H. and Henderson, V. (1989b) *Carl Rogers: Dialogues*. Boston: Houghton Mifflin.

Knight, B. (1986) *Psychotherapy with Older Adults*. London: Sage.

Kroll, J. (1988) *The Challenge of the Borderline Patient*. New York: Norton.

Lago, C. (1979) 'In pursuit of genuineness', *The Counsellor*, 2: 47–54.

Lago, C. with Thompson, L. (1996) *Race, Culture and Counselling*. Buckingham: Open University Press.

Laing, R., Phillipson, H. and Lee, A. (1966) *Interpersonal Perception*. London: Tavistock.

Lambers, E. (1991) 'A person centred perspective on psychopathology'. Paper presented at the 2nd International Conference on Client-Centred and Experiential Psychotherapy, Stirling, Scotland.

Lambers, E. (1993) 'Counselling can be non-directive', *Counselling News*, vol. 9.

Lambers, E. (1994a) 'The person-centred perspective on psychopathology: the neurotic client', in D. Mearns, *Developing Person-Centred Counselling*. London: Sage. pp. 105–9.

Lambers, E. (1994b) 'Personality disorder', in D. Mearns, *Developing Person-Centred Counselling*. London: Sage. pp. 116–20.

Lambers, E. (1994c) 'Borderline personality disorder', in D. Mearns, *Developing Person-Centred Counselling*. London: Sage. pp. 110–13.

Lambers, E. (1994d) 'Psychosis', in D. Mearns, *Developing Person-Centred Counselling*. London: Sage. pp. 113–16.

Lambers, E. (1997) Personal communication. (Elke Lambers directs the PCT Professional Development Certificate in Supervision.)

Levant, R.F. (1984) 'From person to system: two perspectives', in R.F. Levant and J.M. Shlien (eds), *Client-Centered Therapy and the Person-Centered Approach*. New York: Praeger. pp. 243–61.

Levant, R.F. and Shlien, J.M. (eds) (1984) *Client-Centered Therapy and the Person-Centered Approach*. New York: Praeger.

Lietaer, G. (1984) 'Unconditional positive regard: a controversial basic attitude in client-centered therapy', in R.F. Levant and J.M. Shlien (eds), *Client-Centered Therapy and the Person-Centered Approach*. New York: Praeger. pp. 41–58.

Lietaer, G. (1991) 'Authenticiteit en onvoorwaardelijke positieve gezindheid', in H. Swildens, O. de Haas, G. Lietaer and R. Van Balen (eds), *Leerboek Gesprekstherapie*. Amersfoort/Leuven: Acco. pp. 27–64.

Lietaer, G. (forthcoming) 'From non-directive to experiential: a paradigm unfolding', in B. Thorne and E. Lambers (eds), *Person-Centred Therapy: A European Perspective*. London: Sage.

Lietaer, G. and Neirinck, M. (1986) 'Client and therapist perceptions of helping processes in client-centered/experiential psychotherapy, *Person-Centered Review'*, 1(4): 436–55.

Lietaer, G. and Van Kalmthout, M. (eds) (1995) *Praktijkboek Gesprekstherapie.* Utrecht: De Tijdstroom.

Lietaer, G., van Praag, P.H. and Swildens, H. (eds) (1984) *Client-Centered Psychotherapie in Beweging.* Leuven/Amersfoort: Acco.

Lietaer, G., Rombauts, J. and Van Balen, R. (eds) (1990) *Client-Centered and Experiential Psychotherapy in the Nineties.* Leuven: Leuven University Press.

Lipkin, S. (1948) 'The client evaluates nondirective psychotherapy', *Journal of Consulting Psychology,* 12: 137–46.

Lipkin, S. (1954) 'Clients' feelings and attitudes in relation to the outcome of client-centered therapy', *Psychological Monographs: General and Applied,* 68(1) (No. 372).

McLeod, J. (1977) 'The construction of reality in the basic encounter group'. Unpublished paper.

McLeod, J. (1995) 'Engaging with the world of the other: a relational process model of therapeutic empathy'. Unpublished paper.

Maddi, S.R. (1987) 'On the importance of the present', *Person-Centered Review,* 2(2): 171–81.

Mason, J. (1989) *Against Therapy.* London: Collins.

May, R. (1982) 'The problem of evil: an open letter to Carl Rogers', *Journal of Humanistic Psychology,* 22(3): 10–21.

Mearns, D. (1991a) 'The unspoken relationship between psychotherapist and client'. Paper presented to the Second International Conference on Client-Centred and Experiential Psychotherapy, Stirling, Scotland.

Mearns, D. (1991b) 'The phenomenon of "stuckness" within the therapeutic process'. Paper presented to the Second International Conference on Client-Centred and Experiential Psychotherapy, Stirling, Scotland.

Mearns, D. (1991c) 'On being a supervisor', in W. Dryden and B. Thorne (eds), *Training and Supervision for Counselling in Action.* London: Sage. pp. 116–28.

Mearns, D. (1992a) 'On the self-concept striking back', in W. Dryden (ed.), *Hard-Earned Lessons from Counselling in Action.* London: Sage. pp. 72–4.

Mearns, D. (1992b) 'On the dangers of under- and over-involvement', in W. Dryden (ed.), *Hard-Earned Lessons from Counselling in Action.* London: Sage. pp. 77–9.

Mearns, D. (1992c) 'On the balance between tyranny and the appropriate use of power in counselling', in W. Dryden (ed.), *Hard-Earned Lessons from Counselling in Action.* London: Sage. pp. 79–82.

Mearns, D. (1992d) 'On sufficiency and commitment', in W. Dryden (ed.), *Hard-Earned Lessons from Counselling in Action.* London: Sage. pp. 74–6.

Mearns, D. (1993a) 'The core conditions', in W. Dryden (ed.), *Questions and Answers on Counselling in Action.* London: Sage. pp. 1–4.

Mearns, D. (1993b) 'The ending phase of counselling', in W. Dryden (ed.), *Questions and Answers on Counselling in Action.* London: Sage. pp. 36–9.

Mearns, D. (1993c) 'Dissonance reduction processes within psychotherapy'. Public lecture presented in the University of Athens, Greece.

Mearns, D. (1994a) *Developing Person-Centred Counselling.* London: Sage.

Mearns, D. (1994b) 'Using the large unstructured group to develop congruence in person-centred training', in *Developing Person-Centred Counselling.* London: Sage. pp. 41–3.

Mearns, D. (1994c) 'Personal therapy is not enough', in *Developing Person-Centred Counselling*. London: Sage. pp. 34–6.

Mearns, D. (1994d) 'Let the client's locus of evaluation be the guide to your working', in *Developing Person-Centred Counselling*. London: Sage. pp. 80–3.

Mearns, D. (1994e) 'Be aware of and beware the dynamics of self-concept change', in *Developing Person-Centred Counselling*. London: Sage. pp. 88–93.

Mearns, D. (1994f) 'Don't confuse unconditional positive regard with "liking" ', in *Developing Person-Centred Counselling*. London: Sage. pp. 3–5.

Mearns, D. (1994g) 'Extend the core conditions to the whole of your client', in *Developing Person-Centred Counselling*. London: Sage. pp. 12–16.

Mearns, D. (1994h) 'How much of your "self" can you use therapeutically with your client?', in *Developing Person-Centred Counselling*. London: Sage. pp. 17–20.

Mearns, D. (1994i) 'Counsellor "paralysis": diagnosis and treatment', in *Developing Person-Centred Counselling*. London: Sage. pp. 23–7.

Mearns, D. (1994j) 'Assisting the client's focusing', in *Developing Person-Centred Counselling*. London: Sage. pp. 84–8.

Mearns, D. (1994k) 'Concentrate on the quality of your "presence" with the client', in *Developing Person-Centred Counselling*. London: Sage. pp. 5–9.

Mearns, D. (1994l) 'Be "beside" the client, but not "on the side of" the client', in *Developing Person-Centred Counselling*. London: Sage. pp. 53–5.

Mearns, D. (1994m) 'Getting the "power dynamic" right', in *Developing Person-Centred Counselling*. London: Sage. pp. 77–80.

Mearns, D. (1994n) 'Becoming aware of the "unspoken relationship" between counsellor and client', in *Developing Person-Centred Counselling*. London: Sage. pp. 64–8.

Mearns, D. (1994o) 'Tapping the "unspoken relationship" between counsellor and client', in *Developing Person-Centred Counselling*. London: Sage. pp. 69–74.

Mearns, D. (1994p) 'Trouble-shooting "stuckness" within the therapeutic process', in *Developing Person-Centred Counselling*. London: Sage. pp. 69–101.

Mearns, D. (1994q) 'Confronting the client', in *Developing Person-Centred Counselling*. London: Sage. pp. 93–6

Mearns, D. (1994r) 'What is involved in offering wider contracts to clients?', in *Developing Person-Centred Counselling*. London: Sage. pp. 9–11.

Mearns, D. (1994s) 'How to work with a couple?', in *Developing Person-Centred Counselling*. London: Sage. pp. 56–60.

Mearns, D. (1994t) 'The dance of psychotherapy', *Person-Centred Practice*, 2(2): 5–13.

Mearns, D. (1994u) 'What to do if you are not perfect', in *Developing Person-Centred Counselling*. London: Sage. pp. 37–40.

Mearns, D. (1995) 'Supervision: a tale of the missing client', *British Journal of Guidance and Counselling*, 23(3): 421–7.

Mearns, D. (1996a) 'Key issues in professional counsellor training'. Plenary paper presented to the Third Annual Conference of the European Association for Counselling, Vouliagmeni, Greece.

Mearns, D. (1996b) 'The personal development dimension in professional counsellor training'. Paper presented to the Third Annual Conference of the European Association for Counselling, Vouliagmeni, Greece.

Mearns, D. (1996c) 'Working at relational depth with clients in person-centred therapy', *Counselling*, 7(4): 306–11.

Mearns, D. (1996d) 'The existential approach in person-centred therapy'. Paper presented to the Fourth Annual Conference of the Croatian Psychological Association, Opatija, Croatia.

Mearns, D. (1997a) 'Central dynamics in client-centered therapy training', *The Person-Centered Journal*, 4(1): 31–43.

Mearns, D. (1997b) 'Achieving the personal development dimension in professional counsellor training', *Counselling*, 8(2): 113–20.

Mearns, D. and Dryden, W. (eds) (1989) *Experiences of Counselling in Action*. London: Sage.

Mearns, D. and McLeod, J. (1984) 'A person-centered approach to research', in R.F. Levant and J.M. Shlien (eds), *Client-Centered Therapy and the Person-Centered Approach*. New York: Praeger. pp. 370–89.

Mearns, D. and Thorne, B. (1988) *Person-Centred Counselling in Action*. London: Sage.

Mearns, D. and Thorne, B. (forthcoming) *Person-Centred Counselling*. London: Sage.

Merry, T. (1995) *Invitation to Person-Centred Psychology*. London: Whurr.

Mullen, J. and Abeles, N. (1972) 'Relationship of liking, empathy and therapist's experience to outcome of therapy', in *Psychotherapy 1971, an Aldine Annual*. Chicago: Aldine–Atherton.

Natiello, P. (1987) 'The person-centered approach', *Person Centered Review*, 2(2): 203–16.

Natiello, P. (1994) 'The collaborative relationship in psychotherapy', *The Person-Centered Journal*, 1(2): 11–18.

Nye, R.O. (1986) *Three Psychologies*, 3rd edn. Monterey, CA: Brooks/Cole.

O'Leary, C.J. (1989) 'The person-centered approach and family therapy: a dialogue between two traditions', *Person-Centered Review*, 4(3): 308–23.

O'Leary, C.J. (forthcoming) *Family Therapy and the Person Centred Approach*. London: Sage.

Patterson, C.H. (1964) 'Supervising students in the counseling practicum', *Journal of Counseling Psychology*, 11(1): 47–53.

Patterson, C.H. (1983) 'A client-centered approach to supervision', *The Counseling Psychologist*, 11(1): 22–5.

Patterson, C.H. (1984) 'Empathy, warmth and genuineness in psychotherapy: a review of reviews', *Psychotherapy*, 21(4): 431–8.

Polanyi, M. (1958) *Personal Knowledge*. London: Routledge.

Prouty, G.F. (1990) 'Pre-therapy: a theoretical evolution in the person-centered/ experiential psychotherapy of schizophrenia and retardation', in G. Lietaer, J. Rombauts and R. Van Balen (eds), *Client-Centered and Experiential Psychotherapy in the Nineties*. Leuven: University of Leuven Press. pp. 645–58.

Prouty, G.F. (1994) *Theoretical Evolutions in Person-Centered/Experiential Therapy: Applications to Schizophrenic and Retarded Psychoses*. Westport, CT: Praeger.

Prouty, G.F. and Cronval, M. (1989) 'Psychotherapy with a depressed mentally retarded adult: an application of pre-therapy', in A. Dozen and F. Menolascino (eds), *Depression in Mentally Retarded Children and Adults*. Leiden: Logon Publications. pp. 281–93.

Prouty, G.F. and Kubiak, M.A. (1988) 'The development of communicative contact with a catatonic schizophrenic', *Journal of Communication Therapy*, 4(1): 13–20.

Prouty, G.F. and Pietrazak, S. (1988) 'The pre-therapy method applied to persons experiencing hallucinatory images', *Person-Centered Review*, 3(4): 426–41.

Raskin, N.J. (1952) 'An objective study of the locus of evaluation factor in psychotherapy', in W. Wolff and J.A. Precker (eds), *Success in Psychotherapy*. New York: Grune and Stratton.

Raskin, N.J. and Van der Veen, F. (1970) 'Client-centered family therapy: some clinical and research perspectives', in J.T. Hart and T.M. Tomlinson (eds), *New Directions in Client-Centered Therapy*. Boston: Houghton Mifflin. pp. 398–406.

Rennie, D. (1985) 'Client deference in the psychotherapy relationship'. Paper presented at the 16th Annual Meeting of the Society for Psychotherapy Research. Evanston, IL.

Rennie, D. (1987) 'A model of the client's experience of psychotherapy'. Paper presented at the Sixth Annual International Human Science Conference, Ottawa.

Rennie, D. (1990) 'Toward a representation of the client's experience of the psychotherapy hour', in G. Lietaer, J. Rombauts and R. Van Balen (eds), *Client-Centered and Experiential Psychotherapy in the Nineties*. Leuven: University of Leuven Press. pp. 155–73.

Rennie, D. (forthcoming) *Psychotherapy Inside Out*. London: Sage.

Rogers, C.R. (1939) *The Clinical Treatment of the Problem Child*. Boston: Houghton Mifflin.

Rogers, C.R. (1942a) *Counseling and Psychotherapy*. Boston: Houghton Mifflin.

Rogers, C.R. (1942b) 'The use of electrically recorded interviews in improving psychotherapeutic techniques', *American Journal of Orthopsychiatry*, 12: 429–34.

Rogers, C.R. (1951) *Client-Centered Therapy*. Boston: Houghton Mifflin.

Rogers, C.R. (1957a) 'The necessary and sufficient conditions of therapeutic personality change', *Journal of Consulting Psychology*, 21(2): 95–103.

Rogers, C.R. (1957b) 'A note on the nature of man', *Journal of Counseling Psychology*, 4: 199–203.

Rogers, C.R. (1957c) 'A therapist's view of the good life: the fully functioning person', *The Humanist*, 17: 291–300.

Rogers, C.R. (1959) 'A theory of therapy, personality and interpersonal relationships as developed in the client-centered framework', in S. Koch (ed.), *Psychology: A Study of a Science*, Volume 3. *Formulations of the Person and the Social Contract*. New York: McGraw-Hill, pp. 184–256.

Rogers, C.R. (1960) 'Social implications', in H. Kirschenbaum and V. Henderson (eds) (1989), *The Carl Rogers Reader*. Boston: Houghton Mifflin. pp. 436–7.

Rogers, C.R. (1961a) *On Becoming a Person*. Boston: Houghton Mifflin.

Rogers, C.R. (1961b) 'The process equation of psychotherapy', *American Journal of Psychotherapy*, 15(1): 27–45.

Rogers, C.R. (1963) 'The actualizing tendency in relation to "motives" and to consciousness', in M. Jones (ed.), *Nebraska Symposium on Motivation*. Lincoln: University of Nebraska Press, pp. 1–24.

Rogers, C.R. (1964) 'Toward a modern approach to values', *Journal of Abnormal and Social Psychology*, 68(2): 160–7.

Rogers, C.R. (1975) 'A person-centered approach to intergroup tensions'. Paper presented to the Association of Humanistic Psychology Conference, Cuernavaca, Mexico, 19 December.

Rogers, C.R. (1978a) 'Do we need a reality?', *Dawnpoint*, 1(2): 6–9.

Rogers, C.R. (1978b) 'The formative tendency', *Journal of Humanistic Psychology*, 18(1): 23–6.

Rogers, C.R. (1979) Personal communication.

Rogers, C.R. (1980a) *A Way of Being*. Boston: Houghton Mifflin.

Rogers, C.R. (1980b) 'What I learned from two research studies', in H. Kirschen-baum and V. Henderson (eds) (1989), *The Carl Rogers Reader*. Boston: Houghton Mifflin, pp. 203–10.

Rogers, C.R. (1980c) 'Empathic: an unappreciated way of being', in *A Way of Being*. Boston: Houghton Mifflin. pp. 137–63.

Rogers, C.R. (1986) 'A client-centered/person-centered approach to therapy', in L. Kutash and A. Wolf (eds), *Psychotherapist's Casebook*. San Francisco: Jossey-Bass. pp. 197–208.

Rogers, C.R. (1987) 'Client-centered? Person-Centered?', *Person-Centered Review*, 2(1): 11–14.

Rogers, C.R. and Sanford, R.C. (1989) 'Client-centered psychotherapy', in H. Kaplan and B. Gadock (eds), *The Comprehensive Textbook of Psychiatry V*. Balti-more: Williams and Williams Co. pp. 482–501.

Rogers, C.R. and Skinner, B.F. (1956) 'Some issues concerning the control of human behavior', *Science*, 24 (No. 3231): 1057–66.

Rogers, C.R., Gendlin, E.T., Kiesler, D.J. and Truax, C.B. (eds) (1967) *The Therapeutic Relationship and its Impact: A Study of Psychotherapy with Schizophrenics*. Madison: University of Wisconsin Press.

Rombauts, J. and Devriendt, M. (1990) 'Conjoint couple therapy in client-centered practice', in G. Lietaer, J. Rombauts and R. Van Balen (eds), *Client-Centered and Experiential Psychotherapy in the Nineties*. Leuven: University of Leuven Press. pp. 847–63.

Roy, B.C. (1991) 'A client-centered approach to multiple personality and dis-sociative process', in *New Directions in Client-Centered Therapy: Practice with Difficult Client Populations*. Spring Lecture Series, The Chicago Counseling Center, Chicago, IL. pp. 18–40.

Sabbe, B. (1991) 'Cliëntgerichte partnerrelatie – en gezinstherapie', in H. Swildens, O. de Haas, G. Lietaer and R. Van Balen (eds), *Leerboek Gesprekstherapie*. Amersfoort/ Leuven: Acco. pp. 415–32.

Santen, B. (1991) 'Cliëntgerichte kinderpsychotherapie', in H. Swildens, O. de Haas, G. Lietaer and R. Van Balen (eds), *Leerboek Gesprekstherapie*. Amersfoort/ Leuven: Acco. pp. 395–414.

Scott, M.J. and Stradling, S.G. (1992) *Counselling for Post-Traumatic Stress Disorder*. London: Sage.

Seeman, J. (1984) 'The fully functioning person: theory and research', in R.F. Levant and J.M. Shlien (eds), *Client-Centered Therapy and the Person-Centered Approach*. New York: Praeger. pp. 131–52.

Seeman, J. (1987) 'Transference and psychotherapy', *Person-Centered Review*, 2(2): 189–95.

Seeman, J. (1994) 'Conceptual analysis of client and counselor activity in client-centered therapy', *Person-Centered Journal*, 1(2): 5–10.

Shlien, J. (1984) 'A countertheory of transference', in R. Levant and J. Shlien (eds), *Client-Centered Therapy and the Person-Centered Approach*. Boston: Praeger. pp. 153–81.

Shlien, J. (1987) 'A countertheory of transference', *Person-Centered Review*, 2(1): 15–49.

Shlien, J.M. and Zimring, F.M. (1970) 'Research directives and methods in client-centered therapy', in J.T. Hart and T.M. Tomlinson (eds), *New Directions in Client-Centered Therapy*. Boston: Houghton Mifflin. pp. 33–57.

Sims, J.M. (1989) 'Client-centered therapy: the art of knowing', *Person-Centered Review*, 4(1): 27–41.

Skinner, B.F. (1948) *Walden II*. New York: Macmillan.

Skinner, B.F. (1971) *Beyond Freedom and Dignity*. New York: Knopf.

Sue, D.W. and Sue, D. (1990) *Counselling the Culturally Different*, 2nd edn. New York: John Wiley.

Swildens, H. (1986) 'Over psychopathologie en haar belang voor de client-centered psychotherapie', in R. Van Balen, M. Leijssen and G. Lietaer (eds), *Droom en Werkelijkheid in Client-Centered Psychotherapie*. Leuven/Amersfoort: Acco. pp. 65–86.

Swildens, H. (1990) 'Client-centered psychotherapy for patients with borderline symptoms', in G. Lietaer, J. Rombauts and R. Van Balen (eds), *Client-Centered and Experiential Psychotherapy in the Nineties*. Leuven: University of Leuven Press. pp. 623–36.

Swildens, H. (1991) 'De psychopathologie in haar betekenis voor de clientgerichte gesprekstherapie', in H. Swildens, O. de Haas, G. Lietaer and R. Van Balen (eds), *Leerboek Gesprekstherapie*. Amersfoort/Leuven: Acco. pp. 305–31.

Swildens, H., de Haas, O., Lietaer, G. and Van Balen, R. (eds) (1991) *Leerboek Gesprekstherapie*. Amersfoort/Leuven: Acco.

Taft, J. (1933) *The Dynamics of Therapy*. New York: Macmillan.

Teusch, L. (1990) 'Positive effects and limitations of client-centered therapy with schizophrenic patients', in G. Lietaer, J. Rombauts and R. Van Balen (eds), *Client-Centered and Experiential Psychotherapy in the Nineties*. Leuven: University of Leuven Press. pp. 637–44.

Thayer, L. (1987) 'An experiential person-oriented learning process in counselor education', *Person-Centered Review*, 2(1): pp. 64–86.

Thorne, B.J. (1987) 'Beyond the core conditions', in W. Dryden (ed.), *Key Cases in Psychotherapy*. London: Croom Helm.

Thorne, B.J. (1991a) 'The blessing and the curse of empathy', in *Person-Centred Counselling: Therapeutic and Spiritual Dimensions*. London: Whurr. pp. 3–18.

Thorne, B.J. (1991b) 'Intimacy', in *Person-Centred Counselling: Therapeutic and Spiritual Dimensions*. London: Whurr. pp. 143–53.

Thorne, B.J. (1991c) 'The quality of tenderness', in *Person-Centred Counselling: Therapeutic and Spiritual Dimensions*. London: Whurr. pp. 73–81.

Thorne, B.J. (1992) *Carl Rogers*. London: Sage.

Thorne, B.J. (1994) 'Brief companionship', in D. Mearns, *Developing Person-Centred Counselling*. London: Sage. pp. 60–4.

Thorne, B.J. and Lambers, E. (eds) (forthcoming) *Person-Centred Therapy: A European Perspective*. London: Sage.

Tiedemann, J. and Krips, A. (1991) 'De existentiële dimensie', in H. Swildens, O. de Haas, G. Lietaer and R. Van Balen (eds), *Leerboek Gesprekstherapie*. Amersfoort/Leuven: Acco. pp. 169–94.

Tomlinson, T.M. and Hart, J.T. (1962) 'A validation study of the process scale', *Journal of Consulting Psychology*, 26(1): 74–8.

Truax, G.B. and Carkhuff, R.R. (1967) *Toward Effective Counseling and Psychotherapy*. Chicago: Aldine.

Tscheulin, D. (1990) 'Confrontation and non-confrontation as differential techniques in differential client-centered therapy', in G. Lietaer, J. Rombaut and R. Van Balen (eds), *Client-Centered and Experiential Psychotherapy in the Nineties*. Leuven: University of Leuven Press. pp. 327–36.

Tudor, K. and Worral, M. (1994) 'Congruence reconsidered', *British Journal of Guidance and Counselling*, 22(2): 197–205.

Vanaerschot, G. (1990) 'The process of empathy: holding and letting go', in G. Lietaer, J. Rombauts and R. Van Balen (eds), *Client-Centered and Experiential Psychotherapy in the Nineties*. Leuven: University of Leuven Press. pp. 269–94.

Vanaerschot, G. and Van Balen, R. (1991) 'Empathie', in H. Swildens, O. de Haas, G. Lietaer and R. Van Balen (eds), *Leerboek Gesprekstherapie*. Amersfoort/Leuven: Acco. pp. 93–138.

Van Balen, R. (1984) 'Overdracht in client-centered therapie', in G. Lietaer, P. van Praag and H. Swildens (eds), *Client-Centered Psychotherapie in Beweging*. Leuven/Amersfoort: Acco. pp. 207–26.

Van Balen, R. (1990) 'The therapeutic relationship according to Carl Rogers: only a climate? A dialogue? Or both?' in G. Lietaer, J. Rombauts and R. Van Balen (eds), *Client-Centered and Experiential Psychotherapy in the Nineties*. Leuven: University of Leuven Press. pp. 65–86.

Van Balen, R. (1991) 'Theorie de persoonlijkheidsverandering', in H. Swildens, O. de Haas, G. Lietaer and R. Van Balen (eds), *Leerboek Gesprekstherapie*. Amersfoort/Leuven: Acco. pp. 139–68.

Van Balen, R., Leijssen, M. and Lietaer, G. (eds) (1986) *Droom en Werkelijkheid in Client-Centered Psychotherapie*. Leuven/Amersfoort: Acco.

Van Belle, H. (1980) *Basic Intent and Therapeutic Approach of Carl Rogers*. Toronto: Wedge Publishing Foundation.

Van de Veire, C. (1995) 'Steunende en structurerende cliëntgerichte psychotherapie bij een borderline cliënte', in G. Lietaer and M. Van Kalmthout (eds), *Praktijkboek Gesprekstherapie*. Utrecht: De Tijdstroom. pp. 167–77.

Van der Veen, F. (1970) 'Client perception of therapist conditions as a factor in psychotherapy', in J.T. Hart and T.M. Tomlinson (eds), *New Directions in Client-Centered Therapy*. Boston: Houghton Mifflin. pp. 214–22.

Van Kalmthout, M.A. (forthcoming) 'Personality change and the concept of self', in B. Thorne and E. Lambers (eds), *Person-Centred Therapy: A European Perspective*. London: Sage.

Van Kalmthout, M.A. and Pelgrim, F.A. (1990) 'In search of universal concepts in psychopathology and psychotherapy', in G. Lietaer, J. Rombauts and R. Van Balen (eds), *Client-Centered and Experiential Psychotherapy in the Nineties*. Leuven: University of Leuven Press. pp. 381–96.

Van Werde, D. (1990) 'Psychotherapy with a retarded, schizoaffective woman: an application of Prouty's pre-therapy', in A. Dozen, A. van Gennep and G. Zwanikken (eds), *Treatment of Mental Illness and Behavioral Disorder in the Mentally Retarded*. Proceedings of the International Congress, 3–4 May.

Van Werde, D (1994a) 'An introduction to client-centred pre-therapy', in D. Mearns, *Developing Person-Centred Counselling*. London: Sage. pp. 121–5.

Van Werde, D. (1994b) 'Dealing with the possibility of psychotic content in a seemingly congruent communication', in D. Mearns, *Developing Person-Centred Counselling*. London: Sage. pp. 125–8.

Verlackt, P. (1995) 'Helpen bij patstellingen', in G. Lietaer and M. Van Kalmthout (eds), *Praktijboek Gesprekstherapie*. Utrecht: De Tijdstroom. pp. 199–206.

Vitz, P. (1977) *Psychology as Religion: the Cult of Self-Workshop*. Grand Rapids, MI: William B. Eerdmans.

Warner, M. (1989) 'Empathy and strategy in the family system', *Person-Centered Review*, 4(3): 324–43.

Warner, M. (1991) 'Fragile process'. Paper presented at the Second International Conference on Client-Centred and Experiential Psychotherapy, Stirling, Scotland.

Watson, N. (1984) 'The empirical status of Rogers' hypotheses of the necessary and sufficient conditions for effective psychotherapy', in R.F. Levant and J.M. Shlien (eds), *Client-Centered Therapy and the Person-Centered Approach*. New York: Praeger. pp. 17–40.

Wexler, D.A. and Rice, L.N. (eds) (1974) *Innovations in Client-Centered Therapy*. New York: John Wiley.

Wilkins, P. (1997) 'Congruence and countertransference: similarities and differences', *Counselling*, 8(1): 36–41.

Worden, J.W. (1988) *Grief Counselling and Grief Therapy*. London: Routledge.

Zimring, F. (1995) 'A new explanation for the beneficial results of client-centered therapy: the possibility of a new paradigm', *The Person-Centered Journal*, 2(2): 36–48.

Index